HIT SO HARD

HIT SO HARD

| A MEMOIR |

PATTY SCHEMEL

with

ERIN HOSIER

DA CAPO PRESS

Da Capo Press
Hachette Book Group
1290 Avenue of the Americas, New York, NY 10104
www.dacapopress.com
@DaCapoPress, @DaCapoPR
Printed in the United States of America

First Edition: October 2017
Published by Da Capo Press, an imprint of Perseus Books, LLC,
a subsidiary of Hachette Book Group, Inc.
The publisher is not responsible for websites (or their content)
that are not owned by the publisher.

Editorial production by Lori Hobkirk at the Book Factory.
Print book interior design by Cynthia Young at Sagecraft.

Library of Congress Cataloging-in-Publication Data has been applied for.
ISBNs: 978-0-306-82507-1 (hardcover); 978-0-306-82508-8 (ebook)
LSC-C

10 9 8 7 6 5 4 3 2 1

For Beatrice, when she's older.

CONTENTS

1   Come Back When You Grow Up   1

2   Flaming Youth   10

3   One O' the Girls   16

4   New Town   18

5   Credit in the Straight World   22

6   Doll Squad   26

7   Sybil   32

8   Jabberjaw   38

9   Godsend   45

10   Son of a Gun   49

11   Rock and Rio   52

12   Heavy   58

13   Asking for It   64

14   Beautiful Son   72

15   Live Through This   77

16   Loaded   82

17   Playing Your Song   93

18   Take Everything   100

19   How to Buy Drugs in New York City   112

20   Patient Pat   114

21   The Art of the Four-Day Detox   124

22   Sister   127

23   Shut the Door   134

24   I'm Drumming as Fast as I Can   138

25 One Way or Another 141

26 Use Once and Destroy 150

27 Soon 155

28 Taking Care of Business 159

29 Walks Up on St. Andrews 165

30 Buying Drugs in L.A. 171

31 Six Months Gone 175

32 Bringing It All Back Home 180

33 The End of the Line 188

34 Pink Turns to Blue 193

35 Occupational Hazards 197

36 A Day in the Life 200

37 Rock Bottom No. 1 202

38 Back to School 207

39 Re/lapse 213

40 Privilege Set Me Free 217

41 Temperatures Rising 222

42 *Je T'aime . . . Moi Non Plus* 229

43 Walking with a Ghost 232

44 In and Out of Grace 237

45 A Northern Soul 244

46 Something Electrical 250

47 The Difference 259

Acknowledgments 271

Index 273

Photographs follow page 184

COME BACK WHEN YOU GROW UP

I was born recovering. I don't remember a time before I knew the concept. I'm surprised my first spoken sentence wasn't "Hi, my name is Patty, and I'm already an alcoholic." It was the late 1960s, and Alcoholics Anonymous was our de facto church growing up in our community in Marysville, Washington, about 45 minutes north of Seattle. My parents were both in the ranks, and we'd often host meetings in our living room—my brother, sister, and I casually listening in. Somehow I always knew that normal families didn't do this. For one, things were as shrouded in secrecy as they were out in the open.

My religious upbringing was never about God but "God as you understand him" (which is a difficult concept to grasp if you don't know what anyone else understands), and our guidelines for living were based on the Twelve Steps. I grew up hearing about my parents' allergy to alcohol but never once saw them relapse. I understood that when my parents drank, it had been harmful and had caused them to mess up their lives, but I never related how that might have anything to do with mine. In my kid mind, I thought they were like that because they had both come from New York City, a whole galaxy away—and however sick they were before, they'd gotten better.

I'd heard my mother's addiction story many times, as she relayed it to groups of addicts on a regular basis. She had a way of speaking that connected with every person in the room, from the newcomer in the back to the old-timers right up front. She wanted to be an actress, but her mother gave her two choices: become a nun or marry a good Irish catholic. She married an Irish cop, they moved to Brooklyn, and she became an alcoholic housewife of the 1950s. She had her first cocktail at a holiday party and talked about the way it tasted and the warm way it went down her throat, how after that first drink she had many more that night.

She did her best to keep up appearances, hiding bottles and keeping all the lies straight. She ended up in a psychiatric hospital (the way addiction was treated then), strapped to the bed with the d.t.'s. She found AA when a neighbor came over to welcome her home from the hospital. This woman's husband had begun going to meetings and hadn't had a drink in seven months. My mom broke down in her kitchen and asked for help. That evening a stranger came to pick her up for a meeting. In those days they called it a Twelve Step Call. She stayed sober and met my future dad at an AA meeting in 1964. They were both married to other people at the time, but within a year they'd fallen in love, imploded their lives, and camped across America in a Volkswagen bus before settling for a while in Los Angeles.

When an addict in recovery suddenly moves to a different part of the state/country/world, that's called a geographic cure. My parents believed in big life changes and do-overs of all kinds. My sister, Susan, was born on the road. I came two years later. Mom got pregnant again almost immediately after they had me, and we moved north to Washington where my brother, Larry, was born in 1968, forever marking us Irish Twins. My parents wanted to be artists and actors, but a bohemian life was not in the cards. The coffeehouse they tried to open in eastern Washington failed to spark. Instead, Dad would commute every day to Seattle to work at the phone company while Mom would stay home with us kids, packing lunches and organizing AA meetings to be held in our living room. Weekends, we wore corduroy and went camping. It was the 1970s, and we were still a family, learning to fall in line and live out our respective roles. I was in the middle, the one who watched and waited.

WE LIVED IN a three-bedroom rambler-style house in a development on a cul de sac. Susan and I shared a bedroom, and Larry had his own. There were three styles of houses in this development, and that was the extent of the visual diversity there. Thickets of blackberry bushes separated our yard from the neighbors behind us, and fences separated the neighbors on each side. There was a path along the blackberry bushes that cut through the neighbor's yard behind the house to the bus stop we'd take to school until we were all old enough to drive. For entertainment we had a swing set and otherwise played in the street every day with the other kids in our neighborhood or listened to the trains roar down the tracks nearby.

You couldn't say we were poor but wouldn't say we made it all the way to middle class by today's standards either. The family car was an unreliable Chevy Impala with too many miles on it and an engine that would stall if you dared apply the brakes. Consequently, Mom had to teeter on the precipice of stopping when it was time to drop us in front of the school. We had to kind of jump out and hope for the best. I wasn't embarrassed or anything—most of my friends' families were in the same boat. At least my parents' thick accents were a source of fascination for my friends, who were moved to do impressions. They used words like "soda" instead of "pop" or "sofa" instead of "couch." I always wondered why they would want to move from the great City of New York all the way across the states to this grey and boring town where it rained all the time. Brooklyn had personality, and we lived basically Nowhere.

I've always had a reputation for being stubborn and prone to angry outbursts, even as a kid. In fourth grade Mrs. Johnson wrote on my report card that I needed to watch my "redhead hot temper." What can I say? I had a lot of unchanneled aggression. I was probably still angry with other adults I considered assholes, such as Mrs. Goodwin, who the year before had told my parents I was "uncoordinated." I don't know what she meant by that; maybe she meant "looks uncomfortable in a dress," which I will own. The bar for elementary schoolers wasn't set very high; at least I wasn't eating glue like Brent Stoller.

I was pretty androgynous then. Until about 8, Mom had been dressing me like my older sister for school each day: dresses and tights, little patent leather shoes. One day I told her I wanted to wear pants, and she said, "Well, this is what all the big girls are wearing." I remember thinking, *Exactly: no thanks*. She relented when we discovered the genius novelty clothing line called Garanimals, my saving grace. Match the animal tag on the shirt with the animal tag on the pants and you've got an outfit! After that, Mom tried to embrace my inner butch, which I still appreciate. She made sure to point it out whenever there was a woman doing a man's job. "That lady is driving a dump truck." Or "Look, that's a lady climbing that telephone pole! Isn't that neat?" She encouraged me to play soccer, which I loved and needed to blow off steam.

I knew at a young age that I wasn't a typical girl, that in some ways I had more in common with boys. I remember tag was the trendy recess game in first grade, but with boys as the chasers and girls as the chased. I didn't do anything about it, but I wanted to chase the girls, too. By third grade I'd figured out that I had a crush on the prettiest girl in class—Lorna—whom I quickly won over by winning the talent portion of the friendship competition. I discovered that if I could make someone laugh, I was in—they'd want to spend all their free time being entertained by me, and I could spend my time feeling okay about myself.

WHEN WE WERE still kids, our mother was pretty crafty. She had a creative side that she was always encouraging us to explore in ourselves. When Larry and I got it in our heads that we'd like to fly, Mom had an idea. She disappeared from the kitchen table for a few minutes and came back with art supplies: old newspaper, cardboard, some markers, scissors, and duct tape. Within minutes she'd fashioned paper wings to attach to our backs. I thought it was the most magical invention. With actual wings, I could pretend for real.

Growing up, I was a lot closer to my mom than my dad, who was decidedly neither creative nor sporty (though he could be very funny). His fiddling and his ever-present cigarettes were the things that defined him. Even when he took us camping, our hikes were less aerobic activities than gentle walks around the parameter of the tent. He was the type to keep to himself in the garage. You could always find him tinkering with electronics and he had a vast collection of wire spools and screws and odd pieces of metal for soldering, buckets of nuts and bolts, and tools of every kind. He just knew he would "need that someday" for some MacGyver ridiculousness. (C'mon Dad, I thought, *If it works, don't fix it.*)

There was always an overflowing ashtray in every single room of our house. He was a brooder, and maybe that's where I get it from, among other traits. I don't remember him ever exploding at us in anger, though Larry often cowered in his presence if he sensed Dad was in a mood.

It's part of family lore that when my sister Susan was born it was estimated that her soul's age was a confident 27. She knew exactly what she wanted out of life; indeed, she got her first job at 12 in order to save up for the Mustang she'd be driving by 16. It was as if she had never been a kid. I really grew up in her room—musically, for sure. That's the only time we ever really got along, when she would play her records and was feeling charitable enough to include me. Together we memorized Elton John's greatest hits. Thin Lizzy. Boom Town Rats. Some punk rock, too, The Clash. Gary Newman. Music was the only thing we had in common, though. Most of the time it was round after round of raging sibling rivalry— screaming and getting in each other's faces, me getting mad enough to throw a punch, it all ending with a bathroom door slammed and locked. There's a well-known AA slogan: "We're all here because we're not all there."

FIFTH GRADE WAS WHEN IT ALL BEGAN, the beginning of the end of innocence. My aborted preteen love life began with a slipped note from Scott Benson that read "WILL YOU GO WITH ME?" There were two boxes: one marked "YES" and one for "NO." I looked up from my desk and saw he had his head down in a book, pretending not to notice me noticing. I marked the YES box, folded it back up, and passed it to Stephen Markham, whose desk was next to Scott's. Instead of the smooth delivery I'd hoped for, Stephen unfolded the white notebook origami and laughed out loud before showing it to Scott. It was just a joke. I quickly turned back to face the board and tried to ignore their snickering, but my cheeks burned with mortification. I began to feel stupid in public. My social anxiety hit me right in my core, where I began to collect a feeling of heaviness in my chest, a constant physical reminder of my awkwardness.

Mom would tell me often that my curly, auburn hair was beautiful and that redheads were the rarest of the species. "You are *special*," she'd say, pointing out that I was the only one in the family to wear the Irish badge of courage. I strongly suspected she'd rehearsed these pep talks and was generally full of shit. After all, she was responsible for 50 percent of my genetic material, so no matter what I looked like she was going to go easy on the criticism. I secretly rejected her acceptance. It wasn't just the hair, but I wore glasses too, the one-two punch of school picture hell. Unfortunately, my glasses were just like my dad's, the type where the tinted lenses adjusted to the light (but never quickly enough). I thought it was cool that one could go outside and suddenly the glass would go dark like some kind of mood ring. But inside, they never quite registered as clear, especially during picture day, the images of which made me look like I'd been the recipient of recent cataract surgery.

There just weren't any options in those days; the nearby Sears Optical department in 1978 was not getting the fashion memos from Paris and New York. The best I could do for a couple years were a pair of simple silver metal frames. When I broke one of the arms of my glasses at the hinge, Dad insisted he could fix it himself in his workshop. He soldered the metal arm together where the hinge had been. Even though I could no longer fold them, and there was a weird blob of soldered metal by my ear for the rest of the year, they were fixed, according to him. That was my style: parent patented. I didn't know it at the time, but fifth grade was about to get worse.

In our room, Susan had this desk with three drawers—the top one was for pot, the middle drawer for booze, the bottom was full of bongs and random paraphernalia. So it stood to reason that the first time I got drunk it would happen right there. It was the last day of school for all of us, and Susan's boyfriend had procured a fifth of Bacardi 151. Larry was there, too. Susan was 14, I was 12, and Larry was 11. She just wanted us out of her hair, but her boyfriend poured me a double and mixed it with Coke. When I took that first sip and shared some with Larry, I immediately got the appeal. It wasn't the way it tasted—it was the warm blanket effect. It was the way I could feel the cold-but-warm liquid mixing with my blood, moving through my veins, encircling my spine, pulsing in my eardrum, making everything light, then heavy, erasing all that was negative, awkward, and angry. Instantly, and forever after, I wanted to feel that way all the time.

THIS WAS ONLY the beginning. I was finally free of my body, free of myself, everything that made me *me*. An insecure, fearful, clumsy, socially awkward redhead, and very likely a burgeoning lesbian. With that first drink it all disappeared. I finally felt a sense of calm, as if under a spell. I felt fearless and smart and attractive. This story is one I hear from all of my recovering friends. With the first drink or drug we feel finally "at home."

That summer, I began to make a habit of re-creating the experience. Apparently I wasn't discreet. It drove Susan crazy that I couldn't keep from slurring at the dinner table in front of our parents after one afternoon cocktail. Why couldn't I hold my liquor better? She'd whisper-scream to her boyfriend constantly that "Patty can't handle her drugs." At 11 and 12, she felt I should be honing my tolerance in private and protecting the sibling covenant—thou shalt not fuck it up for the rest of 'em. She needn't have worried, though; despite our parents' vast experience with alcohol abuse, no one seemed to notice.

Right around the time I had my first drink, Dad was becoming a regular at the Horseshoe Cafe—his favorite post-AA-meeting watering hole, where everybody went for recovery fellowship. There, in 1978, he met another woman and began an affair. It was a repeat of the way he and my mom had gotten together, but fifteen years and three kids later. Mom found out through the grapevine, and it wasn't long before they'd decided to divorce. When they told us at the dinner table one night, my immediate and lasting impression was fury. Yes, lots of people's parents were divorced—the neighbor girl, Kathy, who Larry and I played with after school, her parents were divorced. It had confused me to know it could happen to other kids (commonly and randomly), and growing up I'd asked my mother if she and Dad would ever consider it. "Of course not!" She'd say, as if she couldn't fathom where I'd even heard such a thing was possible. I blindly believed her and felt secretly smug that ours was an unbreakable family unit, even if I sometimes fantasized that Susan had been kidnapped or ran off with her older boyfriend.

When reality hit that our whole lives were about to change, I felt betrayed and enraged. My parents were liars; we'd all been living a lie. I was the only one I could count on now.

| 2 |

FLAMING YOUTH

It was the summer before sixth grade when Dad moved out. It was a surprise to no one that Susan would go with him—she was a real teenager now—and Larry and I would stay home with Mom. The two of them would move to Seattle and get an apartment, and we would visit with him on weekends. That was the idea anyway. The primary upside to my parents' divorce was that Susan would be out of my hair, and I'd get the bedroom and its dresser drawers all to myself. With her gone I was the oldest in the house—that included my mother, who was as absent from our lives as Dad and Susan.

For the first time in her life, our mother was free to experience her revolution from within. Even though she had to work, it was obvious that she enjoyed it much more than she'd enjoyed staying home with us and playing the role of housewife. Now she was free to reinvent herself once more. She promptly got a job at the General Phone Company (chief rival of Dad's employer, Pacific Bell) and got really politically active in AA. In short order she'd become the delegate for the entire state of Washington. This meant she had to speak at many conferences, and she left my brother and I alone during long weekends, to our great pleasure.

Once school started in the fall, there was a sharp contrast between our old and new lives. I was entering middle school, and it was the first time I was expected to take care of myself—get my brother up in the morning, take a shower, eat something, and get us to school on time. After school it was Doritos and Pepsi in front of "Donahue," then later I would prepare frozen Salisbury steak dinners for us in the microwave. At least there was always an array of processed foods to be found in the kitchen. Mom was good about shopping—it was the way she took care of us.

Whenever Mom was going to leave for a few days, she would take us to Sound City (the record store) and buy us anything we wanted. Larry and I would choose posters and records and issues of *Hit Parader* and *CREEM, Mad* magazine and *Monster Mag.* She stopped trying to dictate our bedtimes, so we stayed up late watching *Saturday Night Live* and monster movies. This is when we discovered KISS. Pop culture as parental penance.

Besides my brother, I didn't really have many other friends, though we did often play in the cul de sac with Jessica from across the street. She was the first girl to confirm for me that I was probably gayer than I wanted to be. At age 10 and 11, I needed a peer to confirm the weirdness of what was happening to our bodies, and Jessica was the same age. Even if she didn't live right next door, even if I'd liked Susan more, I would have wanted to hang out with Jessica. She had boobs and a wild older sister who threw parties with soundtracks by Heart when their parents were out of town. The family came from Texas and had a mysterious dad who'd worked border patrol outside Mexico. Once he'd made the switch to Canada, the family brought the Texas up to Washington. Jessica's mom had a distinctive accent and, like my parents, had different regional names for everyday items—she called a vacuum cleaner a "sweeper." When she called Jessica in from the yard, she'd always yell her first and middle name together: "Jessica Marie!" As if there was another Jessica nearby who needed that clarification.

Their dad had a stash of *Hustler* magazines in the garage that he didn't try to hide and a ton of guns and ammo that he didn't bother to lock up. Whenever I was over there, I came to expect to feel like I was in danger. It made things exciting. One day during hide and seek, Jessica and I kissed. I think for her it was just practice for middle school boys, but for me it was transcendent. It happened a few times and eventually stopped, which made lying near her in our sleeping bags during overnights in the backyard excruciating. We never spoke of it. Once the school year started up in the fall, Jessica got busier, and I saw less of her. I never expected things would go any differently.

That fall, Larry would become my first drug buddy. We liked the way smoking pot made music sound like we were swimming in an 8-track. That sealed it for me; I needed the daily ritual of substance abuse and rock 'n' roll. Vodka and Coke in my collectible Looney Tunes Tasmanian Devil glass went best with the swirly phaser breakdown of "Whole Lotta Love." Thank god the two coincided in my life while I was still young. What a waste of music not to take drugs!

LARRY AND I visited our father and discovered that he was still openly dating the lady from the meetings—and she had two little kids, who we were expected to hang out with. We were pretty disgusted, but what could we do? He was happy. Parts of his personality seemed brighter and more optimistic whenever he had a new girlfriend. He started listening to ABBA! He wore Jovan Musk! He began wearing a sheepskin jacket with a cowboy hat. Our father who hailed from Brooklyn suddenly preferred to listen to Swedish pop music and dress as if he lived in Oklahoma. Larry and I agreed it was easier to just go with the flow, keep the peace, and suffer through some awkward meals. It was worth it for his new relaxed approach to rules and curfews.

We preferred living with our mother because when we were home, we were usually alone. The joys of being latchkey kids! But it took only about nine months before Mom's absences alarmed the neighbors enough that they reported our abandonment to Child Protective Services. One day after school, a strange woman knocked on our door and asked where our mother was and if she often left us alone on weekends. Then more questions: *What do you eat for breakfast? How do you get to school?* I knew instinctively that our mom was in trouble and I should lie for her, but my excuses ("She's working, but we see her all the time") were not convincing enough. I felt betrayed by the neighbors and felt watched and paranoid. *Which one of you fuckers called the cops?*

Dad had to move back from Seattle to take care of us. Which meant Susan was back, too, and Mom moved into a nearby apartment. Susan now possessed a kind of citified worldliness that ensured Larry and I would be corrupted anew. By 13, I was openly carrying a pack of cigarettes—a habit that benefitted the whole family if someone happened to be out. It was a different smoking culture then; I even remember lighting up with Dad at that age *in* the grocery store. Dad remodeled the spare room that he'd used as a darkroom for his photography and made it into a tiny studio apartment with a private entrance for Susan.

He ran a much tighter ship than Mom, which I resented. There was a chart on the fridge that tracked the days and who was expected to do what, when. We each had one week on call for a specific task—dishes, vacuuming the rugs, making dinner—stuff a mom or a wife should be doing. (At least Dad gave me an allowance of $20 a week to buy cigarettes.) Maybe to make it up to me, he bought me a full drum kit.

WHEN I WAS 13, I'd signed up for the school jazz ensemble. Our band teacher suggested I try the clarinet or the flute, since those were the girl instruments. I did get to play a soft treatment of a Karen Carpenter song for the annual performance, but all the real drum parts went to the other drummer, Jason. The following year, I joined the marching band and had been practicing on a rented snare, learning to play "Yesterday" by the Beatles. I had a standard issue, rubber practice pad to put over the top, and I would play the first Cars record over and over on different parts of the drum, even the rim, and I'd play as if I had a full kit in front of me. Now that I had my own kit, I could practice all the time and increase my repertoire. I quickly learned to play "Riff Raff" by AC/DC. I had it on a record—*If You Want Blood You've Got It*—and every day I'd drop the needle over and over, stopping and starting. I kept the drum set right next to my bed and played as often as I was home.

Maybe it was triggered by my parents' divorce, or maybe I was feeling weird and defective at the idea that I might be gay, maybe it was in my genes. Whatever the trigger, I had all this aggression, and I needed to channel it. Anger is just one letter away from danger. I liked the idea that I could play an instrument that girls weren't supposed to, that I could pretend I was someone else. Playing music, I could leave my body. And I loved that drumming hurt.

Drumming is a bloodsport, like boxing. It's not for wimps. Part of developing the necessary stamina is to teach yourself to play through pain, something that women do particularly well. I'm giving this kid lessons right now, and we've been doing a lot of double bass work, and the other day he got his first big blister and was surprised by how much it hurt. He really didn't like it when I told him he had to pop it—that the only way through is to nurture those calluses. Your hands have to be like leather. But that's just number one—that's not even the painful part. When I'm playing I am hitting those things as hard as I can. It's not uncommon to smash a finger on the rim or to open up fresh blisters or old wounds. Some people tape their fingers and ice their knuckles, but I prefer to let it bleed.

| 3 |

ONE O' THE GIRLS

Adolescence. Oh God, red hair, and glasses. That was me in a nut-shell, the dark side of a John Hughes movie. Also: GAY. A bur-geoning lesbian, which seemed like the most embarrassing, obvious thing. When I'd experience a flare-up, such as the time I'd made a pass at my best friend, drunkenly trying to kiss her, stupidly, in-sanely—that's when I'd blame it on being drunk. Alcohol gave me the bravery I needed to obliterate my self-esteem. I came out to my mother, who was supportive but unable to make me feel any better.

The only thing that did, at 14, 15, 16, was this intense sense of connection I felt listening to punk music. I'd discovered a weird Canadian radio station, which first introduced me to the Fall, Wire, and the Butthole Surfers, the bands that would ultimately open me up to the possibility of a career spent repeatedly hitting things with sticks until they break. Punk had a violence that appealed to me. Instead of dancing or jumping up and down, going to shows was an excuse to crash into people or experience the delicious thrill of an accidental black eye. In the pit, everyone was equal. Girls were no different—there just weren't very many of them.

When it came to my blossoming sexuality (so to speak), there weren't enough girls to choose from, so I'd have to make do with boys. I would have preferred not to be different in this regard. I wanted *to want to* spend seven-minutes-in-heaven with a guy. My chance came at my friend Debbie's birthday party in eighth grade. Debbie was hanging out with a kid named Bobby, and Bobby had a friend named Pat, who seemed nice enough and wore the same wire-rimmed glasses as I. Pat and Patty, it was perfectly obvious. As Billy Joel's new wave record, *Glass Houses*, played, the four of us danced awkwardly while attempting to make out without using our tongues. I was not excited about or interested in any of it; I just wanted to be doing whatever everybody else was.

| 4 |

NEW TOWN

You know, it's always the same. Somehow when you're 15 years old, there's always a Matthew McConaughey in *Dazed & Confused*-guy willing to buy the beer. I learned how to procure the party by loitering in liquor store parking lots with Susan, who was herself 17. It was 1982, and all you had to do was slip the guy $5. My sister was back, and Mom was out—she moved to an apartment ten minutes away in a town called Everett. We saw her on the weekends, and everything changed. At least when Mom had been around, she'd compulsively cleaned up after us.

Now I spent a lot more time partying outside the house. It was the time of ragers in the woods with the other children of divorce in town, the heshers, and the rockers. The heshers were identifiable by their Pink Floyd T-shirts, their ubiquitous roaches, and their Pontiac GTOs. The rockers wore leather jackets and Reebok high-tops with their jeans tucked in. All of the farm kids were into their Country and Western, hardcore. I swear I've seen some line dances, a little do-si-do in a parking lot. Chewing tobacco was the great equalizer; in the woods, we were all hicks.

My social life really opened up when I started playing music. That was the common thread for all my relationships. If you liked the Ramones, you could come over to my house and I could play you all the songs on the first record. That's how my first band Milkbone came to be. It was made up of five like-minded weirdos—my friends Joe, Erica, Danny, and Kevin (and also sometimes Erica's sister, Michelle, would hang out and dance, just cause). Band practice launched in my bedroom, but eventually we moved my drums over to Dan's house where we were able to spread out and record a tape of all our original songs (and our lone cover of a Ventures song). We were pretty confident about our songs and started playing all over town: at house parties, in basements, a barn, and the high school cafeteria. Everybody loved us, even the goths, which was surprising considering we had kind of a B-52s vibe.

Despite the fact that I was typically a person who isolated, I wasn't nervous when I was playing in front of a crowd. Of course, I was drinking before and during shows. It was beginning to be something I would become known for: up-for-anything-Patty, who didn't mind a trip down a flight of stairs if there was more to drink at the bottom. I was always taking it too far. Making a fool out of myself, hurting myself in order to prove that nothing was really that painful. My senior year of high school was a turning point, the year I really chose alcohol above all else.

I had a crush on one of my friends, Lucy, who I had a few classes with. Lucy was a cheerleader and had blonde hair and blue eyes. She laughed at my jokes and expressed interest in Milkbone and good music in general. I knew she probably wasn't gay, but a girl can dream. It was hard not to fantasize about being with her when she was so easy to talk to, and we both liked the same bands. She wasn't much into drinking, though. That was okay—I could drink enough for both of us.

One night that fall, Lucy and I went to Seattle together to see the Ramones. Her sister went to U-Dub (the University of Washington), and we'd planned to crash on her dorm room floor. I couldn't wait to see the show, as the Fastbacks were opening, and I idolized Kim Warnick, the bass player who made punk sound so musical. That night, we should have been able to enjoy our slumber party. Instead, I would spend most of it in jail.

It didn't even take that long. When the show was set to begin in fifteen minutes, I went out to the parking lot with Lucy and a few friends to smoke and down a 40-ounce beer. It was a ritual I craved, almost as fun as the part where we'd drink inside while the band played, and then drink some more after it was all over. Within minutes an unmarked police car rolled up, and two plainclothes cops started barking orders at us. "IDs, IDs . . . We're gonna need to see IDs!"

In the late 1980s in Seattle there was a movement against the all-ages rock show—part of a crackdown on the teenage "riots" people feared were incited by punk music but were actually the product of kids being menaced by the police. As soon as they descended, most of the kids in the parking lot dispersed, not wanting to miss the show. But I held my ground, not wanting to put my bottle down. I didn't want to not have it just because of these clowns.

The cops turned their attention on me. "How old are you?"

I looked them in the eye but didn't answer. "Why don't you put your drink down and show us your identification." I was emboldened not just by alcohol but by the small crowd that stayed to watch, including Lucy. "What's your name?"

I came up with a clever answer: "Fuck. You." And that was the first time I was ever handcuffed and arrested.

At the precinct they called my mom. I seem to remember choosing her over my dad for that conversation, thinking defensively that maybe this wouldn't have happened if I weren't the daughter of a professional recovering alcoholic who hadn't been much of a disciplinarian to begin with. Plus, she might not be as hard on me since she herself was in trouble with CPS and was now living alone. She was pissed, but she did come to pick me up, and while I would be grounded for more than a month by my parents, my punishment from the county was minimal. I had to write a letter of apology to the officer who I'd offended with my use of the F-word. That was all it took to get that cleared from my permanent record, to ask nicely.

I could tell my mom anything, but I would never tell her how much I drank or what drugs I'd started using. When I started to realize that I was gay and the pain of that secret was too much, I had to tell her. I got my chance when I got drunk on New Year's Eve and made a pass at a straight friend and was so full of shame and humiliation that I let it all out. I sat on my mother's couch and put my head in my hands and cried. I wanted to disappear and then kill myself (in that order). Mom sat close and listened to me tell her that I was in love with a girl and it would not be reciprocated.

She hugged me tight and told me that it was okay and there was nothing wrong with me, that there was a whole wide world out there outside the small town of Marysville, and I would find my people.

My greatest fear was that everyone would *know*, that people would talk. I just hoped that if people were gossiping, it would be about my drinking and not my being gay. After all, only one of those things was socially acceptable.

| 5 |

CREDIT IN THE STRAIGHT WORLD

When I met Raegan Butcher (not a pseudonym) at Railmakers warehouse in Everett, I was inspired to make him my boyfriend. We had mutual friends who were starting a punk band; Raegan would be the singer, and I would play the drums. The guitarist Danny had a Fender Telecaster and played a lot of Clash and Husker Du songs. Tommy, the bass player, was a great musician but had only ever played jazz. He thought that punk rock was funny and a bit beneath him. These guys grew up together in an even smaller town than Marysville called Snohomish; it's all farms and football there. We called ourselves the Primitives.

It was the summer of 1986. Our first real show where we were paid actual money was at Industrial Noise in Tacoma. We were on a lineup with the Melvins and were paid $6 apiece (or $24 for gas). To celebrate after the show we did speed and drank forty ouncers outside. Afterward, the guys went back into the club, and Raegan and I made out in the van. He was cute and funny, and I loved playing music with him, but most of all I was determined to be straight. Sex was awkward, but that seemed to be expected based on what I'd heard and imagined; the first Stooges record was playing, and when Iggy sang "No Fun," I agreed. So I went on birth control and just accepted that this was the way it would be for me.

One night the guys and I went to Seattle to see the Beastie Boys during their "Licensed to Ill" tour. We were there to see the hardcore band Murphy's Law open for their friends from NYC, but the show wasn't what I'd expected. It was my first experience with what I guess you could call feminist rage. The Beastie Boys were pouring beer on the floor of the stage and telling the girls in the audience they could come on stage too, if they mopped up the beer. The guys in my band all thought it was hilarious, but I was furious. During the drive home they kept telling me to chill out and lighten up — "It's only a joke, and it was funny."

I liked being one of the guys, but these situations kept coming up for me. I realized that I'd grown up just accepting that if you were a girl, especially a girl drummer, the guy at the music store was gonna talk down to you. The guys I worked with were going to make gross jokes and call their ex-girlfriends bitches, and I would go along with it because that was the way of the world, just the reality of being a woman. Raegan and I stayed together for about six months, and when we broke up, so did the band.

Ultimately, I wanted to be in a band that stood for something, a band whose songs weren't about the joys of pizza day in the high school cafeteria.

BEING IN A BAND is like having a girlfriend, and when you break up you think you'll never find another person like that again, but then you do. When I'm in between bands I feel lost, like I'll never have that again, but then the phone rings.

I was living in Everett, sharing a place with my mom and working as a subcontractor installing telephone wiring into commercial buildings, carrying on the family tradition of working for the phone company. I hated the way guys would talk about women on the jobsite, hated being the only one that had to pick up the lunch order, hated being talked down to. I wanted to play drums in a new band. Playing drums made all the shitty jobs a little bit less shitty.

Finally my friend Helen called—she was getting an all-girl thing together, would I be willing to make the commute? She and the guitarist, Cathy, both lived in Seattle, and Mara and Annette (vocals and bass) lived in Tacoma. I packed my drums into my convertible Volkswagen and happily made the long drive to Annette's house. We tried out a few ideas, found that we clicked, and started practicing every weekend. I liked the fact that we were all girls, but I wanted our band to be heavier, like Mudhoney. If it couldn't be heavy, I preferred something bigger, or more atmospheric, like Galaxie 500. Our sound was lighter, more pop, but it was better for me to be making music than not.

Doll Squad's first show was at Community World Theater in Tacoma, opening for our friends in Girl Trouble. On the way home from the show, I was drunk and driving back to Everett when I hit a light pole getting onto the freeway. Totaled my car, lost my drums, and of course the police came. I was charged with driving under the influence and had to pay the city for the light pole. This was the second time I'd been arrested in regard to my drinking, and I wasn't even legally allowed to consume it.

Now that I didn't have a car, Cathy was my designated driver to and from practice. She lived on Capitol Hill in Seattle, had a lime green 1960s Nova, and her apartment looked like a kitschy vintage shop—she was the queen of collectibles. She worked nights as a lab tech at the blood bank but was one of those people who always expressed herself with clothes; she would usually finish off an outfit with a hat. I would go to her apartment before practice and listen to records while she got ready to go. I was sitting down on the floor in front of her records holding that first Psychedelic Furs record when the phone rang. It was Helen saying that practice was cancelled.

I put on the Furs record, went to the refrigerator, grabbed a beer, and drank it fast. There was always a six pack of some imported beer in Cathy's fridge, which puzzled me. *Who keeps a six pack of beer sitting in their fridge for weeks?* Beer was meant to be obtained and consumed in the same night. I wouldn't hold it against her, though; I felt safe with Cathy, like I could tell her some secrets and it would be ok.

"What do you want to do now that there's no practice?" I asked.

"I guess this is it," Cathy looked at me, half smiling. "Drink beer and listen to records?" We kissed against the wall, and as the drums kicked in on "India," we tripped backward over her guitar case.

I moved in a month later.

| 6 |

DOLL SQUAD

It was 1987, and I was living in Capitol Hill in Seattle. When I moved into Cathy's, I didn't have much, just my clothes and drums. A friend of my mom's sold me his MG convertible, a small two-seat sports car (probably not the best choice considering how I totaled my last one). It had a cassette player but no room for drums. Instead we'd loaded my drums into Cathy's Nova. I got a job as a flagger for a construction company. I would get up early and drive out to wherever the work site was, always in some rural area on these country roads. I liked being out in the middle of nowhere most days, and it was an easy job to do with a hangover, which I always had. When I got home each day, I'd see Cathy for an hour before she would leave for the blood bank. While she was gone, I'd grab a bottle of vodka and tomato juice and make giant Bloody Marys to drink through-out the night.

I wouldn't turn 21 until April, and I had never been to a gay bar, so Cathy suggested we go to Canada, where the drinking age was 19. Our neighbor Jake was from Vancouver. He was always in a chair in the courtyard garden listening to Barbara Streisand. We would stop and talk on the way to our car. "*GIRLS*, you will love it up there!" He took out a pen and notepad and gave us the address for a gay club called Numbers Cabaret. That weekend we made the two-and-a-half hour trip across the border, and we found our way to Davies Street and the club.

I was really nervous. There were a lot of men and just a few women. We found a booth to sit in and watched the dance floor and the pool table. The music was all disco, Madonna, and Janet Jackson. There were leather daddies in chaps, the straight-up Tom of Finland style. There were a few Don Johnson wannabes, with their perfectly coiffed hair and pastel Izod shirts. A few new wave boys with full makeup would only dance during a Communards or Marc Almond song. I brought a pillbox filled with cross top speed (ephed-rine) that I'd purchased from one of the guys at work. Over the course of the night, I took about ten of those just to stay up. This was tech-nically the first time I smuggled drugs across a border.

After I came out and started living with Cathy, I got really in-spired by activist groups like the Lavender Ladies and ACT UP, and I attended my first gay pride parade. It made me feel like part of a huge community instead of a small one. Gay pride also meant day drinking. The parade would start before noon, so everyone would meet beforehand for breakfast and Bloody Marys. When I started drinking, I couldn't stop. Everyone else had a mimosa and eggs benedict, and I had a Bloody Mary, four shots of bourbon, and a couple beers. When the parade ended, it's more drinks and preferably some speed or cocaine. I never made it to work the day after.

DOLL SQUAD REHEARSED at Music Bank, a well-known rehearsal space for bands in yet another warehouse. Inside there were a bunch of practice rooms, and we shared one with the Sub Pop band Catbutt. Music Bank was later known as the home base of Alice in Chains and Mother Love Bone (later Pearl Jam). Layne Staley and Jerry Cantrell practically lived there; they definitely had all the keys. The scene at MB was more metal than punk and what would be called grunge, a kind of hip-ified garage metal that became synonymous with Seattle in the early 1990s. One day we were loading our gear into our room, when a sweaty, long-haired rocker guy sticks his head into our open door, and says, "Oh, hey, you guys are all girls." To which we said, "Yes."

I looked at this skinny rocker with unfortunate facial hair (his beard had a braid), who was also wearing a conch belt that was holding up shorts over long underwear—it was Layne Staley. Not long after, Alice in Chains bass player Mike Starr made an appearance. He was almost too pretty and had this soft, flowing hair down to the middle of his chest. After that first meeting, I started to see a lot of those guys, but especially Layne, since we also shared a number of mutual friends.

Our band sometimes played at the Community World Theater—this great big old converted movie house in Tacoma—and that's where I first saw Nirvana at one of their early shows. They performed this incredible set, where they memorably closed with a cover of CCR's "Bad Moon Rising." (This was pre-*Bleach*, their debut on Sub Pop.) The drummer then was this mustached guy named Dave Foster, who looked like a 1970s porn star or a cast member of *Magnum P.I.*

I'd known Kurt Cobain from around the scene since probably 1986. He'd roadied for the Melvins when the Primitives opened for them in Tacoma, and we went to a lot of the same shows in Seattle and Olympia, where he lived. Kurt was easy to be around, and we were the same age. We shared a legacy of broken homes and high school alienation in working-class Washington, getting jumped in the Dairy Queen parking lot, being outcasts. And we liked the same bands and movies from the 1970s—*Over the Edge, Times Square,* and *Foxes*—all about hell-raising teenagers, all best friends; we knew all the lines. As much as I liked him, I don't think anyone was like, *There's a prophet among us,* or anything—we were too in the middle of it. At that point, Nirvana was amazing in the same way the new Mudhoney record was amazing. Kurt was great, but he was no Mark Lanegan.

I should clarify that Kurt was just like anyone else until he picked up his guitar. There was definitely a buzz around his abilities. Back then the way insiders traded music was with duplicated cassette tapes. Larry had a Maxell tape of Nirvana playing a live set on "Audioasis," a radio show on KCMU—the UW college station. They played "Paper Cuts," "Floyd the Barber," and some early *Bleach* outtakes. There was something about his singing voice— when you heard it clearly, you could feel it physically.

Doll Squad was set to open for Nirvana at the Central Tavern a little later that year when Chad Channing was playing with them. I remember watching the band unload their equipment. Chad's drums were notable because they were North drums, which have open-ended toms that look like upside down pieces of elbow macaroni and filter sound outward. I'd only ever seen them in magazines. Anyway, as soon as they got everything out to set up, something happened that made it impossible to play, and the whole lineup was cancelled. It was okay because this affected the night of about forty people.

One night I went to see Black Flag with a couple of girlfriends, and afterward, in the parking lot, we met three big, imposing dudes wearing trench coats over flannel shirts. They told us they were in a band called Screaming Trees. We listened to their cassette on the way home, and it was like, holy shit, these guys are awesome. Then I saw them play not long after with Beat Happening. This was a typical Thursday night in Seattle—it was just that easy to be blown away.

I knew this couple, Faye & Tad; they lived in Capitol Hill, aka the "gayborhood." I found out soon after our first meeting that Layne lived right upstairs from them. A bunch of us would hang out at Faye & Tad's, just drinking and getting high. After my tween years, pot lost its effect. I considered it a waste of time, like if there was nothing else, I guess I would maybe give it another go (and I would feel sorry for myself as I did). Layne was a classic stoner, and I was a classic drunk. It all seemed so innocent then. Of course, even when it happened to Nirvana, nobody could imagine that any one of us would ever go on to have any impact ourselves.

THE FIRST TIME I took heroin I injected it, or I should say my friend injected it for me. One night Angela and I went to a show in Seattle, and after we felt safely drunk, she mentioned that she had some dope, but nowhere to take it. I knew that Helen, our singer, had her own place—we immediately went there and shot up in Helen's bathroom. I had never taken heroin before, but for some reason I didn't think it was a big deal, even injecting it—I don't think I was aware that there are other ways to take it. I was an equal opportunity substance ingestion specialist. I asked Angela to do the honors since I didn't want to mess it up, but she seemed nervous about the dosage and ultimately gave me just a little bit. I would have characterized the experience as just okay, nothing mind-blowing. Just another thing to do in Seattle.

I met Bruce Pavitt, the founder of Sub Pop records, when Doll Squad played one of his Sunday showcases at the Vogue (3 bands, $2 at the door). I was 20, and he was in his 30s at the time, but somehow he didn't seem so old. We became fast friends, and he invited me over to his apartment, which was a few blocks away from ours; I went over a few days later. Bruce had just quit his job at Muzak, which is a company that distributes background music for stores, offices, and elevators. (In the late 1980s in Seattle, Muzak was *the* place to work if you were in a band. Mark Arm from

Mudhoney worked there, Ron from Love Battery, Tad Doyle). Now he could focus full-time on promoting the bands he championed.

He had more records than anyone I'd ever met—vinyl in every color covered every wall. He showed me the first Soundgarden EP called *Screaming Life;* the cover image was by Charles Peterson, who would go on to become a notable photographer of the scene. Next Bruce handed me the latest Green River record called *Rehab Doll.* They had just broken up, but Mark Arm was already in a new band, Mudhoney. He showed me the cover art for their upcoming first single "Touch Me I'm Sick," which was destined to be a hit.

"See, it will be on brown vinyl, and the cover art is a toilet." Indeed.

After talking about the sonic virtues of producer Steve Albini from Big Black, I was given a stack of stuff to take home: the very first White Zombie record (before they signed with Geffen, back when they sounded a lot like Pussy Galore). Dinosaur Jr.'s "You're Living All Over Me," the Vaselines's EP, "Dying For It," and the Pixies's debut *Surfer Rosa.* The days spent at Bruce's were like college courses in rock.

Doll Squad started playing fewer shows. Cathy wanted a change. She had some friends in Portland and liked it there. She decided to move and asked me to go with her. I loved her, but I loved Seattle, too, and hadn't burned too many bridges yet. I helped her pack her apartment. We would stay friends.

| 7 |

SYBIL

In the stack of records Bruce gave me was the first Spaceman 3 record, *The Perfect Prescription*. I sent it to Larry, and he became obsessed with the cover art, which prominently featured a Fender Jaguar. When we were just starting a new band called Sybil, I bought Larry a cheapo guitar, a no-name brand, and he made good use of it, but once he saw the Jaguar, he started saving up for the real thing. That's when I knew he was really serious about being in a band, and by the time we'd booked our first real show, he had the Fender of his dreams.

Sybil was Larry, me, and Tammy Watson, who lived across the hall from Nil's Bernstein—future publicist for Nirvana and Sub Pop, in a old house made into four small apartments on Howell

Street where everyone hung out and passed through. Then there was Dale who had moved from Denver—she had a car. Then, this guy Robin was our bass player—so talented. Our first rehearsal was in an abandoned house everyone called the Black House. It was on a street called Denny Way right off 15th. We don't know why it still had electricity, but it did. We eventually moved out to George-town—an industrial neighborhood alongside the trains and the Boeing Field.

For as long as I could remember, Olympia had been a hub of the music scene in Washington. A city known for its DIY record labels (like K. Records since 1982, and in 1991, Kill Rock Stars), it also had a reputation for breeding crafty feminists and sex-positive bee-keepers. Influential bands like Beat Happening, Bikini Kill, Sleater-Kinney, and a hundred predecessors all came out of Olympia. I'd been going there to see shows since 1986, and it was always a scene, but we couldn't have known then that anyone from Olympia would be remembered, let alone iconized.

There was a group of us who would make the hour-long commute between Seattle and Olympia every week to see and be seen. The usual suspects: Kurt of Nirvana; Dylan Carlson of the heavy, droney band Earth; and his friend Slim Moon, who would go on to found the label Kill Rock Stars. Together they had a side project called Lush. All the guys seemed to have long, wavy hair then, and the girls liked theirs short. A couple years before Bikini Kill came together, their drummer Tobi Vail was known for her fanzine, *Jig-saw*—one of the more prominent zines to have influenced the riot grrrl movement. At the time, Kathleen Hanna was in another band called Viva Knieval, and a fixture of the scene.

Sybil's first 7-inch was for a song called "Olympia," which was our hit, you could say. *In Olympia, where the boys are lonely / In Olympia, where the girls don't know me*. It was a song about the difference between our two cities. Olympia was where all the straight-edge punks lived, and Seattle laughed in the face of its sobriety. We made fun of those "good kids" from Olympia and their "cuddle core" or "pal rock," as we called it sometimes—could you really call yourself a punk if people went to your shows for a hug?

IN 1990 I was living in Capitol Hill with Larry and stuffing things in boxes at Microsoft just before the scene blew up. Most nights Sybil would practice in a crappy space in Georgetown, which was then an industrial wasteland. We shared it with another Sub Pop band called Blood Circus (which would later label themselves as the band that Nirvana once opened for), and Tree People (which ended up becoming Built to Spill). Pretty much everyone hung out there. One night after one of our practices, I went to a house party in north Seattle and saw a girl dancing by herself (or maybe I couldn't see anyone else around her). She'd put on a Saints record, which might have been enough on its own if she weren't so amazingly hot. When I was introduced—her name was Jenn—I noticed she was wearing a piece of masking tape with the word "Phranc" on it, who was a self-described Jewish lesbian folksinger and longtime member of the punk scene. Another lesbian! I instantly became fixated by the idea of us together. She worked at a diner called Mae's, which quickly became my new favorite restaurant.

The very next day I went to Mae's, and Jenn wasn't working. I covertly asked one of her colleagues for Jenn's number. I then proceeded to call her about nine times in twelve hours, only to hang up from nerves. Eventually, I gathered the courage to ask her to come see Sybil open for Mudhoney. I kept looking for her in the crowd and felt that anxious suspense you get in your gut. The relief when she showed was orgasmic. I think the drums sealed the deal for her. Our first date was on the 4th of July, and we were pretty inseparable after that. Jenn made me look at things differently. The music I listened to, the artists I liked. She was constantly reading, and when I wasn't in her bed, she had her head in a book.

But very quickly my drinking started to get in the way. Jenn had a normal relationship with alcohol and no real problem with hangovers. She could take LSD once in a while, maybe if we went camping or something, but she couldn't relate to my habits. Since I had early mornings at Microsoft, I stayed out as late as possible just so I could have more time to drink. Consequently our sleeping schedules weren't in sync. She started to complain that the effects were noticeable.

Six months into dating, Jenn told me she wanted to take a break. It was an agonizing three days apart. I drove past her house a hundred times. It wouldn't be the last time I made a promise to a girlfriend that "this time" would be "different." I told her I'd stop drinking so much, just drink beer, only on the weekends, whatever I had to say.

After a year of dating, Jenn was getting antsy to leave Seattle. She was okay during the summers, but once the grey rain took over the other nine months of the year, her mood really suffered. We both had friends in San Francisco, and it was a city where we could work. It was hard to leave Sybil behind—it was a band I loved and believed in—but I couldn't risk losing Jenn. And it would be good to ditch Microsoft.

We moved in November and got a place in the Mission District. She got a job pretty quickly, teaching ESL, and I got a job working in the shipping department at a medical supply warehouse. I went out every night to scout bands to join. It made me anxious whenever I wasn't playing drums. I eventually ended up in a band called Dumbhead with Dale Crover's girlfriend, Debbie Shane. Debbie and I shared a similar taste in music, and we got to use the Melvins's practice space. I practiced on Dale's drum kit, which was unique. It featured a huge marching snare with a woven Kevlar drumhead, attached were odd metal pieces to hit. Sitting behind something so majestic felt more like being in the cockpit of an industrial tank.

It was good to be around familiar faces. The last time I'd seen the Melvins, the Primitives were opening for them, and Kurt was their roadie. Now Kurt was on the cover of *Rolling Stone* in a T-shirt that said CORPORATE MAGAZINES STILL SUCK, discussing the fact that his new record had sold 3 million copies in four months. Everyone in Seattle had gone to the record release party at Re-Bar—it felt like a totally normal level of success, the occasional limo ride or the band's name in lights. Now MTV was playing "Smells Like Teen Spirit" at least once an hour (not that I had cable to see it), and Nirvana was on a six-week European tour. Being in S.F. made me homesick for our friends and the scene back home.

At my job my responsibilities included enduring a constant barrage of Phil Collins's "Sussudio" seemingly on repeat for hours while I stuffed boxes. That's what I got for skipping college (not that college was ever even discussed as an option in our house). It wasn't what I wanted to be doing for money, that was clear; I needed my future in music to start now. The monotony of the days made it easy for me to justify the fact that I drank as much as ever, if not more.

Things were getting increasingly messy between Jenn and me because of it. She resented picking me up drunk from bars on Mission Street at least once a week, and if she wanted to see me most nights, she'd have to pull up a stool. We did try to mix things up. We made friends with a couple other dykes who were really into speed. In order to even out the effects of the alcohol, I started taking crystal meth with them. I thought of it as a shot of espresso, a real cheerer-upper. I was convinced it made me look sober to Jenn. Whenever we'd get into an argument, I'd yell, and she always seemed pretty calm. Then I'd leave and get drunk and come back in the middle of the night. I started most of the arguments just so I could have a reason to leave and get drunk.

I think we both believed that I would stop overdoing it once we moved out of Seattle, that the move would be my geographic cure. You figure it's everything or everyone around you that makes you drink, not what's inside of you. But that's how you know you're an addict, when the fresh start never stops. That year marked the first time I would be forced to consider I might have a problem with alcohol. I knew it was fucked up, but what could I do? Overdoing it was in my genes, and I had plenty of good years left of socially acceptable inebriation before I'd ever seriously consider stopping after two or three beers.

WHEN MY FRIEND Dylan Carlson called one day that spring to tell me that Kurt had recommended me to his wife, Courtney Love, who was looking for a drummer for her band, Hole, I didn't hesitate to say yes to an audition in L.A. I knew a little bit about Hole—Sybil had opened for them once in Seattle at Off-Ramp before their debut album was released, but I'd never officially met Courtney. Though Nirvana was now on track to sell millions of records, Hole was the band I'd been hearing about for years. Courtney was already notorious and surrounded by myth; the stories about her were legendary: she was Jerry Garcia's illegitimate daughter, she was the heir to the Bausch & Lomb Corporation, she'd burned a house down but made sure the cats got free. Every rumor about her seemed to be worthy of an exclamation point.

Eric Erlandson sent me a tape of the first record and some live bootlegs of new songs they played during a recent tour with Mudhoney. I thought *Pretty on the Inside* was all right, but I tended to like less noisy songs with more structure. I really liked the new songs, though, especially "Violet." Not to brag, but I knew I had a lot to offer this band. I had a good feeling.

Dale wasn't worried about me passing the audition, but he did give me a pointed warning: Kurt and Courtney weren't afraid of heroin, and heroin was bad news.

| 8 |

JABBERJAW

I packed my drums in the back of my car and drove down to L.A. to meet with Eric Erlandson in a coffee shop. We talked things through—he and Courtney wanted to produce a more melodic sound for a new record with more structure than the first record, *Pretty on the Inside*. Eric was looking for a drummer who could keep time amid Courtney's chaotic transitions. We got together immediately after to work on some of their catalogue. I liked the songs. (I also noticed that the main riff to "Mrs. Jones" was copied verbatim from "Dark Entries" by Bauhaus.) And Eric seemed to respond to me, too. I'll never forget when I sent him a demo tape of a bunch of my work, and he called and said, "Is this really you? Playing drums?" It was as if he couldn't believe it.

It was April 24, 1992, my twenty-fifth birthday, when we set up at Jabberjaw, a coffeehouse turned all-ages nightclub on Pico. The first time I saw her she was wearing a blue gingham dress and knee socks. It's now a Courtney cliché—the bleached blonde hair, red lipstick, bruised knees in a prom dress, chronically late—certainly no one you could ever forget even if you wanted to. I set up my drums, took off my shoes, and played three of their songs on the sweat lodge of a stage for Eric, who stood brooding with his guitar against the Tiffany blue walls of the bar. Kurt had come with her, but I think he listened from the other room, not wanting to be too much of an influence. Even with the fan Courtney insisted he purchased from Rite Aid down the block, I was sweating all over that place, and thought I'd faint from dehydration. After a rousing version of the Wipers's song "Over the Edge," we finally went outside to get some air.

"What kind of drugs do you do?" Courtney asked first thing, dragging on a Winston.

"Speed, I guess. And alcohol," I said, leaving out the rest of the truth. "But I don't play when I'm fucked up."

"Braggart. Do you want to be my drummer?" I told her I did.

"Fine, it's settled," she said, "You'll come stay with Kurt and me."

It became obvious really quickly that she was going to become a significant person in my life.

WHEN I RETURNED home to Jenn a few days later, I had already been invited to join the band and had plans to move immediately to Los Angeles. During the drive back, I saw it all very clearly. I would move into the spare bedroom at Kurt and Courtney's place on Alta Loma Terrace in Hollywood. I knew I'd spend half my time in Seattle, where Nirvana and Hole were co-based. I suspected that Jenn would decide she would stay in S.F., and we would have a long-distance relationship for a while until it was no longer feasible. I knew

I would visit a few times but mostly call her when I was drunk in the middle of the night. She would come down to L.A. or up to Seattle to see me, but how long could that really sustain itself? I knew what I wanted was to travel, to play all over the world and meet my favorite musicians, and to make out with beautiful strangers.

But the day after I got back to S.F., the verdict in the Rodney King case came down, and the subsequent riots shut down the city—L.A. was burning. We devised a new plan to reconvene in Seattle once the dust settled. In the meantime, Courtney called me at least once a day to talk. I soon learned that she was notorious for her phone calls (and her phone bills). At first I thought it was a bonding exercise and an extension of my audition—it was important that we had the same pop and punk references and that she trusted her drummer and vice versa. But I soon discovered it was more than that. Courtney had to talk like some people have to smoke a cigarette; she was always fiending for conversation. She never slept, so most of those calls would come in around 2 or 3 in the morning.

I've heard Courtney's conversational style described as playing pinball. The subject matter would shift from a new idea for a song, to industry gossip, to reflections on something she'd experienced earlier that day, to a story about herself at 5 years old—all in three minutes or less. Sometimes she'd ask a question of whomever she was talking to, but the focus wouldn't stay there long. With us at first there was a lot of talk about music, and had I seen the new issue of *NME*? What did I think about Blur? She could quote something Morrissey said in a 1987 magazine profile and come up with the source material just as quickly.

MY GEAR WAS in L.A. full time, so when in Seattle I borrowed from a friend. Everyone seemed to have a house with a basement in the U district near the university, where there were always many houses to rent. It was pretty common for a group of six friends to share a house/practice space, and there was a punk rock version a lot of bands would use. I went over one afternoon to practice, and while I was taking a break in the kitchen, I saw a girl coming up the stairs from the basement. She had just finished practicing with her band, Sour Puss. *A drummer*, I thought—she was holding her sticks. She sat on the couch with a beer.

"Hi, I'm Patty, and Eric said I could use his drums." She looked at me, all big eyes and blue-black hair, and didn't say a word. I took that as a challenge. I sat down on the edge of couch next to her, waiting as the rest of her band finished packing their gear. I picked up a magazine with Pearl Jam on the cover and asked, "What are they wearing? Are those shorts, or are they pants?" They were wearing long shorts over long underwear.

"They're Shants!" She looked at me and smiled a little, then laughed. Swoon. (Her name was Polly.)

We started hanging out, and I'd go watch her band play, or Larry and I would go visit her at her job at Pagliacci Pizza, eat lunch for free, and wait for her to get off work. She had the best sense of humor, and we made each other laugh a lot. She had a really clever style and would sew clothes and alter them, make new dresses out of old ones. Polly was also someone I could drink and take drugs with. This was when heroin became a daily habit for me. I wanted to get fucked up and be surrounded by other fucked up people, and I didn't want to ever be alone. We moved in together on Capitol Hill summer of 1993.

Hole did some interviews for *Live Through This* at that apartment. It was neutral territory—no one could rifle through Kurt's garbage. The only press we did at their house was with Pamela Des Barres for *Interview* magazine, because of course she is PAMELA-of-the-GTOs-des Barres. Courtney would show up after we'd been waiting for at least an hour, talking to the journalist. She'd typically walk in and sit down in front of my records and start flipping through them.

Grabbing my Strawberry Switchblade record, "OOOHH, Pat, put this on!" She'd launch into a story about David Balfe, who managed them, who she knew from her friendship with Julian Cope back in the Teardrop Explodes days.

Holding up my Cactus World News record, "Oh *no*, Pat, really? Is this good?"

"Yes, I like them. It's Irish guitar pop."

She held up a Glen Branca record. "This is more Eric and Kristen." Eric and Kristen agreed. The journalist would try to keep up.

IN APRIL, NIRVANA came home from touring and recording. By then they were the number one band in America, and Kurt needed to take a break to cope with the reality of their success. There was no question that it made him physically uncomfortable. One night when I was staying with them on Spalding, we'd been hanging out with all the windows open, and a neighbor had the radio on. Kurt was in bed, I was in the hallway, and Courtney was in the kitchen. Suddenly we could clearly hear the opening chords of "Smells Like Teen Spirit."

"Kurt! Kuurrttt! They're playing your song . . . " Courtney yelled across the apartment.

He didn't respond except to curl into the fetal position and sink his head further into a pillow, which he then folded over his head to block out the sound.

HE AND COURTNEY came back to Seattle so Hole could record our first EP together. For all of the many properties they'd either rented or bought, the two of them would most often stay at one of three luxury hotels between Seattle and L.A. Transience and seclusion was their thing. By then I'd moved myself back to Seattle, where I would share a two-bedroom apartment with Larry. Most of my things were somewhere else, either in storage in another city or in a different rehearsal space or about to be. I ended up using Dave Grohl's kit for those sessions. The studio was called Word of Mouth, formerly known as Triangle Studios, the same place where Nirvana's first album, *Bleach*, was recorded, with the same producer, Jack Endino. Eric and Courtney had recently signed a seven-album contract with DGC/Geffen, but this EP was contracted for UK indie label City Slang.

I hadn't been inside Word of Mouth since my days with Doll Squad, so I remember feeling extra excited about the opportunities that lay ahead. I did let the thought cross my mind: *I'm gonna get a house with a pool*. I had no real basis for thinking that, other than the fact that my friends couldn't go anywhere without being recognized. And this recording session would mark the first time I'd experienced a team of chiropractors being summoned to the studio to give us all adjustments. It was very Madonna.

We wrote two new songs in the studio—"Beautiful Son" and "Twenty Years in the Dakota"—and recorded a third called "Old Age," which had been one of Courtney's ongoing collaborations with Kurt (there were a couple of songs they passed back and forth to each other, same melody with different lyrics by each). We didn't yet have a bass player, so Jack and Courtney alternated those parts. Courtney also had the basic verse and chord progression for "Miss World." Though we didn't do anything with it then, I could tell it had a strong hook, and it later became our lead single on the full-length record.

One night I ran into Kim Warnick of the Fastbacks, and she was telling me a story about a Make-a-Wish foundation event she was trying to organize. A neighborhood kid with a terminal illness wanted to meet Eddie Vedder, but he wouldn't be available in time. She was wondering if Kurt might be willing to meet with him instead. I told her I'd ask him, and two days later the kid and his family came to the studio to meet Kurt and watch Hole record. It was another reminder that the scene in Seattle was making an impact; at 25, millions knew the songs we played by heart.

While Kurt and Courtney stayed behind in a newly rented house in the Hollywood Hills, Eric and I went up alone to practice the Hole catalogue at their place in the woods in Carnation, Washington. In June of 1992, Eric and I moved up there ahead of them and turned it into a rehearsal space. One day, early on in our knowing each other, Eric came over to the house in the early afternoon, and as was the custom of the day, I offered him a beer. There was a pause and he looked at me like he wasn't sure he'd heard me correctly. "Not now," he said, eyeing me with what felt definitively like judgment, "I'm working."

It was a stark contrast to Courtney's professional philosophy at the time, but I got the message quickly that there was room for only one person's chaos in Hole. When I'd first started playing in bands I would usually drink beer before a show. There's so much adrenaline and anxiety that it felt natural to want to take that edge off. But over time, I had to admit, even I'd begun to notice that just one or two could indeed affect my playing. A couple of Schmidts weren't worth the risk of Eric's disappointment or a less-than-great performance, so knowing how he felt about it, I opted for Pepsi instead. That public showing made me feel in control of things for years. Then of course once I'd walked off stage all bets were off.

| 9 |

GODSEND

When Courtney gave an interview to *Vanity Fair* (where she posed for a photograph, smoking a cigarette while pregnant and talked openly about her heroin use), everything exploded. Now she and Kurt were being watched by authorities and openly judged in the press, and the attention didn't have anything to do with the music. Kurt's inclination was to retreat, to shun the media and keep his head down, but Courtney's style was to attack and defend. She wanted him to take control of the family public relations and defend her honor. "Fight for us!" She'd scream at him sometimes. "You have to fight!"

Kurt didn't want to fight—it took too much out of him, that angry masculine posturing. But at the same time, it was in him.

Misogyny and homophobia disgusted him, especially when it was perpetuated by other rock bands, which was then reflected by the fans. There was that infamous feud between Kurt and Axl Rose that was officially kicked off at the MTV Video Music Awards later that year. Kurt and Courtney were backstage with Frances, and Courtney said something sarcastic to Axl, and he told Kurt to "Keep your bitch in line," or something to that effect. In a way, it had a good outcome because Kurt got to talk shit about Axl and men like him, and separate Nirvana from that kind of macho bullshit. They could be just as angry or angrier than anyone, but they were angry about the right things.

But on the other hand, the fact that a big part of Nirvana's audience was responding to Kurt's own rage without understanding why he was angry weighed on him. The smashing of instruments at the end of shows was part of that. Kurt was creating something beautiful, then destroying it, giving it just to take it away.

I'd imagine one of the reasons Kurt preferred not to draw attention to himself was because he wasn't interested in cutting down on his drug intake, which made everything he ever said to the press a lie. He hated himself for the hypocrisy. *We're not on drugs. We used to be, but we're clean now. We're good parents. Life is worth living.* When Courtney wanted them to clean up, I think Kurt felt betrayed. I imagine he felt pressured and abandoned in his addiction. That's when the drugs aren't working anymore and nothing feels good. It's the loneliest feeling in the world.

Once you're an addict, heroin use isn't necessarily debilitating or noticeable to others. In the right doses it can be energizing. You feel great! Kurt was often really lucid and hilarious on drugs—but he was also sullen and withdrawn without them. By then, though, it was about maintenance, just using, even to function. Once Frances was back home with us in L.A., the heroin use continued—of course it did; we were addicts. Kurt and Courtney did what they had to do to prove to CPS that they were sober enough to have custody, and when she moved home, everyone did the best impression of a parent that they could at the time.

Kurt was the silly one. We spent hours a day down on the baby's level, in a kind of pillow fort they'd made in the nursery with all these mattresses on the floor. We'd lie on our stomachs with Frances in between and talk to her in funny voices. Kurt's sense of humor had always been pretty fecal-based, and babies were a perfect audience for him. I took a lot of video of the two of them interacting. Frances bonded easily—she was a wide-eyed and curious baby, and Kurt made her laugh. He had several characters that he liked to invoke. He could do Donald Duck, and there was his animated frog voice. He had this bit he did where he narrated whatever was going on from Frances's point of view, in her voice, which was always bitchy and above-it-all. And all the while she'd just be totally blissed-out and transfixed.

One sweet ritual revolved around an antique rocking chair Courtney had in the house. We each took shifts rocking Frances and singing little songs. The song I played whenever I rocked her was "Godsend" by Beat Happening, a ten-minute pop lullaby that always seemed to do the trick. There was always music then, if not always harmony.

I'D SPEND THE DAY practicing with Eric, learning all the songs from that first Hole album—*Pretty on the Inside*—the singles, the new stuff, some covers. At night I'd go to see bands with Polly. I would drink every single night and bring the party back to my place. Whoever was in town playing a show would end up there.

I didn't ever really say no to anything then. Even though I was in a supposedly monogamous relationship, I would make out with other girls if the opportunity presented itself. Sometimes it presented itself more than a few times with the same girl. One found out where I lived and left a note on my door saying she wanted to get together later. Polly found the note, and when I got home she went off. "YOU are cheating on me!?" She threw the note at me and fled to her friend's. I went into Pagliaccis and waited for her to go on break. *"I'm sorry." "I miss you." "I was drunk!"* I wanted to stay together. She came home that night, and we made up. We stayed together, but this wouldn't be the last time I hurt her like that.

| 10 |

SON OF A GUN

"Pat, do you want to go to Jet Rag with us?"

The door opened, and Courtney peeked her head in through the bathroom door that separated our rooms. Jet Rag is a vintage clothing store on LaBrea. I got up and got dressed. It was just before noon, so I was doing okay—as usual we'd all been up most of the night. Kurt was downstairs with Jackie, the nanny. He was holding Frances and dancing her in his lap while singing, "Jad likes Coca Cola but I like Pepsi," a Stinky Puffs song. Stinky Puffs was one of Kurt's favorite bands at the time and featured Simon Fair Timony, a then 7-year-old songwriter. Kurt handed Frances to Jackie who brought her over to a blanket on the floor in the living room. She sat down with her and gave her a bottle.

"You coming with us?" Kurt asked, and I said yeah and grabbed my cigarettes. Kurt yelled up to Courtney who was forever upstairs getting dressed. She came down, said bye to Jackie and Bean, and we piled into their grey Volvo. Kurt always drove because Courtney had never wanted to learn. The three of us often went shopping: antique stores, thrift stores, record stores. Courtney would buy vintage quilts, dresses, and baby clothes. Kurt would always look at old toys and curiosities—globes and medical equipment. If he bought clothes, they were often vintage pajamas. My thing was ironic T-shirts featuring slogans like "#1 Grandpa." After Jet Rag, we went to a store where Courtney bought furniture to have delivered.

When we got into the car to leave, Kurt asked me, "Have you ever shot a gun?"

"If a bb gun counts, sure," I answered. I remembered my childhood friend's dad's gun collection in the garage and told Kurt about the machine he had that would load shotgun shells. It seemed a little over-the-top to me at the time.

"There's a shooting range nearby. Do you want to go?" he said. Courtney had no interest; she had her *Melody Maker* in her lap and car window down, smoking cigarettes with her feet on the dash of the car. This particular issue had a photo of Brett Anderson of Suede, and Leslie Rankine of Silverfish on the cover. As Kurt drove, Courtney chain-smoked and occasionally read aloud amusing quotes from the features.

At the range, Kurt paid for me, and they gave us safety glasses and four boxes of ammo. Walking into the place reminded me of being in a hardware or auto parts store—wood paneling and neat little rows of ammunition for sale. The air had a certain smell, like firecrackers and WD-40. I used a handgun that looked like it came straight out of *High Plains Drifter*. I don't even remember what kind of gun Kurt used. I knew he was into shooting targets in the woods of Seattle with Dylan. It was an activity I associated more with Dylan, though, whose apartment was memorable for its ubiquitous back issues of *Guns & Ammo, Shotgun Sports*, and *Precision Shooter* magazines.

I was given goggles and noise-canceling headphones, and we were led to what looked like a bowling lane for privacy. It was difficult to imagine handling these things all the time and without protective gear. The sound—even when I wasn't hearing it as powerfully as you might without headphones—was unforgettable. The movies don't do it justice—it's so much louder than the heaviest of Melvins songs performed live. There are lots of steps you have to remember in the handling of the weapon itself, and I found the checklist of safety precautions to be nerve-racking.

I wasn't very good at hitting my mark. Kurt took his targets with him when we left. He said he wanted to make something out of them.

WHENEVER KURT, COURTNEY, and I were together, we'd make new music. Kurt loved playing drums, so I'd switch to guitar, then he'd play guitar and I'd take over the drums, with Courtney on bass. Living together, there'd be times when I'd witness Kurt write a new punk anthem in ten minutes in a closet. A thin wall separated the guest room where I slept and the room where Kurt most often liked to write and work out melodies in the Alta Loma house. I'll never forget lying in bed, listening to him work out the vocal for the song that became "Rape Me," over and over for months. It was an intensely creative time, so I didn't question the darker truths Kurt's writing clearly revealed.

ROCK AND RIO

In January 1993, Courtney and I went to Brazil with Nirvana, which was there to play a couple shows for one hundred thousand people, and record some demos for their next album, *In Utero*. The festival was called "Hollywood Rock" and covered two cities—the first night in São Paolo, the second in Rio de Janeiro. The headliners were Nirvana, Alice in Chains, Red Hot Chili Peppers, L7, and yes, Simply Red.

It was my first time in South America, or anywhere, really, and I was thrilled to be able to go on a weeklong vacation with my friends. Our relationships were about music and partying—it was rare to break the routine of playing shows, seeing shows, hanging out backstage or after hours, barely remembering what you were doing the last time you saw each other. Another thing we rarely did while on tour was actually experience the cities we were visiting. Outside of buying drugs on the Lower East Side, I never knew much about NYC. I knew the beds were comfortable, the room service better-than-average, but I wasn't taking the draft horses out for a spin in Central Park to do a little sightseeing. But Brazil was different. It was almost absurd, the culture shock of a bunch of grungy junkies from L.A. and Seattle in a town known for its tropical temperatures and monuments to Catholicism.

Kurt and Courtney spent a majority of their time isolating themselves from the group. Despite the cracks that were beginning to form in their relationships with Dave and Krist and their wives, Nirvana Inc. was overall a great group of people to be around. The band had been working with the same touring team since the beginning—there was Big John (Duncan), a Scottish punker with tattooed arms the size of thighs who Kurt had recruited to be his guitar tech. In the 1980s, John had played in the hardcore band the Exploited. Then there was Ernie Bailey, another guitar tech who was a genius at rebuilding the broken ones. He lived in Seattle, same as Craig Montgomery, the sound guy.

On the way to the stadium from the hotel we all rode together in a passenger van. As soon as we pulled out of the hotel, the van was mobbed by kids. There was a motorcade of police who cleared the way, and a police escort to and from the shows in Rio and São Paolo. The first show at São Paulo was notoriously crazy. Nirvana wasn't playing the crowd pleasers for the ninety thousand people in attendance, and there were enough false starts to songs that Krist threw a guitar at Kurt and stormed off. From the wings, Ernie tossed a cantaloupe at Kurt, who picked up the mess and smashed it into his guitar strings and proceeded to play that way. Krist returned to the stage and they all switched instruments: Krist on guitar, Dave on bass, Kurt on drums. The whole thing ended in a lot of smashing of equipment that would have to be rebuilt or replaced within the week before the next show.

The plane to Rio was too small, just big enough for the bands and crew. I was feeling nauseated, so Courtney gave me a Valium. It was the first time I'd tried it—pills never appealed to me as vessels for a high because they seemed to take too long to work. It couldn't be denied that our plane's trajectory was sketchy as hell. And then the landing was brutal. The plane seemed to skip on the runway way too fast, then skidded, and turned sharply, before coming to an abrupt stop. It was as if the pilot was landing a plane for the first time. Anthony Kiedis stood up first and stomped to the front of the airplane. He was wearing huge steel-toed combat boots, and we all watched as he pulled back and kicked the cockpit door as hard as he could, all while screaming, "YOU MOTHER-FUCKERS!" That started everybody else yelling—this could have been some kind of Buddy Holly situation. All I could think was, *Valium works.*

THE GUYS IN the Chili Peppers were sober, and it showed. Their *Blood Sugar Sex Magik* performances were always high energy—Flea played in his underwear and Anthony in a skirt, and for the final songs, the entire band wore hard hats with tall flames shooting out the tops of them. It was like a circus act. While some of us were staying up all night and sleeping well into the afternoon, Chili Peppers were hiking for hours to see the Christ the Redeemer statue or making memories at a museum. Flea hadn't done heroin since the previous year, and he somehow made it look easy to stop. He had this sweet tone of voice and an air of total positivity. He undoubtedly knew that most of us were spending a lot of our time high on various substances, but he didn't have any judgment about it.

I had planned to drink to excess, and I rightly guessed that cocaine would be readily available, but I hadn't guessed that Layne

Staley would arrange to have Maria, one of our dealers in Seattle, fly down strapped with lots of heroin and paraphernalia. I don't know how she did it—maybe she had friends or relatives in Brazil, maybe she told them the needles were for her diabetes. After that first night in São Paulo, Kurt, Courtney and I, Alice in Chains, and all the girls from L7, would hang out in one of the hotel suites, getting fixed up by Maria. At one point Kurt announced that he wanted to do a speedball (a mix of coke and heroin).

"Oh no, you don't!" Courtney wasn't fond of the idea of him mixing his drugs, having dealt with the consequences of having to revive him in the past.

I defied her, though, and left Kurt a bottle cap full of cocaine hidden in the bathroom. It was a weird impulse, given that I wouldn't have done a speedball at that time in my life, but he was my friend, and I wanted him to be happy.

We did manage to go on one adventure when we all went hang gliding together. I was probably hung over—I'm sure we all were—but the idea of actually flying was too thrilling to pass up. *With actual wings, I could pretend for real.* The trip lasted about three hours and involved hiking to the top of a mountain, getting strapped into a sleeping bag underneath a similarly strapped-in pilot who operates the flying machine made of tin and polyester, then running to the edge of a cliff, fly for ten minutes, and land on the beach below. Somewhere I have a picture of Courtney strapped in and wearing a helmet. I'd never seen Kurt so happy. There's a picture of him online that shows him in a promotional brochure for the hang gliding tour group, where he's referred to as "Nirvana's popstar." I'm positive no one ever gave them permission, but it seems like a fitting endorsement.

Courtney and I used Nirvana's studio space to work out new Hole songs—that's where we came up with "Miss World" and "She Walks." Earlier that day, Nirvana had recorded the nameless song that would eventually become "Scentless Apprentice." It reminded me of that rhyme I played as a kid called the Name Game (the one that goes, "Bo-na-na fan-na, fo-fa-na"). I mentioned it to Kurt and Dave, and that night it showed up on the set list as "Chuck Chuck Bo Buck."

With Kurt on bass, the three of us recorded a new song we called "Drunk in Rio," which got its name from our dedication to lyrical accuracy. (Apparently this song is sometimes referred to as "Closing Time" on bootlegs.) Courtney had this pretty verse guitar part, and we were trying out different ideas for a second part. I started playing this fast, hammering beat on my snare, and when Kurt heard it, he started playing guitar over it. Even after we stopped recording, the two of them kept playing it and playing it. Courtney often had trouble figuring out how to end a song. New songs were her thing, shiny new songs and pretty parts without endings. I think she wanted to stay inside the song, the way you never want a feeling to end.

WHEN WE RETURNED to Seattle, we set about finding a bass player for Hole. I was excited about how productive we'd been since I'd joined Hole and moved back, but I had to admit—though only to myself—that my heroin habit was intensifying. I was using about $100 worth a day, which covered me morning and night. The three of us were using the same drugs, but we all tried to keep it a secret from each other. That was hard to do when everybody got their supply from the same source: Caitlyn on Capitol Hill. She carried Seattle's best black tar and catered to musicians. If you stayed at her place for an hour, it was hard not to run into someone you knew. One day not long after we all returned from Brazil, I went to Caitlyn's and was sitting on the couch, when Layne came out of the kitchen. I had just seen him at the shows, but when he saw me, he was so excited. He always seemed like he was about to give you some great news.

It was the dead of winter, and Layne always wore a lot of layers, no matter the weather. He wore gloves year round to cover up the track marks in his hands. He was talking a million miles an hour, and as he spoke he unwrapped the scarf from around his neck and set it down on the arm of a chair. We watched as he pulled out a needle from his jacket pocket and put his other hand to his throat. Then mid-sentence, he strained to pump up his neck so a vein would pop—and I'm talking, and he's totally listening—and he put his finger up to the vein as if taking his pulse, felt it, then put the syringe in, and shot up in his neck. I'd never seen anything like it! A casual neck injection.

A moment later he was done and barely paused before he said, suddenly in an even better mood, "It's so good to see you, Patty. Do you want to go somewhere and get some coffee?"

Coffee? "No, that's okay, Layne. I think I'm just gonna do this." I couldn't imagine—at that point—how it was possible to do something like that without a mirror, much less with such nonchalance. Layne, unlike so many heroin users, just didn't want to be alone.

I couldn't even shoot up unassisted yet. The first time I came to Caitlyn's by myself to score, I ran into Kurt. It was awkward, and he was a little standoffish. I felt like I had disappointed him in some way. "What are you looking for?" He asked.

"I came to buy a little dope," I said, no big deal.

"Don't," Kurt said. "You shouldn't do this." I didn't want to hear it. I was still in the beginning of the whole experience. Surely he could remember what it was like to be an amateur. After a few minutes, Kurt had a change of heart when I told him I'd only tried heroin a couple of times and that I didn't even know how to give myself a shot. With that, he took some of his stash and shared it with me. Then he shot up my arm for me. I was impressed with his small gauge insulin needle and his practiced efficiency—it made for a less uncomfortable pinch. After that I started to go to Caitlyn's every day.

| 12 |

HEAVY

This was the ad Courtney posted in her zine, looking for a new bass player: *"I want someone who can play ok, and stand in front of 30,000 people, take off her shirt and have 'fuck you' written on her tits. If you're not afraid of me and you're not afraid to fucking say it, send a letter. No more pussies, no more fake girls, I want a whore from hell."*

We'd auditioned so many girls, and no one was right. But then Eric began telling me about this band out of Minneapolis he'd been scouting, Janitor Joe, and its bass player, Kristen Pfaff, who played so heavy and made it look effortless. He felt so strongly that she was the one. We got together to play one day, and she picked everything up really quickly. Kristen was hands down the best bass player I'd ever worked with. She was classically trained and knew how to play the piano and the cello. She was a super butch with her bass—I once saw her repair the neck of her bass with toothpicks like some kind of punk rock Girl Scout. She understood rhythm so well and could just lock in and propel songs. Kristen could launch into Echo and the Bunnymen or the Germs on demand. She knew Unrest's "Skinhead Girl" by heart, and this just elevated our cover options. Our song "Plump" was inspired by one of her ideas.

We officially became a band that spring when we played a few European shows and festivals. In late March 1993, we went to England and played "Beautiful Son" on BBC's *The Word*, the first time I was ever on television. Crowds were already going crazy for the songs we hadn't even released yet—we knew we were onto something. Unfortunately, though, we had a lot of downtime with which to take an abundance of drugs and do our best to hide it from Eric, the only person in our band at the time who was immune to heroin's charms.

In London I took Ecstasy with Kristen and Eric. We went to a club, and it was the definition of *ugh*. Everybody seemed to be enjoying an ecstatic, sensual experience, but the drug had the opposite effect on me. How could people want to dance on this stuff? Luckily we ran into Deb Googe from My Bloody Valentine, a longtime personal hero, who stayed with me and tried to make it normal. I didn't want to move and was stunned with paranoia that I might have hurt my brain by messing with its chemistry. It probably didn't help that I was drunk on top of it.

In addition to everything else I was taking, I'd recently opened my mind to pills, especially since I'd had that good experience with Valium, and I didn't usually have to pay for them. One of the perks of the job. There were pills you could get only in Europe, such as Rohypnol, which was easily procured there but risky to bring back home. Maybe it's because we were in a band, but we were always subject to searches at airports, which made common medicine a more viable option than needles and baggies of powder. Also known as the date rape drug, Rohypnol is illegal in the United States but was freely prescribed in Europe at the time. They came in individual blister packs that felt very satisfying to pierce through, especially if I was experiencing any symptoms of withdrawal. It's similar to but about ten times stronger than Valium, so even if you're uncomfortable, you probably wouldn't remember it later.

Triazolam was another pill we could always get in Europe. It's another benzo that completely sedates you but only for two good hours. Perfect for short flights, or if one needed to come down off speed. For heroin detox there was Temgesic, which is buprenorphine, a tiny pill that dissolves in your mouth so you don't have to wait as long. If there's one thing a drug addict doesn't have a tolerance for, it's patience.

After the London shows, I boarded a flight with Courtney and Frances back to Seattle. Flying with Courtney was always an adventure. At that point we often went from playing dingy clubs with gross backstage areas—with bathrooms that had no door on the toilet stalls—to five-star hotel suites (or, Courtney insisted on a suite—I was thrilled to have my own room), and first class. She demanded the same level of luxury wherever she was and was generous about sharing the wealth, especially when someone else was footing the bill. That flight started out like any other, with a complimentary beverage to wash down the Rohypnol.

I had just tucked in and waited for the sweet relief of unconsciousness, when the plane jerked so violently that I was almost knocked out of my seat. Courtney and I looked at each other— Frances was in her lap. The turbulence was unlike anything I'd experienced and seemed to go on forever, jolting me out of the chemical stupor that would have otherwise kicked in by then. It was different from the flight to Rio. Courtney held Frances to her chest. She was just seven months old. Suddenly, there was an announcement that we would be attempting an emergency landing (!), and the plane made a sharp descent. An alarm sounded, and the flight attendants began shouting at everyone to "Assume crash position! Brace for impact!" That meant folding over with our heads to our knees. Courtney held Frances tight, then was told to "Put your baby on the floor!" (Apparently this was the emergency protocol at the time.) Courtney screamed back, "I'm not putting my baby on the floor!" Eventually she had no choice, and somehow Frances remained calm—she never even cried.

I wasn't sure what to do with my arms. Should I smash them over my ears to drown out the impending screaming as we plunged to a fiery death? Should I hold hands with Courtney; is that what was expected in these situations? In the end I think I grabbed my ankles and stared at Franny. I couldn't tell if the pill was at all protecting me from the sharp edges of terror, or if it was the shock. I think Courtney felt it, too. At one point during the descent she leaned over and whispered to me the plane wouldn't go down because she was pretty sure there was a member of Parliament sitting in front of us.

And then everything evened out and the plane landed safely back in London. As soon as we realized we'd survived, I knew before Courtney ever said the words, "We're going to the fucking Ritz," that we'd most definitely be staying somewhere expensive to recover from our ordeal. Massages, crème brûlée, maybe even a bidet in the bathroom. Before I passed out from pure exhaustion, Courtney and I half-watched a tribute concert to Bob Dylan at Madison Square Garden on television. When Kris Kristofferson began to introduce the next performer, Sinead O'Connor, we turned the volume way up and prepared to be moved.

Courtney was already speculating about which song from what era Sinead might perform. "She has to do a Dylan song—it's a Dylan tribute," I said, when we were both suddenly silenced by an unexpectedly intense roar of the crowd as Sinead walked on stage to meet her band. At first, it sounded like the home team had just won the World Series. When she came out with her earpiece and stood before the crowd, she looked shy and slightly embarrassed

and began to say thank you. But then, the screaming failed to disappear after too-long a pause, and it was soon clear that what we
were actually hearing were angry boos of protest from the
audience.

The look of shock and confusion on Sinead's face was so jarring
that Courtney stopped talking mid-sentence, then stayed quiet for
a long time. The camera scanned the arena's audience, and we could
plainly see that a good chunk of the crowd was jeering at her with
their fists in the air. It had been a couple weeks after she tore the
picture of the pope on *Saturday Night Live*. I had only been vaguely
aware of the scandal. She looked completely vulnerable up there,
very young and so, so beautiful—perfect, really—as classically feminine as one can be with a shaved head.

The band started to play, but the crowd was an angry mob. Kris
Kristofferson came over and whispered something in her ear. She
nodded, and the band started up again. This time, Sinead cut them
off herself, took out her earpieces, and started in on an a cappella
version of Bob Marley's "War," the same song she'd played that
night on *SNL*, its lyrics a transcription of a speech about racial in-
justice by Ethiopian president and Rastafarian religious icon Haile
Selassie. She was screaming the lyrics, the jugular vein in her neck
threatening to burst. Anything could happen. I held my breath.
Sinead stopped and stared hard at the crowd, not backing down,
then turned and ran into the wings and Kristofferson's arms, where
he held her as she broke down.

"Jesus," Courtney said, taking the words out of my mouth. "I
thought *I* was hated."

"What just happened?"

"I think we just learned a valuable lesson, Pat. Don't ever fuck
with the pope."

IT WAS THE INAUGURAL year of the four-day Phoenix Festival
at an airfield in Britain. It was the biggest crowd I'd ever played for.

I sat behind my drums and took in the scene, as far as I could see, the expectant masses waiting for us. It was both scary and exciting, a total adrenaline rush only matched in intensity by the roar of the crowd. We played fourteen songs, including three covers—"Credit in the Straight World," a Young Marble Giants's song, "Do It Clean" by Echo & the Bunnymen, and "Pennyroyal Tea," a new Nirvana song they hadn't yet performed live. I'm not sure why we got it first—that would have been between Kurt and Courtney, but sometimes couples share.

In the hotel it was Eric and Kristen in one room, Courtney and I in the other. As confident and strong as she was, there was also an undercurrent of insecurity. The title of the zine she made then was "And She's Not Even Pretty," based on something a female fan said about her in a fan letter to Kurt. I think she trusted me initially because he did, and of course being a lesbian meant that I wasn't a threat to her marriage.

| 13 |

ASKING FOR IT

I'm not sure what Kristen's experience was, but as the drummer in the band, I was paid $6,000 to co-write and record *Live Through This*. From there, I received a personal check from Eric for $1,000 a month that came from the DGC advance they received when they signed. Since my rent in Seattle was $500 a month, when I ran out of cash and asked Eric for more, nine times out of ten he'd say no. He'd only relent if I could produce receipts for musical equipment, which he would then reimburse me for. (Did I mention that Eric had once worked as an accountant in the royalties department at Capitol Records?) I used to joke to Kristen that whenever Eric busted out his wallet you could hear rusty hinges and a spider would crawl out. I didn't really need to buy equipment anymore anyway, as it was now being designed for me by DW to the exact dimensions I wanted, and I'd get sticks from Promark.

In October 1993 we went to Marietta, Georgia, to record *Live Through This* at Triclops, the studio where the Smashing Pumpkins had made *Siamese Dream*. Our producers were Paul Kolderie and Sean Slade, who'd worked with Radiohead and Dinosaur Jr. We buckled down in the studio and took advantage of our new major label perks. My experiences with recording were one step above DIY, very punk, poor-person bootlegs. I never had the luxury of many takes—of time—of trying different cymbal tones on for size. This time our instruments would be shipped and delivered to the rehearsal space for us. Now I'd have my own tech whose job it was to set up and tune the drums and arrange all the mics before I arrived. Now I would participate in conversations about the size and quality of the room we were in and how it would affect the sound.

Courtney showed up at rehearsals a couple of days after the rest of us did. When she got to the studio, she came in and asked Sean first thing, "What's that drum mic on the snare?"

"It's a Shure 57." Courtney said something about Steve Albini. I sat down at my drums, and Sean left the room and went back into the control room. Courtney leaned over my kick drum and asked me about the mics.

"How do your drums sound?"

I liked the way things were sounding. "Pretty good. Come in and listen." I was sure they could hear us in the control room from all the mics overhead.

"Well, is it Pixies or Dinosaur Jr?" (Which I interpreted as "Does it sound like Steve Albini or J Mascis?")

"What does that mean?"

"What I mean is, is it *Bug* or *Green Mind*?" This made me laugh.

"Maybe just listen?"

She called Butch Vig and talked about drum mics. I think she called Billy, too, and then talked to Kurt. After her consults, she put together a drum map on paper—a combination of Kurt and Billy's suggestions. She brought the drawing into the control room, and Sean and Paul quietly listened to her talk for ten minutes. When she was done they suggested she listen to the sounds we already had. She lit up a cigarette in front of a NO SMOKING sign and sat back on the couch while I stood in the doorway. Sean played a bit of a rehearsal take of "Jennifer's Body" that we'd done earlier. They isolated the drum track. She listened and decided that it was good.

"Okay, it's Jimmy Chamberlain."

"Violet" and "Doll Parts" were written right before I joined the band.

"Miss World," "Jennifer's Body," and "Plump" we wrote together in the practice space on Capitol Hill. I added a drum part to "Doll Parts." The original was acoustic and I added a longer, louder ending with drums. "Plump" had a different bridge originally. I have cassettes of the demo versions.

"Gutless" had a different bridge in an earlier version, and I changed the drum part. "I Think That I Would Die" was originally called "Baby"; Courtney gave it that title when we finished recording it. We finished writing it in the studio right before recording it.

"Credit in the Straight World" is a cover of a Young Marble Giants's song. I loved covering it because I love Stuart Moxham and that record so much. The mellotron intro part right before it was originally part of the song "Old Age," which we recorded but never used on the album. "Softer Softest" was originally titled "Pee Girl." I added the drum part right before we recorded it. It had always been played without one. "She Walks" was already written, but "Asking for It" was created entirely in the studio. I don't even recall the guitar part being played before Eric put it together the day we recorded it.

Having a real budget to record made such a difference. I learned that different takes could yield two or three parts of one finished song. On one take, the beginning came in like thunder, but the ending wasn't as explosive as it had been on the take I did an hour ago: no problem, splice two separate pieces together by literally cutting the tape with a razor blade then reattaching it to another take. Or "punching in," which means starting the song a few measures before the part you want to record and then "punching" record right at a spot to record the second half. Ultimately the goal is to get one amazing take of a song, and that happened with "Jennifer's Body" and "Miss World." I can detect differences in the snare drum sounds on "Doll Parts" still today. I can hear the two snare drums that are on that song: a 1970s-era Ludwig Black Beauty at the beginning, and my DW Black Oyster, which was a deeper snare drum and has a big, loose room sound.

We were always writing, extending parts, changing lyrics; Courtney liked playing new things. She got tired of songs after playing them awhile, which is why we changed the live versions of songs constantly on tour. When we wrote songs together, we developed a language. Courtney had endless musical vocabulary, even when it came to drummers. She knew who Cozy Powell was, for instance, who was a session drummer that worked with bands like Whitesnake and Black Sabbath. That really impressed me and was also pretty funny.

Her directives were heavy on references to other bands to explain her structure ideas. "Let's Peter Buck 8 times," (the verse), "into a short PJ Harvey," (chorus), "the bridge should be Bunnymen," etc. If Courtney couldn't execute one of her ideas on guitar but wanted Eric to, all she would have to say was, "Make it like 'Seasons of Wither'" (referring to an Aerosmith song with an arpeggiated guitar part).

When I was recording the drum parts, Eric and Kristen would play along with me, and Courtney would sing, so it was so much easier to maintain that energy. Even though it was just a scratch, she'd go all out for the power vocal on "Violet" or "Jennifer's Body." Eric kept boxes and boxes of tapes of every rehearsal or jam session. At the end of every day, I felt really confident that I was right where I needed to be.

WE WERE STAYING at some corporate rentals in the suburbs, me and Courtney in one, Eric and Kristen in another. We'd go into the studio around noon, have some lunch, then start the session. We'd have dinner nine hours later, stay there until late at night, then go back to the impersonal efficiency apartment. Kristen and Eric were just ending their relationship, so things were a bit tense between them. After a few days, Courtney decided to move over to the much more comfortable Nikko Hotel, so Kristen would come over to my place after recording. We went to Blockbuster in town and rented every single episode of the 1967 British television series *The Prisoner*, which was seventeen VHS tapes. Every night after recording, Kristen and I would watch them.

Sometimes we'd go to the Nikko to hang out with Courtney. Mostly she made calls while I had dinner. One night after a long session, Courtney called Nirvana's tour manager so he could hold the phone up to the stage so we could hear the band play their version of the Vaselines's cover "Jesus Wants Me for a Sunbeam" live. She put the phone on speaker. There was so much crowd noise, I could barely hear Kurt singing. So far we'd only had a taste of that kind of performance opportunity. Needless to say we felt ready.

On Friday night after our first week in Georgia, Courtney and I ended up leaving and going up to New York to see Nirvana play the season premiere of *Saturday Night Live*. I started drinking on the plane, which was a clear indication that I wouldn't be able to stop until I was unconscious, then I would carry on the same way the following day. In fact I was so drunk at *30 Rock* that I could not see straight, the whole thing was like a dream. I have a vague recollection that RuPaul was there. And Chris Farley and Phil Hartman. A basketball player was hosting—Charles Barkley—never really heard of him (when it was Hole's turn to play *SNL* the following year, the host that night would be another athlete, George Foreman).

The experience of performing on *Saturday Night Live* is an all-day activity. We got there in the afternoon to meet up with the guys. There were sound checks and a lot of waiting around. I must have watched some sketches being rehearsed. I recall roaming around in the corridors backstage, wandering into random rooms like I was on a private tour. That night Nirvana played "Heart-Shaped Box" and "Rape Me," and Pat Smear borrowed my Farrah Fawcett-in-a-bikini T-shirt to wear on stage. But through it all I was stumbling. I had the sensation of awareness that I was engaging in a once-in-a-lifetime experience but not knowing how that was supposed to feel. *Maybe I should have brought my camera.*

I DO NOT RECALL coming back from NYC, getting off the plane in Atlanta, or going back to the studio. I do remember thinking, *I gotta pull it together.* Eric hadn't wanted us to go in the first place, since we were still in the middle of laying down basic tracks. What I do remember is sitting on a leather couch in an empty office while a neighborhood dealer cut up crystal meth on the desk. When you snort meth, it burns your nose and throat—it brought me right out of the blackout though. When I walked out of there, I went to the live room, sat at my drums, and Eric and I ran through some practice takes of "Miss World," then recorded it.

After work one night we went to the Masquerade to watch an AmRep showcase, which was the label of Kristen's former band, Janitor Joe. We got drunk at the show, and Kristen and I made out in the club. Was this our Fleetwood Mac period? Courtney and Eric had been a thing long before Kurt or I ever came along. Eric and Kristen had moved in together very soon after meeting and were now in the midst of negotiating their breakup. I don't think anyone saw us then, or afterward, in the car ride home, while Eric drove, with Courtney in the front seat. We didn't go to third base or anything, but there was heavy petting, hands on legs, hands up legs.

As far as I could tell Kristen was still straight, but I also knew she'd dated at least one woman in college. I knew her ex-girlfriend

Jenny Olsen. Kristen was well-read in lesbian lit, for instance; she knew her Leslie Feinberg. It was great to be able to talk with someone who also loved the novel *Stone Butch Blues*, the story of a transgender identity crisis. Kristen was one of those people who made you feel smarter by association. She'd already lived nine lives before joining Hole. She was actually from Buffalo, had quite possibly been married before, and had told me she'd already experimented with dope and kicked it. We connected on many levels, besides the physical attraction and the way we played music together. We had heroin in common, too, but it hadn't taken her long to figure out the code of silence and privacy that needed to surround a habit.

WE'D FINISHED RECORDING, so in November '93, Hole joined the Lemonheads for a few dates of the West Coast leg of their tour. There was still mixing to be done for the record, and the cover art—which became the famous beauty queen image, photographed by Ellen von Unwerth—but now we needed to get used to playing the songs live. Our band budget for these shows was very modest. We rented a van, had a couple of crew people to help with gear and merch, and that was pretty much it. Courtney and I shared a hotel room, and Kristen and Eric each had their own.

Portland was Courtney's old hometown. After we did our sound check at the Pine Street Theater, she wanted to go thrift shopping, so a runner from the venue drove the two of us to a store downtown. I assumed he would wait with his car, but by the time we came back outside, he was gone. Courtney knew the area really well and said casually, "Let's just take the bus."

The bus? Public transportation was the last thing I would have guessed she'd be willing to utilize, but she didn't seem to mind and knew the routes by heart. When the bus pulled up, we stepped on, and she took a handful of change out of her purse and dropped it in the coin collector, not bothering to count. I followed her to a seat and sat down. There were maybe five people on the bus and not one of them recognized her. We were dropped off three blocks from the venue, and that was that.

By the time we got to San Francisco, Kristen had started a little road hookup with the Lemonheads' guitar tech. Backstage, before that show, our tour manager came in to announce we had five minutes until showtime. My pre-stage ritual includes a stretch, a bottle of water, and a pee. I went to the bathroom and opened the door and there's Kristen and the guitar tech in the stall, smoking heroin off some foil. By Seattle, Kristen was strung out. We played the Moore theater right before Thanksgiving, and Larry showed up backstage, high out of his mind—he'd started shooting up. That night I went over to his place with Polly and started my heroin habit in earnest. That was the night I decided I was all in.

| 14 |

BEAUTIFUL SON

I went to Kurt's intervention high, not so much in solidarity, but just because I always was then. Courtney had summoned me to the house to convince him to go to rehab. In early March, she had gone to Europe to meet up with him during the Italian leg of the Nirvana tour. I was at home when Eric called to report that Kurt was in a coma in Rome—he'd overdosed. At the time, I thought for sure it had been an accident. I didn't hear any of the details until much later. But when he came home after his recovery, I could see that he was in bad shape. He looked sick and had been withdrawing from other people and cancelled a leg of the tour. There were a lot of concerned whispers.

A week before, Kurt had locked himself in the bathroom with some guns, and the cops had come. Things probably couldn't have gotten much more public. I knew there would be people there, but it was jarring to see how many and who. Dave and Krist, and Dylan, but also Nirvana manager Danny Goldberg, our manager, Janet Billig, somebody's lawyer, all sitting around the dining room table. Kurt had already lashed out at everyone in the room, particularly Courtney, who wasn't sober herself. By the time I'd arrived, Kurt had already locked himself in the bedroom, refusing to come down. The whole house was somber. Courtney was in the kitchen, crying. "Go up and see Kurt. He'll talk to you."

At the top of the stairs I knocked on the bedroom door. "It's Pat."

Kurt and Pat (Smear) were lying on the bed. I lay down alongside. Pat, Kurt, Pat. We laid like that for a while, not talking. I tried to project support. I wasn't there to be part of the tough love brigade—who was I to say anything about getting clean—I was high myself. Kurt was ashamed. He didn't want to stop; he couldn't imagine stopping. We'd gotten into the habit, as addicts, to go through the process of detox before important life events. Doing *Saturday Night Live* in a week? Detox. Having a kid? Detox. Saying dumb things to the press and need to rein it in? Detox. I did it so often myself—maybe twelve times in a few years—it was standard addiction maintenance: go to the clinic, pay $4,000 to lie in a bed for a couple days, sedated and hydrated, taking other drugs in order not to crave the worse drugs. Then it was a semi-clean slate—I just switched back to drinking "normally" until things got sloppy again. But now things had reached the point of no return for Kurt; he was scaring people. He'd OD'd in New York City; he'd almost died in Rome; he'd given up trying not to die, and surviving didn't change anything but made him feel even worse.

"If I don't go, Courtney's saying I'll never see Frances again," he said, sounding bereft.

Rehab wasn't detox—it was a public admission of guilt that implied a promise to try. It was isolating. Geffen intended to send him to Exodus, which was where all the rock stars went to clean up then—Anthony Keidis, at least, and the guys from Jane's Addiction. I'd end up there myself within the year. There were worse places to go, but it didn't matter where they were sending him. Being a junkie was an inevitable truth, his destiny. He was done making an effort when failure was inevitable. It never occurred to him then that he could stop.

Kurt was like a sister trapped in a brother's body. He had a feminine side, and with his stomach issues, he often looked like he was in the throes of menstrual aches. Sometimes his resting posture was to clutch the hollow cavern of his stomach while gritting his teeth. His insides were chronically inflamed, but I would guess the addiction had been exacerbating his pain. He was really small and tried to hide it, and often wore two pairs of mangled jeans at a time, and those on top of thermal underwear, which he wore underneath two long-sleeved T-shirts, with a flannel shirt on top of that. He had these clear blue eyes swimming in an ocean of pain, and that day they were never bluer.

Kurt smoked another cigarette and looked around the side of the bed for Courtney's makeup bag, which held a tube of concealer. Looking in the mirror over the antique iron headboard, he dabbed the makeup under his eyes and tried to erase the dark circles that now shadowed his face and asked me how he looked. He was so fragile in that moment, trying to look a little better for the room. He was so much thinner than he'd been just two years before. Of all the times I'd seen Kurt playing dress up in Courtney's slips, or with green nail polish chipped on one hand, and barrettes in his hair, this was a sadder kind of drag—he was trying to make himself disappear, already fading to ghost.

"Do I look ready to face the music?" He said with trademark sarcasm.

"I think we both look a little tired these days," I said. "But you still look better than any of those assholes downstairs." I could feel his resignation; he'd lost his sense of humor. Kurt was already running.

Pat and I tried to encourage him. We were on his side; we loved him.

"I'm strung out, too," I told him. "Starting tomorrow, I'm going to go to my sister's in Portland." My unspoken plan for this particular DIY detox was to simply drink myself into such a stupor that I would eclipse the dope-sickness with an alcoholic blackout.

I hugged my friend, his skinny body. I told him to hang in there and left them both in bed. Not wanting to stay for whatever might be coming next, I left the house with Dylan Carlson. This seemed as good a time as any to go get high one more time at my place. As we were leaving to make the ten-minute drive, I saw there was a cop trailing one car behind, and I remembered in a flash that the tags on my car's license plate were expired. Dylan was rummaging through our drug kit, seeing about the syringes.

"Oh shit, a cop is right behind us. The drugs—" I was sure we were going to get pulled over. How do you like that, fleeing the scene of an intervention.

"Fuck." Dylan crammed everything in the bag, and as I took a turn on a windy, tree-lined street, he tossed everything out the window. I had to remember to get the tags renewed; Jesus Christ, I was getting sloppy. Instead of feeling elated that we'd safely disposed of the drugs, I couldn't stop lamenting their loss. (Who would find them in a ditch? Would the drugs go undone?)

I knew I had to pull it together. We had an album coming out soon with a tour to follow. The very next day I called my sister, Susan, in Portland and told her I needed some time away from Seattle. As luck would have it, she had a conference she had to go to near the ocean—I could come stay at the hotel with her for a while, which was on the beach. It was exactly the environment I needed to set about detoxing from heroin with nothing but alcohol to help me through. This would be the beginning of my time on the hamster wheel of detox, replacing one thing for another.

I WAS AT THE hotel sweating and drunk exactly fourteen days later, my sister blessedly away at her event, the TV blaring in the background. That's how I heard that Kurt was dead. A body had been found in the room above the garage, "an apparent suicide."

That was the room they called the greenhouse, even though there weren't any plants in there. In fact, I always knew the room to be completely empty, with a cold linoleum floor. The image of him lying there, I just couldn't allow myself to picture it.

I grabbed the phone and called Eric, who confirmed the awful news. "You'd better come home," he said. In a blur of disbelief I got a message to Susan, who helped me get a plane ticket. Within three hours of hearing the news, I'd be back at Caitlyn's in Seattle where I immediately got loaded—no fucking way I was going to be sober for this.

Driving to the house was surreal—news vans lined the narrow street leading up to the driveway for blocks. Walking into the house was even more surreal. A giant swath of mourners, bewildered and staring at each other, so many of us obviously high. I huddled in a corner for a while with Mark Lanegan and Dylan. The strangest people were there—for one, Courtney's famously estranged mother, Linda Carroll, who had flown in for support. I'd never seen her before or since. She had a terrible aura. Courtney stayed upstairs shooting dope with an old friend she usually called an enemy. She stayed sequestered for an hour at a time, then emerged in Kurt's fuzzy green sweater, her face swollen from crying, to spend time outside with mourning fans. I couldn't help but think about the last time I'd seen Kurt, when we'd lain there on the same bed during that stupid intervention.

There was a memorial service. It felt formal, not long enough. Krist spoke. Dylan read Buddhist passages. Courtney read from the Bible, then Rimbaud. Danny Goldberg and Michael Stipe said things, their voices swirling together to further remind us that the only voice that mattered now was gone.

| 15 |

LIVE THROUGH THIS

In the aftermath of Kurt's death, we all went our separate ways to try to make sense of what had happened and, privately for each one of us, figure out how we were going to proceed. Already there were conspiracy whispers that Kurt was murdered and would never have been able to inject the amount of heroin he did and still have the consciousness to pull the trigger of a gun. I knew for a fact that he could, and did, on a regular basis. He always pushed it to the edge in his addiction. Yes, he could be hilarious, and at times I saw him full of joy—especially when he was with Frances—but Kurt was also clinically depressed, and clearly felt he couldn't stop using heroin. He'd overdosed many times; he'd tried to kill himself a month before.

Live Through This was released less than one week after they found his body. Already it was getting rave reviews, but the shock of what had happened was too fresh; nobody could predict when we would come back together, or even if we wanted to. Kristin was leaning toward quitting the band and immediately went back home to Minneapolis to try to kick opiates there, doing a few weeks at Hazelden. There was a feeling that we both needed to get away from Seattle in order for it to stick.

I went to my first real inpatient rehab at a place called Sundown in Yakima, Washington. Larry decided he would go to the same facility, so our father drove both of us to it. I don't recall any meaningful conversation with Dad on the commute, which I was partly grateful for and partly annoyed that he seemed to be able to dole out the words of addict wisdom to his A.A. family but not to his actual family of addicts. I couldn't blame him, though—in his day, rehab didn't really exist. It was more like getting locked in a psych ward, or at least going to the hospital (or jail). He'd never been.

The program lasted twenty-one days, which was not enough, but it was all that was available. When we checked in, Larry and I were separated, as the addicts were split up according to gender. The women's facility housed thirty. It would be my first experience detoxing cold turkey. Sundown was pretty bare-bones, and it wasn't equipped for anything medical. I recall you could ask for aspirin, but no benzos or relief for the shakes, vomiting, intestinal distress, panic, insomnia, pain.

On the fourth day, I opened the sliding glass door of my room and went outside to sit on one of the plastic chairs on the patio. I had my pajamas on and my Black Flag hooded sweatshirt. I lit up a cigarette, my only pleasure.

I saw there was someone doing the same on the patio right next door.

"Hi! I heard I got a new neighbor but haven't seen anyone over there," the woman said cheerfully. "I'm Nancy."

I couldn't really get how she could be so friendly and perky. After all, we were in fuckin rehab. As far as I could tell, my bad mood was the new normal. I looked over and managed to form a sound like, "Hi."

She looked at me and saw I wasn't really in any shape to form a sentence yet, but soon enough we'd make friends. We were in the same group therapy, and she made jokes during her shares that made me laugh. It had been a while since I thought anything was funny—I was so grateful just to feel anything, even for a split second, that wasn't sick. The focus of our recovery was the twelve steps—it was a straightforward A.A. curriculum. Everyone was assigned a counselor, and everyone participated in group. That exercise was meant to teach you to confront yourself with the truth of your addiction with the help of a sounding board. Everyone had to tell their story at some point, then the group would call you out on your bullshit, and you'd be forced to call the bad thing you did what it was. For instance, if you had used your sexuality in any way to obtain drugs, even with your regular significant other, you had to admit you were a prostitute.

Soon enough I did get used to standing in front of a podium, saying my name, that I was an addict and an alcoholic, and that I knew I had a lot of work to do.

The shame-based treatment was meant to discourage any of us from distancing ourselves from our behavior, even if it was a socially sanctioned activity. Nancy told me she was there because she was a big wine drinker and didn't think that was such a bad thing until her husband, John, got a call from the police saying she'd gotten into a car accident she had no memory of.

"Not so bad one time, but after FIVE times John started hiding the car keys. His friends at the sheriff's department said they couldn't keep pulling me out of ditches," she told me.

"He asked me to get some help, take a break for a while, and that brings us up to date."

I told two people about Kurt: Nancy and my counselor. I wanted to deal with my grief, to have this be the time in my life when I learned a lesson, when the death of my friend made an impact beyond terrible sadness. I knew what could happen if I kept drinking or using heroin, and I wanted to believe that this was the end of the line for me. But I worried about what would happen when I left this place. I hadn't spoken to Courtney about our next steps as a band. As far as any of us knew, we were on indefinite hiatus, at least as far as a tour was concerned. Luckily, Nancy had a job for me painting houses when I got out. A month previous I had been on the cusp of finding real success as a musician, and now I was just happy to be alive, much less sober. One day at a time was definitely real to me now.

In June the rain in Seattle finally stops, the sun comes out, and summer finally begins. I'll never forget that first time leaving rehab, how I could smell and taste things again, feel my body again. I'd learned to breathe there, a deep inhale of hope and an exhale of anxiety. It was good to see Polly, too, who had also stayed clean and was going to meetings. Every day I'd drive to the pier, park the car, and walk on the ferry, nice and simple. Most mornings it was still cold, so I'd sit inside and look out the window with some coffee. The ferry ride from Seattle to Bainbridge Island took thirty-five minutes. Nancy would pick me up on the other side.

I'd just managed thirty days clean when Kristen called and told me she'd come back home just long enough to collect her stuff and move back to Minneapolis to stay, at least for a while. She needed more time away while the band decided what to do next. The U-Haul was already packed and ready to go. She wanted to get together one last time before she went and tried to get me to bring over some of her stuff. Did I have her Sebadoh record?

I knew myself, that I couldn't go over there and not fuck up— this was a classic let's-get-high-one-more-time opportunity, and I was newly serious about this job I'd taken painting houses in the mornings. I didn't want to slip. Polly ended up dropping off the re-cords at Kristen's place at the Swansonia while I watched O. J. Simpson flee in the white Bronco down the 405.

The next morning I was up on a ladder scraping paint from an old Victorian on Bainbridge Island when Nancy told me I had an urgent call—it was Polly. That's how I found out that Kristen had died that night; she'd overdosed in her bathtub. *No, no, no.* The sun beat down on me on the deck of the ferry ride home, even as I shiv-ered with the news. *She had just been here. We had just made a record. We were just 27.* I knew what had happened—just one more hit of heroin for the road, maybe this time she'd get back to the way it used to feel in the beginning. I thought about her there, the warm water turning cold in the bath, her long hair wet and tangled, the way she must have looked when Eric found her.

Before that phone call, I'd been contemplating a new beginning, a sack lunch existence, a life away from the self-loathing and the feeling like shit on the regular. I had the sense that I wanted to live. But afterward, a kind of fresh terror washed over me: What if I couldn't? When I got home, I was in shock. I came back to the house, sat down on the couch, and didn't move until the next morn-ing. I could feel everything, and it was excruciating. The next day I turned on the news to, "Sad news out of Seattle. Courtney Love's band member, Kristen Pfaff, died last night," and then they showed a picture of me.

The phone started to ring almost immediately. Friends, journal-ists, everyone had questions. Could it be another suicide, was it re-lated to Kurt? "This was an accident!" I said, "This was not supposed to happen—Kristen didn't kill herself!" From that day forward, O. J. Simpson news would eclipse everything—not that there was anything more to say. Not enough people had gotten the chance to meet her or hear her play. She was too young. I wanted her back.

| 16 |

LOADED

Kristen Pfaff, May 26, 1967, to June 16, 1994

After Kristen, it was grief layered on top of grief. When Kurt died, it changed the landscape of rock 'n' roll itself, but when Kristen died, it just changed our band. And her lack of fame meant that few people knew. I'd show up at someone's house looking depressed, and I'd be offered condolences for Kurt. It was surreal that her role in Hole was so interchangeable with mine that people got us confused. *Kristen Pfaff died, too*, I'd find myself saying, then not wanting to explain if they didn't know who I was talking about: *our bass player, my friend.*

What were the odds of losing two close friends in so short a time, in the midst of the release of our first record, the one that just happens to have the title *Live Through This*? The shock and anger of it rallied our band, as if we were fighting back against whatever forces in the universe had conspired to end us. I don't remember a lot of time between Kristin's death and the unanimous decision that we would find a new bass player in time to play the Reading Festival on August 26, then ultimately go on the previously scheduled world tour. Before that we hadn't even had a plan in place to reunite, but suddenly it felt mandatory. The worst possible decision would have been to give up.

It was Billy Corgan who recommended Melissa Auf der Maur, a 22-year-old musician from Montreal, whose indie band Tinker had opened for Smashing Pumpkins. Unlike the crazy audition process that necessitated Kristin's hiring, it was all decided before we even met Melissa in person. She would come to Seattle to learn the songs, staying in the guestroom at Courtney's house, before we went to England just two weeks later.

I went with Courtney to pick up Melissa at the airport, and I liked her immediately. We naturally felt for her because the chaos she was walking into would be a lot for even the most seasoned musician. It's a special kind of pressure, learning so much material in so short a time in the exact style of the person who wrote the parts. It helped that she exuded a genuine positivity and optimism and had a kind of spiritual quality—even now I joke that she would be the type to thank the microphones used to record her last album. I don't know if she kept a gratitude journal, but I wouldn't put it past her.

Her personality was consistent, too, which was refreshing: no darkness, serious about her musicianship, a hard worker. I liked that she had a strong sense of herself and didn't look like anyone else, like the Botticelli painting, the Birth of Venus (which I like to call "Venus on the Half Shell"), like she was from another time entirely, or another dimension where fairies and sprites wear miniskirts and leave pixie dust in their wake. Another thing that I'd never experienced in a person before: she had a real patriotism for Canada. I'd never given much thought to "Rah rah America!" but dammit, she was proud to be from Quebec.

Once we had our bass player, we began rehearsals for Reading, which meant I was with Courtney every day and spent a lot of time at the house. I began to notice Frances's new live-in nanny, Annie, who had moved into the attic, which I thought of as the Fonzie suite. She wasn't necessarily my type, but I thought she was cute. Short blonde hair, blue eyes, vegan, and had never smoked a cigarette in her life. Annie had a girlfriend, a real Indigo Girl, but she was no match for me. One day after practice I found myself lingering in the kitchen with her a little longer than I normally would. I absentmindedly talked about the muscle-ache in my back, how I was pretty rusty from being weeks out of practice.

"Oh, I can help you with that," Annie said, echoing the 1970s porn music in my mind, as she started to rub my shoulders, and I felt the telltale physical stirring that comes with attraction. I knew it was cheesy to receive and enjoy a massage on the living room floor by a lesbian with a girlfriend, but I was a lesbian with a girlfriend, too, so maybe they cancelled each other out. After that day, I'd spend a lot more time in the kitchen with Annie and Frances, and a lot less time with Polly.

The actual performance at Reading was fucking scary and emotionally loaded. I couldn't help but look out from behind my drums at Melissa and think about Kristen, who had just been there three months before. We got through it and played okay, but I felt pretty vulnerable and was glad to have sober people around. I was determined for rehab to stick and to honor my friends by not fucking up and dying. I'd brought the Big Book to have with me backstage and listened to A.A. speaker tapes on the plane. I vowed to go to meetings on the road whenever I could.

After England, we flew straight to Cleveland, Ohio, for two nights at Nautica Stage, opening for Nine Inch Nails. We stayed in a hotel that was connected to a hospital, and I wondered if that was a deliberate decision by management. The day before the first show, Courtney was really agitated. That afternoon in her room she casually mentioned that she'd made the decision to fly back to L.A. to get something—presumably drugs—and that she'd see us tomorrow. Coming from a freshly sober place, I begged her not to go.

"Don't do this, Courtney. You know if you do this, you won't make it back in time . . . " I was worried for other reasons than just fucking up the first leg of the tour, but she wasn't having it.

"DON'T, Patty—Stop menacing me!" She shut me down and left that night.

The next day was hectic. No one knew where she was or if she would return. People were worried and annoyed. Eric sulked, and Melissa tried to keep it light, but I'm sure she was confused. I focused on talking to members of NIN and hoping for the best. I was learning about setting boundaries for the first time, especially with other addicts: I couldn't control another person's behavior, and they couldn't control mine—a simple and painful lesson. Courtney missed our sound check but showed up in time for the performance, high. Then I was angry. The sloppiness made me mad. She was all over the place, slurring and yelling, talking too much and trailing off, changing parts midway through the songs, taking her shirt off. There was no reining her in. SPIN magazine's critic said that watching the set was like watching your drunk sister strip at a party.

Afterward, Eric couldn't hold back his contempt. He'd known Courtney the longest and never hesitated to speak up or go off on her. They often screamed at each other like a couple on the verge of divorce. This made me crazy, too. I wished he'd stop trying to rock the boat. It made me feel like a kid again: *Can't we all just get along?*

I WAS GRATEFUL to have a distraction in the form of a new relationship. In early September we played a show in Chicago, and

Annie flew out with Frances. That first night alone together we went to a bar called Berlin and kissed for the first time. It was basically *on* after that. I fixated on her like a drug, my new, better-for-me drug. Music and sex were all I had left, and Annie was so easy to be around. She had a serious maternal quality that I was inherently drawn to and made me feel safe. She was truly gifted with Frances, really loving and attentive, just a natural caregiver. Not too long into the tour, Courtney decided that Cali should be Frances's stay-at-home nanny, and Annie should go on the road with us and work as Courtney's assistant. That decision had a lot to do with me, I'm sure; you couldn't have missed the attraction.

By Halloween, the chaos and the repetition were getting to me. We did a couple of nights in New Orleans, which was a town where I really wanted to make a good impression. Reps from Promark drumsticks, who I had a sponsorship with, were going to be there the first night. And wouldn't you know that was absolutely the worst show—at least at that point in my career—that I'd ever been a part of. There was a lot of talking between songs, and consequently nothing for me to do. It felt like forever before we could get off stage.

Once we did, I rushed the dressing room and dramatically grabbed my bag (one of those regrettably 1990s, stuffed animal-shaped backpacks for four-year-old ravers) and proceeded to stomp back to the hotel. I locked eyes with Courtney on my way out.

"Where do you think you're going?" She eyed me. "We have a couple of radio interviews yet to do."

Radio interviews. Would she never stop talking? I thought I'd signed up to play in a band, not back up someone doing a monologue every night, like *ba-dum-bum* after a joke.

I snapped and threw the backpack (a puppy!) as hard as I could against the nearest cement wall, and everything inside flew out onto the floor. Unfortunately, there was a lot of crap in there—souvenirs from our recent travels, swag from a party we'd just attended at Ann Rice's gothic mansion—including a rubber rat she'd autographed—packs of Marlboro Reds, various CDs that kids would hand to me in bars, Hole stickers and merch from other bands, matchbooks from fancy bars, tampons—too much to collect in a nonchalant manner in front of the crowd that was now gathering to watch. The rage I'd felt when I was a kid, the temper that made me *me*, was back full force.

"Fuck! You!" I screamed as loud as I could, feeling my face turn red and hot.

I felt their eyes on me, the hush that fell over the room when I got angry, the collective *holy shit* of the crowd.

"Whoa, okay, Patty needs a break." I was finally speaking Courtney's language; I could skip the interviews. "Everyone give Pat some space."

In December we got a three-week break for the holidays, and Annie and I went home to Seattle to stay with Courtney. The house had changed since Kurt died, and ever since, it had been rare for Courtney not to be surrounded by people. There had been problems with intruders, kids hopping over fences or hiking through the woods, trying to cut into the yard or catch a glimpse at the place where Kurt had killed himself. There was now a small army of security guards that roamed the parameter of the property and a gate at the driveway with a code.

That year in particular there was always a bunch of people in the house, a revolving group of friends and staff—Joe Mama, Roddy Bottum, Stephen—an old friend from Portland and another assistant, me and Annie, Dylan and his girlfriend, Kurt and Courtney's longtime friend and sometime nanny, Cali DeWitt, sometime nanny Jackie, and sometime nanny Amra, the 22-year-old daughter of an eccentric Hollywood punk, who had been one of Bean's on-the-road nannies.

On Christmas Eve we all gathered at the house for a party. In the months leading up to the holidays on the road, Courtney would not be seen without her Victoria's Secret catalogue. She took it everywhere and circled things she wanted obsessively. The thing was so grimy and dog-eared that once someone tried to toss it out, and she fished it out of the garbage to remind everyone not to fuck with her catalogues. Now I could see that she had been ordering Christmas presents. Mine was a green satin comforter. But Joe Mama got the exact first edition copy of *Valley of the Dolls* that I'd given Courtney for her birthday in July.

Annie and I got Frances ready for bed. That day she'd received an adorable chicken costume as a gift. It became a game to try to get her to put it on.

"Frances, would you mind if I went and got the chicken costume?" I said.

And she'd wait a beat and say, "No!"

"Just once, just this once?"

"No!" and then she'd laugh and laugh. Everything was funny to her.

I sang her the Christmas carol I'd made up for bath time: "The weather outside is frightful, but the tub is so delightful, when you've got really dirty toes, where's the soap, where's the soap, where's the soap!"

It would be Amra's first overnight at the house, and she was invited to stay in an attic-turned-guest room on the floor above. I knew that was the room where Kurt had stashed a lot of his collection of mannequins, dress forms, and various anatomical dolls. He had this one waxy-looking old lady in full makeup and a prairie skirt—she looked like a real person—and Amra couldn't deal. I volunteered to remove it and took it down into the basement, an old wine cellar. This was where Kurt kept his old drum kit, a worn-in Ludwig. I made a mental note to use it whenever I was there to stay fresh between shows.

On Christmas day I went down and played "In Bloom." Maybe for him, maybe for me. I loved the way it sounded. When I was done I went up to the kitchen and Courtney was there alone, looking solemn. "For a moment there I thought that was Kurt."

MY FIRST ORDER of business in town was to break things off with Polly and move out of the apartment we shared. It was an unpleasant reminder that I could completely shut down my emotions for a person I'd loved just a couple months before. We sat down at the kitchen table to talk, and I told her I didn't want to be in a relationship anymore, not while I was on the road. I did not mention the burgeoning affair with Annie. I didn't need to.

"You're breaking my heart," Polly said to me through tears, while I looked down at my hands. I wanted to feel the same level of emotion and sadness, but all I could focus on was the immediate promise of being with Annie again—it took up all my energy. All I could feel was cold to Polly's pain. I don't think karma is a boomerang of experiences but a shitty feeling I carry around still today, the feeling of knowing that I hurt people.

IT DIDN'T TAKE long before Dylan came around to Courtney's to drop off her usual order, and it seemed like a waste not to get in on that. Relapse was as simple as walking downstairs. That first time was actually inspired by Annie, who announced one night during the break that she wanted to see what heroin was like. It was the same old story. If I was going to fall off the wagon, it wasn't going to be for beer—here was the best drug of all being delivered by a friend who knew how to keep quiet, and now my new girlfriend was insisting on him shooting her up, just a little, kind of casually, against my warnings and her usual health regimen and better judgment. Watching her do it, there was no way I could say no, and suddenly I was right back in that place I'd sworn I'd try my hardest to avoid. It felt really good.

For a few days we chipped and had sex while blissfully high, which is a special kind of bonding experience that can be just as addictive as the drug itself. Time stops. During those hours I felt really connected to my body, even though I was also floating outside of it. I was glowing. I didn't mind how thin I was when I was using. I liked the idea of such a small body being capable of making such a big sound, and I felt like I had everything under control when I had those sharper edges. I liked staying up all night having ideas and sleeping off the heroin hangover the next day, then getting up just in time to eat a salad and play music. A part of me felt guilty that I'd essentially introduced Annie to this dangerous and potentially life-altering vice, but a stronger part felt like it was some kind of destiny that we deserved, and maybe we could help keep each other focused on heroin as an occasional vice and not the crutch it had become for some of our friends.

As long as Dylan kept the knowledge of my habits to himself (which I knew he would), and I was only ever buying it when the band was on a break (certainly my plan), it was almost as if it wasn't really happening (if a tree falls in Seattle . . .). I didn't talk to Courtney about my drug use, and she didn't talk about hers with me. She openly took hospice meds in pill form, and we all knew why Dylan was coming over—she didn't have us around so we could tell her what to do, but more likely to drown out the absence of Kurt.

Annie and I could watch out for each other, hold each other accountable, it didn't have to be a big deal—just a once in a while thing. During off days. Maybe on somebody's birthday. Or if I got hit in the head with a mike stand or something during one of the shows—that's a totally legit use for an opiate. I promised myself that if chipping turned to more, I'd simply enter into an outpatient detox and emerge clean and ready to sin again.

After moving out of Polly's, I secured a new apartment in Capitol Hill—my first real adult place. It was in a pre-war building with a nice lobby with painted murals in the hallways. There were hardwood floors and a little room for an office and a place to store my instruments. I bought my first bed with a wrought iron frame and a mattress and box spring and otherwise filled the apartment with furniture I'd inherited from Kurt and Courtney, a well-loved couch and a Formica kitchen table from the 1950s. My favorite feature of the apartment was its original working icebox in the kitchen, separate from the modern refrigerator. I would use it for one thing only and that was to hold a welcome-home syringe full of my reward for those days when I was returning from a long journey. I felt very grown up.

Our first show in January was the Big Day Out music festival in Melbourne, Australia. Now that we were back, I stuck to my regimen of pre-show sobriety, and now that I shared Annie's vegan diet, I could be extra smug on the road (which is funny now, considering all the cigarettes I'd smoke between meat-and-dairy-free snacks, even on a sober day). I wanted my drumming to be above reproach, and knew it would likely be a battle to get through two songs in a row during our set. From the beginning, people were coming to see us hoping for the train wreck. The stress of that was enormous. I felt exposed onstage and often didn't look in the direction of the crowd until three or four songs in. I had a small table set up next to my drums each night, which had a towel, a bottle of water, an ashtray, a lighter and cigarettes, and a newspaper from whatever city we were in at the time. I'd learned from the last go-around that these items were essential to my sanity.

I lived in fear that Courtney would stop playing and yell at me like she so often did with Eric. She expected him to be a mind reader, to follow her all-over-the-place lead. You never knew what was going to happen next. Sometimes she'd stop in the middle of a song to confront someone in the crowd. Sometimes she'd stop in the middle of a song to dive in, taking minutes to reemerge onstage. Sometimes she'd bring a member of the audience up to walk them through the chord progression for "Miss World." Sometimes she'd throw her guitar and walk off. If Eric came in before she was ready, trying to keep it about the music, it could lead to an eruption between them or some smashed equipment.

The violence of the crowd could be scary. In Melbourne, Melissa was hit in the head with a shoe someone threw onstage and got a concussion. The image of Courtney with her leg up on the monitor, her dress torn, screaming—a radiant nightmare—is now forever burned into my consciousness. Performance after performance it seemed to repeat—the ritual of throwing herself onto the willing masses of the pit, who ripped her dresses off and stuck their fingers into her and tore at her thighs with their teeth. Inevitably the guys in yellow shirts would have to rescue her from the frenzy, and she'd emerge triumphant, naked, and mad as hell. At first it was alarming, but by now I'd come to expect drama pretty reliably between "Asking For It" and "Jennifer's Body" (just to name one example). Courtney needed to feel as much as possible in the moment, even when it hurt.

These nightly assaults persisted through Australia and Japan—there was nothing to do but sit there behind the protective wall of drums, smoking a cigarette or reading my newspaper while she ranted about Eddie Vedder or Trent Reznor. When I wasn't losing myself while playing, that meant I was losing myself while just sitting there, waiting for it to be over. I guess Courtney felt she had to do more than play guitar and sing. I always felt that our music should have been enough.

| 17 |

PLAYING YOUR SONG

In February, we flew to New York City to prepare for MTV's "Unplugged," which would be performed live at the Brooklyn Academy of Music. Rehearsals would take two weeks at SIR, a recording studio in Chelsea. The low-fi nature of the show meant we'd have an unusual opportunity to play with a full orchestra. I was also excited to work with producer Hal Willner, who had been the music director of *Saturday Night Live* since the 1980s and was a close collaborator of Lou Reed and Laurie Anderson. It was a real "we've arrived" experience for our band to get to work with luminaries.

When I walked into the room, my drum kit was set up and waiting and chairs for the orchestra lined the wall. I sat down on the black leather couch, lit up a cigarette, and watched the musicians file in. The string section sat down first, taking off layers of coats, scarves, and gloves, and quietly setting up their music stands with sheet music. A tech rolled in an enormous instrument under a canvas bag, which turned out to be a harp. Soon the sound of instruments being tuned filled the air. Finally, just one empty orchestra chair remained, and in walked a guy carrying a pretty large hard case. He sat down, opened the latches, and revealed a baritone saxophone. *Interesting,* I thought, *could be cool.* Then another tech rolled in another large instrument in a case meant for the same player. Inside this one was a tuba. A tuba! I knew this would never fly with Courtney, and I was already wincing imagining her reaction.

I took my place behind the drums. Eric and Melissa came in and greeted everyone. Once we were all set up and ready, Courtney made her entrance. I took a sip of my coffee and waited for the inevitable outburst to come. She walked right up to her chair, took off her coat, grabbed her guitar, and said only, "Hi Hal." After almost two weeks of rehearsals, she never once mentioned the tuba. I stood corrected.

There were four studios at SIR, and one day we heard that Madonna was using the one next to ours. After the musicians had gone home that night, Courtney and I went exploring. It was easy enough, the door open a crack, practically an invitation. The only evidence of Madonna was in a small garbage can next to the grand piano, which contained just two items: a browning banana peel and a used teabag.

"This is for her throat," Courtney declared, picking up the garbage can and tipping it so I could see. "This is part of her vocal warm-up routine."

"You think?"

"It's definitely ginger tea."

That was as punk rock as Madonna got in 1995: a healthy snack. The next day Danny Goldberg comes in and announces that Madonna would like to meet us. "Courtney, I would like to introduce you to Madonna," he declared, as if a great fantasy was being fulfilled. The whole exchange lasted about three minutes. There were handshakes; she was wearing a very fuzzy coat. After Madonna left, Courtney leaned in and whispered to me that she'd seen that coat on sale at Fred Segal.

WE HAD A LOT of interviews and photo shoots in New York. Courtney was simultaneously appearing on the cover of *Vanity Fair*—the very publication she swore she'd sue for slander—and all the major rock magazines in England and the States. We were being shot for a fair amount of video as well. We had stylists and makeup artists—a whole crew we traveled with whose job it was to keep us in lip gloss and looks for performances and shoots. Roz, our regular makeup person, would often joke that the best way to do makeup was to wait for Courtney to nod off—it was the only way to keep her still and give Roz time to fit us all in. I struggled with how I would define my character, style wise, within the context of the band. Courtney was doing her thing—half-naked doll with ripped stockings. Melissa wore the 1970s leather platform boots, mini-skirts, and somehow made a half-shirt look ethereal. Eric was just a curtain of hair in Vans.

Overall I felt pretty good about how I looked in shoots—they gave me a chance to express myself and try different things. I wanted to move beyond the "TOO FAST TO LIVE, TOO YOUNG TO DIE" T-shirt and maintain a kind of soft-butch-on-the-cusp-of-fiscal-responsibility look, with a mod, Richard Ashcroft-y approach to haircuts. I always aimed for Mick Jagger but often ended up with Katie Couric. My playing barefoot was probably the most notable thing about my look, not that anyone could see.

I wasn't overly concerned with looking like the ultimate lesbian or anything; I tried not to play into the categories. You'd never see me in a dress, but I liked lipstick sometimes. I never thought about my breasts as they related to playing drums—ever—until one random night after a show, when a middle-aged dad-type came backstage to compliment my playing. He explained that he was a friend of a friend and had come to the show not knowing what to expect.

He started to gush that I was the best musician in the band, and then he said, "Wow, it's incredible to watch you up there—your breasts are just swinging free when you play—it's a beautiful thing."

Less than twenty-four hours later I was doubling up on sports bras.

It was an odd thing to live like a rock star, being paid in room service and nice sheets, and *experiences*. No cash flow but the chance to be featured looking bloated in the pages of *NME*. My personal rider included ginseng supplements and energy drinks, blank CDs for my discman, and Marlboros. Melissa asked for film for her camera. It wasn't rose petals in toilet bowls—it was just regular rock 'n' roll. Whenever I traveled I used it as an opportunity to try on a new identity. It's an odd thing for a person who grew up in a working-class home—whose idea of success was getting to drive one's own white van—to be suddenly driven around every-where in black town cars and limousines.

Whenever the driver would make small talk, I could not stop myself from creating a completely false identity. What kind of rich person did I want to be during this ride to the airport? Sometimes I was an architect on my way to Spain. I'd ask the driver, "You know those tunnels you walk through to board airplanes? I help design those." Once in Georgia: "I'm a hand model." Then the questions would start, and I would just make it all up as I went along. I looked forward to it sometimes. I wanted to be anything but myself.

THE UNPLUGGED REHEARSALS went relatively smoothly. It was an interesting challenge to learn to play softly and with re-straint. I thought it was good for me. I was learning to listen and pay attention to the quiet spaces between the loud ones. We worked on a couple of covers—Donovan's "Season of the Witch" and "He Hit Me, and It Felt Like a Kiss" written by Carole King. We rear-ranged some of our old songs, "Sugar Coma" and "Old Age," that

Courtney, Kurt, and I had played since we lived together in the house in Seattle.

"Sugar Coma" was more of a song fragment that Hole played to bridge songs during live performances, but a new version of it would appear later as "Boys on the Radio" on the next album, *Celebrity Skin*. Another song that had been in play since the early days, and that we often played a chorus or so of live—but wouldn't be recorded until the following year—was "Best Sunday Dress," that Courtney had written with Kat Bjelland in 1984 for their band Pagan Babies. Courtney's lyrics tended to evolve constantly, and this version took on a new tone since Kurt's death. Almost every song felt like a conversation between them. The set list was something of a tour through the five stages of grief, and I'm sure it was no coincidence that the show would be taping on Valentine's Day.

"Old Age" was another song that the two of them had collaborated on for several years. Kurt had written the melody and had tracked a version of it during Nirvana's *Nevermind* sessions, though at the time it had nonsensical lyrics, and never made it to the finished record. Courtney often brought notebooks and journals full of her writing to rehearsals, and changed choruses and verses while Eric worked through the guitar parts, but when it came time to perform "Old Age" live that night, she had new lyrics completely memorized and sang them clearly. I felt this version was her strongest and most personal. She added the refrain "I'm Sorry" at the end, which is a nod to "South Central Rain" by R.E.M., a song Kurt and Courtney both loved.

There was one cover I resisted taking on and performing live— "You Know You're Right," one of the last songs Nirvana had ever recorded, which had never been released or heard by anyone outside our circle. Eric was against the idea, too. It felt wrong that no one had asked Dave or Krist about it, and if Kurt had wanted the song out there he would have released it before he died. But there was no arguing with Courtney about this, or any, subject. The chorus of "You Know You're Right" is one protracted word, which Courtney sang incorrectly as "Hey." Years later when Nirvana's version was finally released, it was revealed that the word Kurt was extending into five syllables and six seconds, was "Pain."

We finished with "Drunk in Rio," the song that Kurt, Courtney, and I wrote during our trip to South America. I was happy with the way the final performance turned out (though if I had to do it all again, maybe I wouldn't have chosen the button-down shirt with a twirling ballerina print). My mother called to say that I had sounded great, but she wished I had smiled more.

While we were in town, management mandated couples therapy for the band, and we were assigned multiple sessions with a hybrid therapist/certified drug intervention specialist, a kind of rock 'n' roll fixer, which is a side business for former addicts with advanced degrees (or not—they could have just been from Los Angeles). We would eventually go through a few of these people, but this one was memorable for Melissa's nickname for her, Agent Cooper (after the detective in *Twin Peaks*). Cooper had a mannered way of speaking and seemed like the kind of person who would regularly ask for a high five, or worse, a hug. Our job with this therapy was to get to the bottom of the familial dynamic in the band—the ways in which we fell into old habits and turned to coping mechanisms that reminded us of our childhoods. I wondered how much this was costing us. Couldn't we just do some trust falls and call it a day?

At the first sharing circle, Eric and Courtney openly fought—they were definitely the parents, and Melissa and I were their redheaded stepchildren. In the interest of cooperation, I ended up telling Courtney that she scared me, speaking up for the first time in front of everyone, and trying to state the obvious. She was of course incredulous and pissed off. I left there feeling lame. I never had a voice—not growing up and not now in this band. It was why I played the drums and didn't stand out front or talk to the crowd. I was managing a sober path, so as I saw it, avoidance was the name of the game: avoid drugs, avoid trouble, avoid temptation. Avoidance was bliss.

A month later was the one-year anniversary of Kurt's death, and we were in Paris to perform on a TV show. Nobody acknowledged it out loud, but it was definitely in the air; we were feeling it. Courtney was in bad shape and isolated herself completely. We had to reschedule a number of shows so she could convalesce. I spent most of those days with Melissa, who by now had reached her breaking point—she was done. The inconsistent performances, Courtney not knowing what city we were in and shouting a random one onstage while we cringed, the terrible performances, the depressing performances, the endless interviews that had nothing to do with the music (or our part in the making of the music), the physical condition of our lead singer, what we would all call The Darkness—had all conspired to ruin Melissa's natural optimism and love of music and performing. I empathized and felt a responsibility to her; I wanted us both to laugh again. We naturally developed French alter egos and spent a lot of time in Europe making funny videos and talking in snooty accents. Meanwhile our stage manager started to write what city we were in on Courtney's monitor.

AFTER TAPING "DOLL PARTS" for Canal Plus, a French cable channel, Melissa and I slipped out the back. There was a boy with a little book in his hand—he seemed desperate for me to have it, and kept saying something in French, saying "Patty!" over and over. He wanted me to read it. I picked it up and put it in my bag. Later, back at the hotel, Melissa, who speaks perfect French, read it aloud. It was a music fanzine that featured an interview with Kurt in support of *In Utero*. The interviewer talked with him about the new songs and eventually asked about Courtney and Hole. Kurt said, "I don't talk about my wife in print anymore, but Hole just made a great really great record, and Patty Schemel is the best musician in that band." It was like he was talking to me again. And having Melissa right there, able to read it to me, that meant a lot.

| 18 |

TAKE EVERYTHING

By that summer of 1995, after a grueling European tour, we joined the Lollapalooza lineup, which was thirty cities in thirty days. Things got off to a terrible start on July 4th in George, Washington. I didn't actually see it happen, but just as we were about to go on, Courtney hauled off and clocked Bikini Kill's Kathleen Hanna just off stage. It was a horrible start to our set and the tour in general, and I'd always liked Kathleen, who I'd known since the early days when Kurt and I were hanging out in Olympia. Kurt had always been friends with bandmates Tobi Vail and Kathleen, who had inadvertently coined the title for "Smells Like Teen Spirit" when she compared Kurt's natural scent to the popular deodorant of the same name. And, in general, it's not good form for one feminist to punch another, especially if you don't like her. Kathleen wasn't even there to play, but as a guest of Sonic Youth's, a band she'd long been friends with and we all respected.

Courtney ended up having to get her arm bandaged and couldn't play guitar in Vancouver the following day. She spent a lot of the set yelling at Eric to start the songs. Courtney's tempos were always different, but that day Eric played her guitar parts and every song was perfect. In footage I can see I'm wearing a Misfits T-shirt, who I remembered was one of Kathleen's favorite bands. It was my little silent protest in support of her.

This tour would be completed on a bus for the band and crew, always a strange experience, even though I'd grown used to it. The tour bus encourages a kind of intimacy that can feel claustrophobic. There's not a lot of privacy (headphones become your best friend), and there are a lot of rules (no shitting on the bus, no sleeping on the junk bunk where everybody threw their souvenirs, no loud sex). Courtney lived in the back lounge, the main room at the back of the bus. This is where she spent most of her time. My bunk was closest to the back, so I would often hear her watching movies or playing music (sometimes both at once).

She and her assistant, Stephen, had gone on a binge at Block-buster and bought stacks of movies for her to watch on the road. Her tastes were eclectic, and she was always referencing a lot of obscure pop culture and movies in particular. I remember seeing the French biopic *Camille Claudel* with Isabel Adjani, and the best film of 1986—*River's Edge* with Keanu Reeves and Crispin Glover, and my personal favorite—marathon episodes of Season 1 of *Sister Wendy's Odyssey,* where an art historian that just happens to be a nun gives the viewer a tour of different art mu-seums. Courtney was obsessed with the new PJ Harvey record. She played it over and over again that July—if she was on the bus for four hours, she was playing *To Bring You My Love* for four hours. Her favorite song was "Down by the Water," which I soon memorized by osmosis. "*Little fish, big fish swimming in the water/Come back here, man give me my daughter.*" She was studying it.

Drew Barrymore was going out with Eric at the time, and there were so many musicians and celebrities passing through. By far the most interesting bus sighting of my life was when Sinead O'Connor came over to see Courtney a couple weeks into the tour. She hadn't played shows since we'd seen her get booed at the Bob Dylan anniversary concert a few years before, but the Lollapalooza crowds loved her, and she sounded great. Everyone always watched from the wings whenever Sinead was up. So when she showed up on our bus one night, I was completely starstruck. She and Courtney had plans to watch a classic Irish movie, *Ryan's Daughter*, just the two of them. I remember thinking they were in the back for a really long time.

When Sinead emerged hours later, she lay down in the empty bunk across from mine—Sinead O'Connor was just an arm's length away. The next day I woke up and she was gone. The news at the show was that Sinead quit the tour early, left that very morning, in fact—in bare feet—and took a flight back to Ireland. Courtney said she was surprised but for once didn't elaborate. What had the two of them talked about for all that time? Elastica would take her place in the lineup.

The crowds at Lollapalooza could be awful—people yelling at Courtney to show them her tits, Courtney complying, then jumping into the pit to punch a kid who said something rude. These diversions could go on for ten minutes. I played as hard as ever and was receiving the best reviews of my career, but as our shows had turned into spectacles, I found I didn't care to be sober anymore—almost five months clean on the road was good enough. We were in Chicago when I used for the first time since New Year's. It was as easy as ordering up a few bags from Blackie Onassis, the drummer of Urge Overkill, who had a regular hookup in town. Annie was in, too. We figured we deserved an escape from the bleak drudgery of this tour, and if Courtney wasn't going to make an effort, why should I?

HERE ARE A BUNCH of ways I've heard the physical effects of heroin described: like that moment when your dog is getting scratched in just the right place, and it's just heaven to the point of orgasm. *Orgasm.* The physical sensation of someone telling you your lost puppy has been located. *Relief.* Like slipping into a warm bath. Warm. Sedated. Unconscious. "Hopeful." Heroin at first blush makes me feel connected to sunshine, but then the more you take, the darker it gets. "It's the best drug because it makes you feel the best." It's like falling in love for the first time and finding that missing piece, and it's that moment when you reach the top of the highest hill on the rollercoaster, and you take that breath to prepare for the scream as you drop back down.

If you've ever had a colonoscopy or been put under for any kind of medical procedure you'll basically have an idea of what it's like to nod off. It literally happens in 3, 2, 1 . . . and you just feel your head roll back, or forward—maybe you'll be aware enough for the roll—but after that it's lights out. If death results, then oh well, and if you live long enough to merely overdose, you can always take some speed to help you feel more awake.

As for me, I felt it in my back first. A warm wave throughout my core like a relief I'd never known. It was as if I'd been breathing wrong my whole life; all this time I'd only been breathing in, and had never properly exhaled. Until heroin, I'd never known what it felt like to let go. In the beginning, it reminded me of the before-and-after sensation I had as a 12-year-old kid getting glasses for the first time. Slipping them on and really seeing. All this time I'd been missing it, the words on the board, the objects in the distance while in the car (*Oh, all this time I thought that blue thing was the roof-top of a building, but it's actually a body of water*), the way I looked in the mirror. That's the way the dope made me feel, which is ironic, since one lens brings things into focus, and the other one makes it all go away.

The drug is a series of moments: the moment you put the needle in and draw back the plunger. The moment you see your blood in the chamber. The moment you plunge the drug back in, there's that momentary rush of pleasure. The moment you nod into unconsciousness. The first, anxious moment you're aware you're not high anymore. The moment you realize you feel sick. The rage that comes and will only intensify, until you do it all again.

The immediate shot I'd be getting back in my bunk after a show made all the bullshit worth it. I'd play so hard, almost with the intent of hurting myself, just so I could feel that much more blissed-out when it was over. I'd soak in the anxiety of each performance as raw, unmedicated anger rose in my chest, because I knew that the heroin would blot out everything soon enough. The lower back pain and the throbbing in my arms, that thing in my neck, the screaming nerve endings of my permanently bruised wrists and fingers. I lived for that contrast —the dull ache of a pulled muscle and a bad mood, washed away in just moments by a radiating heat from within. (Talk about waiting to exhale.) Heroin, my heroine, yes please.

Word was out that I was a mess, and when we had a three-week rest between shows in L.A., I got a call from management on day two. The message was that my health problems were apparent to everyone, and the addicts in the band had to clean up. I'd have an opportunity to check into Exodus in L.A., the very facility that Kurt was pushed into and had fled from right before he killed himself. I wasn't in a position to decline, but I resented the assignment with everything I had. I was not in the mood to go through it all again, the vicious cycle. Self-medicating constantly to ward off the sickness, then the hell of the physical weaning process, the sleeplessness, the long, inevitable depression that's likely the result of the chemical imbalance in the brain brought on by the heroin (but had also likely been there to some degree all along, which is why an opiate felt like the cure for me). Then I'd have to repair all my relationships that had suffered from what an asshole I'd been for the last several months. Then once I was sober, all that would be left was awkwardness and shame, and for me, too many memories I could never forget.

Who has the time?

I did check into Exodus, but the whole charade ended before it began. Annie came to visit on day two and busted me out. It wasn't a locked ward or anything, and patients aren't forced to stay, but I felt really persecuted and here was an opportunity for a spontaneous adventure. We drove to my L.A. dealer's, then we holed up at Annie's parents' house in Orange County like a couple of teenagers. I think they were out of town. I recall that we had dramatic arguments about our future with drugs. It couldn't last. Management (emphasis on "the man") was paying attention, I was gonna get fired, blah blah. I remember flushing drugs down the toilet and then really regretting it.

For Labor Day weekend we were one of four bands asked to perform in the Tuktoyaktuk settlement of the Northwest Territories, above the Arctic Circle. Arranged by Molson beer and our shared management company, Q-Prime, the plan was for us to play with Metallica, Veruca Salt, and Moist for five hundred North American contest winners who'd been shipped in by Molson for a once-in-a-lifetime promotional experience in a village inhabited by less than one thousand Inuit people. Before we'd left town we'd been given a very stern talking to by our management, as if we were about to go on a field trip to China, not Canada.

"We are about to enter a foreign country where there are strict laws against drug use, and especially drug *smuggling*. If any of you are traveling with anything that wouldn't pass inspection or is suspect in any way, there will be harsh consequences for *everyone*."

No one mentioned the irony that a beer distributor was putting on a rock show in a notoriously dry town—alcohol could be consumed, but not legally sold.

"Holy shit, why not just tell us not to bring any drugs on the plane?" I complained to Annie the night before the flight, as we were packaging all the heroin I'd just purchased into tiny bundles and taping them into little squares at the bottom of a makeup bag.

"Do you think it's okay to put what's left over in the compact?" I asked Annie. "It basically looks like loose powder." Annie shrugged her shoulders—why not.

The syringes were each individually wrapped and placed inside a deconstructed travel hair dryer—my invention. (Crafty like Dad. *If he could see me now.*) In truth I was extremely nervous, mostly because I felt guilty that it wasn't an option for me not to bring the heroin. I was less worried about ending up in prison for drug smuggling than I was for getting busted with my band—letting everyone down was unfathomable.

We all met at Sea-Tac airport. All the bands, lots of management and assistants, some friends, Annie brought along her older sister. One of the big cheese industry execs was accompanied by his girlfriend, who should not be confused with his wife, the one we'd see on his arm at award shows. James Hetfield wore a Viking helmet. There were dogs everywhere, but they turned out to be the bomb-sniffing variety, and we made it through. Even once the flight landed there was still an incredibly long bus ride to go; the only view for miles was cracked mud, earth, and snow. Not even any trees. We heard there'd be caribou.

The makeshift housing meant for the bands was the most rustic I'd ever seen, made of corrugated tin. I wouldn't call them mobile homes, but the structures seemed portable. If this was the good shit, I wondered where the promoters were putting up the contest winners.

"I've had better rooms in rehab," I commented during the tour. Some people laughed knowingly.

Finally, finally we were left alone to unpack. As soon as the door shut behind me, I tore into my luggage and removed the drugs and supplies from their carefully assembled containers. Having gone without for so many hours, my body was reanimating, remembering itself muscle by muscle. It hurt. I looked at my works spread out in front of me on the modest nightstand: needle, dust, fire. *Fuck*. No spoon to cook with, no cotton to filter. There was no time to find someone in the know enough to fetch me some metal cutlery, and I didn't have the energy to make up a story about my sudden desperation for a spoon. Desperate, I looked around the room and settled on a basic glass ashtray with which to cook and used the cotton from my cigarette filter. The process took forever, but I was soothed by the sound of the lighter sparking and the smell of the heroin slowly cooking. Every action to get there was a promise to myself: *as soon as I get this in my system, I won't have to worry.*

Hours before the show all the bands filled the town's high school gym to sign merch for the village natives and contest winners. Members of Metallica were being followed around by a film crew, and Courtney stuck close by Lars Ulrich, telling an interviewer the two of them had just gotten engaged. "How long will the marriage last?" a journalist asked Lars. "Probably until we get to know each other," he said.

We played to the crowd of five hundred under the clover-shaped tent with the just-big-enough stage. Afterward I went back to my room with Annie and took a massive shot. I wanted to be high to see my first Metallica concert. A small group of the other musicians and crew watched from the side of the stage in front of enormous heaters that blew warm air in every direction. I found myself standing next to Courtney and head-banging to "Seek & Destroy." Then as we both swayed to the power ballad "Nothing Else Matters," I noticed an odd odor that seemed to waft from behind us. Catering gone wrong? I turned to whisper to Courtney and noticed that the whole back of her head was trailed by smoke. Her hair extensions were melting in the heat stream. Somebody put a drink out in her hair, and Annie ran over and cut out the offending sections. Just another night in the tundra; I couldn't feel a thing.

THREE DAYS LATER we were booked to perform the MTV Video Music Awards in NYC. I was strung out, and Courtney was also in bad shape, and I remember I tried to get her to call it off. How many times had we played "Violet" live? It wasn't like we had anything more to prove—maybe they'd just let us attend and not play ("Doll Parts" was nominated for Best Alternative Video). Our manager, Peter "Hand of Power" Mensch, laughed out loud when we tried to convince him how unimportant that show was to play. "You're absolutely performing onstage at the VMAs—it's your *job*." Infamously, the evening would not go well.

Indeed we played "Violet" toward the very end of the night, sandwiched between performances by Hootie & the Blowfish and Green Day. Seeing video of it now is a horror. Though the shots of me are mostly from behind and from the side, I can just tell that my pupils are pinpricks. I'd sent someone out to score and shot up before the show, but all I felt was awful. I'd reached that point where the drugs had begun to fail me; the frequency of my use could no longer squash the anxiety of just being alive, not to mention having to appear on television. At that point I felt as if I was injecting fear straight into my arm. I was alone when the drugs stopped working.

In the footage my mouth is open—I can scream and no one would hear over the distortion, but I refrain and bite down, gritting my teeth like the single-minded fiend I'd become. I only have to be effective for four minutes—after that, I'm done. Courtney is screaming the word fuck. Token idiots-for-hire are slam dancing in the "pit" of Radio City Music Hall, and our TV moment ends in our now ubiquitous display of wrecked equipment and punk posturing. Eric kicked his mike stand, and it crashed down on my head.

Intent on getting back to our dressing room and the bathroom with a door that locked, I took a wrong turn backstage and stumbled into a clusterfuck of someone's entourage. I pushed my way through the mass, and there was a bedazzled Michael Jackson, who had opened the show with a fifteen-minute set of greatest hits. This was the moment when he and his then-wife Lisa Marie Presley stood on stage and declared their undying love for each other. They were using that moment on MTV to show everyone that Michael Jackson was a straight, married man in love with the king of rock 'n' roll's daughter—it was exactly the kind of show Kurt and Courtney had put on a few years before with Frances at the VMAs: *See, we're a healthy family.*

I just played on the same stage as Michael Jackson, I thought, *and I could give a shit.* Instead of fulfilling my duties to the press (and participating in the promotion that led to Courtney's infamous interruption of Kurt Loder's interview with Madonna), I walked out the front door of Radio City Music Hall and back to the hotel where I could finally, finally take enough drugs to nod out.

The next morning I had an early flight back to L.A. and a full schedule once I got there. Less than two hours after landing, I needed to be at an interview with *Modern Drummer* magazine, as part of a featured roundtable discussion about the state of our industry and our experiences drumming while menstruating. (Actually, the stated purpose of the article was "to discuss drumming from a feminine point of view.") I had just enough dope to last me the flight.

PRE-9/11, I SIMPLY carried a preloaded syringe in my pocket so I could use on the plane. On any flight longer than four hours, I had to use mid-trip so I wouldn't get sick by the time I landed. The fear of getting caught was overwhelming. I considered a Midnight Express–type sentence to a Turkish prison a better alternative to facing my band and management's wrath. Me being the reason we cancelled a show instead of Courtney? Unimaginable. And yet, here I was again boarding an airplane, casually locating my seat, then heading straight to the bathroom to shoot up. I slept all the way to LAX.

A car was waiting for me outside baggage claim. I told the driver we had to make one stop and directed him to my dealer's house in Silver Lake. I went in and got well, then went straight to the interview at a nice lady's sprawling house in Agoura Hills, arriving in a town car like a rich person too high to drive. The interview had been in the works a long time, and before the previous night I'd been looking forward to it, but photography was involved, and I couldn't fathom how I would get through the day (hour), without continuing to use. I decided to shoot up again in the bathroom just before the interview. There I was, sitting in a director's chair next to six other women, among them Shiela E and Kate Schellenbach— all these personal heroes. Here was my chance to relate and be a person, and instead I'm out of my mind, all the while thinking I'm hiding it.

In one picture I look like Carrie White in the midst of a telekinetic episode: too much of the whites of the eyes; I can tell I'm trying hard to focus and look alive. We were all sitting in these director's chairs, so my legs were crossed. While other people spoke I concentrated on my lap, making sure my hands were resting in a normal, casual way on my knees. Another questionable decision I made that day was to wear a white shirt with long sleeves, probably chosen for its ability to cover my messy arms. Even though it's Prada, the way it's rumpled makes it look a little slept in. Another problem was the blood plainly visible at the cuffs of my sleeve from my recent hasty administration of the needle. This was my opportunity to become legitimate, professional by appearing in a magazine I'd grown up reading. Every once in a while Courtney would introduce me as "Patty Schemel, the first woman on the cover of *Modern Drummer* magazine." (This was not true, nor was I ever on the cover of *Modern Drummer* magazine.) That was her way—if she said it, it might come true, and then she would have known all along. Nobody was fact-checking her from the stage.

I rolled my sleeves strategically, failing to stop the trickle of blood still coming from my arm onto the fabric. Looking down at my hands, I noted their grey pallor while I listened to Roxy Petrucci from the 1980s novelty metal band Vixen talk about her back problems after years of playing drums in heels. I prayed to a god of my understanding not to be called on.

Sheila E was sitting right across from me talking about her collaborations with Prince. Back in 1985, my sister had taken me to see them in Seattle during the *Purple Rain* tour. When Sheila came out and played "Glamorous Life" on stand-up timbales with glow-in-the-dark sticks, I truly got the meaning of the word showmanship. And when she played drums with Prince on the next album, *Sign O' the Times*, her playing on "The Cross" was pure grunge. Once an idol, now a peer.

I answered only three questions that appear in the finished piece and very briefly: yes, my parents were supportive of my drumming, I like to be able to adjust the height of my snare, and I feel it immediately if I have to go in and play hard without warming up ahead of time. Even if I hadn't been high, it's not my nature to take up a lot of space talking about myself, so I was careful to look engaged in what other people were saying. Maybe this article would ultimately help solve gender inequality in music, but in the moment I would be keeping my eye on the prize of the solitude that would finally come when I left.

| 19 |

HOW TO BUY DRUGS
IN NEW YORK CITY

Whenever I was in the city and needed heroin, I went to the Lower East Side and just walked around until I found a street with an alley that looked familiar. Inevitably there'd be a guy who'd step out of a doorway, and as soon as we'd make eye contact, I knew where to follow. Sometimes it was into an elevator in an apartment building, but often I followed the man into the alleyway and he would pause underneath a fire escape, then whistle up. Usually a bucket would plop down on a rope from the sky produced by a dealer out a window above. (One time the bucket was in the form of a sock.) I'd put the money in the bucket, someone on the other end would pull it back up, then send me down $100 worth of bags of heroin.

In New York, they're always branded—a popular designer label at the time was the Playboy bunny stamp. Sometimes, there'd be other people hanging around waiting for their turn. It was a pretty efficient system. The heroin I'd find on the East Coast was usually a white powder, and in L.A. it was a black tar (which isn't a powder but a sticky substance or a small rock). Either one has to be mixed with water and boiled on a spoon in order to dissolve it into an injectable form. There was something about the white stuff that seemed cleaner somehow. I guess it reminded me of the light at the end of the tunnel.

| 20 |

PATIENT PAT

When Hole finally finished the tour, I flew back to Seattle with Annie, Courtney, and Frances. Courtney and I were both strung out. There'd been so much heroin, pills and booze, bad food, cigarettes, and not enough showers. We were skinny and pale and mentally ill with grief and exhaustion; it was hard to come home to a house without Kurt when reminders of him were everywhere. I felt a sense of real doom in Seattle: something had to change or I would use myself dead.

That didn't mean I was planning to clean up just yet. As far as I was concerned, I was on vacation and that meant vacating my responsibilities to my band. We were on hiatus, so I was gonna be high. I was looking forward to daily trips to my icebox.

Courtney had other plans for me. She called one day and declared that we would team up and go on a first-class trip to Hawaii to detox. Annie could come, too. Stephen would be there, and we'd stay at the Four Seasons. It would only suck for the first week, but we'd have the sun and the ocean and volcanoes to help bring us back to basics and make a fresh start.

"That's okay, I'm good," I said.

"Patty, you're strung out. It's obvious. We both need to get clean, so let's man up and do that." She was using her this-is-not-a-negotiation tone of voice.

"I'm not strung out—I'm exhausted from the tour!"

"Hang on a second, Patty. There's someone on the other line—" Courtney clicked over to the other call, and I gestured across the room to Annie that I was in deep shit.

"She knows I'm strung out," I whispered.

"She doesn't know. How could she know? She's the one who's strung out!" Annie was still on my side.

"I'm not going to fucking Hawaii this week; I just need some space from her—"

"I'M BACK!" It was Courtney. "And I heard everything you just said because I was on mute, not the other line. We're going to Hawaii, and that's final. A car will pick you up Tuesday morning—see you on the plane." And with that she was gone. I cursed her phone games, which I'd been burned by before.

WE WENT TO HAWAII, and Annie and I brought the last of the dope, about two days' worth. When it came time to withdrawal, Stephen gave us pills—Demerol and Dilaudid—in a limited supply. These were meant to help us taper off, but he only gave us enough for the first thirty hours, and being time-released, they barely put a dent in my discomfort. I didn't see any of Hawaii besides the inside of the hotel room, and specifically its bathroom. I'm not even sure on which island we were staying. On the third day I begged Stephen for more and stronger pills, and instead he announced that he'd given us all he had. I couldn't believe this amateur operation! Some safe, physician-assisted vacation this was turning out to be! We would be taking the first flight out to Seattle, and we would leave without saying goodbye.

Before we left, I took the last of the pills. I mixed everything— the sedatives and the painkillers, and somehow the combination counteracted whatever opiate was still in my system and threw me immediately into full-blown withdrawal. I had booked us in first class because I knew I would need as much comfort as possible and less competition for the bathroom. We sat down and, as if on cue, I started sweating and couldn't stop. The nausea was unbearable. For six hours I shivered under a blanket, Annie trying to cover for me through her own sickness. "It's the effects of chemo," I heard Annie whisper to the flight attendant. . . "She has cancer. . . . It's not con-tagious. . . . I'm taking her straight to her doctor's when we land." I worried I might have a seizure. Annie covered me with several too-small blankets. It was the worst six hours of my life.

As soon as we landed the driver took us straight to the U-District to get well. The moment it was in my system again, all was right with the world. It was eerie to be so quickly reanimated. My very next thought after I felt right again was, *I've failed again, and ev-erybody knows*. I had to face it.

TAMMY FROM SYBIL found the Patient Pat doll at a thrift store in Seattle. Pat is squishy with red hair and wears blue pajamas with white polka dots, her name printed across her back with her own trademark. She stands about 7 inches tall and is from the 1970s, meant to comfort new patients in children's hospitals. When I moved to SF with Jen, Tammy gave the doll to Larry to keep as a replacement sister, and then he gave her back to me when I moved back to Seattle. I took her with me on every tour, in every country, every video shoot, every drug detox, and every single rehab. She was always in my backpack. Pat reminded me of home and family, and of course to be patient.

I checked myself into a twenty-one-day program in eastern Washington, the same place I'd gone after Kurt died. I didn't want to do it, but I knew I had to bide my time underground, lay low, and gain 10 pounds so I looked healthier in the face. The whole point of rehab was to emerge looking like I'd had a long, restful vacation at a Bible camp. There were many times throughout the decades when I genuinely wanted to get better and feel better and be better, but this was definitely not one of those times; this was about keeping up appearances.

This time away from Annie was supposed to be good for us. Coming off the tour and the failed attempts at getting sober, she was still trying to manage me, but it didn't feel nurturing anymore. It's difficult to be in a relationship that started out sober, then escalated to two people using heroin. We were stuck in the same argument, and we both had trust issues; on some level I must have resented her for choosing to take the drug that made her unable to care for me the way she used to. I'm sure some part of her resented me for introducing her to the feeling of withdrawal.

Admittedly I hadn't been the best girlfriend. If there was an opportunity to hang out with models or musicians I had crushes on, I'd take it. If there was a big party where booze was flowing and drugs were plentiful, I'd take them. Annie had lingering doubts that I could overcome the temptation to cheat. It didn't help when I was photographed with a supermodel in the party pages of *Out* magazine. Nothing had happened between us—the model wasn't even gay—but I wouldn't have put it past me if the situation had presented itself.

I had a sinking feeling while in detox, and then as I moved into week two of treatment, the intrusive thoughts that my sobriety couldn't save us persisted. I wondered what Annie was doing, who she was with. After the first week, I was finally allowed to use one of the four phone booths on the ward. I called our house, and she didn't pick up, so I took the opportunity to check our voicemail messages. As soon as I heard this guy's voice leaving a message for my girlfriend, I knew that my suspicions had not been a product of my high but an unpleasant reality: she was sleeping with him. He was an actor with an unfortunately memorable role in a very popular movie that had come out the previous year, and like me, he was a junkie who took breaks for work. Not very original relationship dynamic, except for the fact that I was a woman and he was a man.

I seethed with rage for ten more days, the whole time lying on a glorified cot dreaming of the all the horrible things I could say to her when I saw her again. I wrote long monologues in my head and wrote about it when I was supposed to be journaling about triggers. *She's not interesting enough to trigger me*, I thought. *The boredom our relationship inspires leads me to use.* It wasn't really true, but it felt good to pin it on someone.

The culmination of twenty-one days of treatment is "Family Day," which is similar to what happens at the end of summer camp. Whoever still loves you comes to the facility for some group therapy and to see the fruits of your arts and crafts workshop. You make amends, then there is a graduation ceremony of sorts. I'd been through this drill before, so I was just relieved that it meant I'd be going home soon. It would be good to see my mom, who was something of a celebrity at this rehab since she had been the A.A. delegate for Washington State and knew the couple who had opened the place.

When it came time to meet my primary counselor, Mom had come prepared with visual aids. She brought in an issue of *SPIN* magazine with a picture of the band, and me looking unkempt, as a kind of show and tell. The counselor, another recovering heroin addict whom I liked, took a quick look at the photo and looked at me pointedly.

"You know the only way you're going to remain clean and sober, is if you're not in this band."

I protested strongly—what a shitty thing to say! There was no way I was going to *not* live my dream just because my dream happened to pair well with the drug culture.

The counselor wasn't backing down. "But it's the same thing over and over. The dynamic of the band is not going to change. The people surrounding you are not sober. Temptation is everywhere. Your schedule is erratic, when what you need now is structure."

I wasn't listening. As each point was made, I'd shoot it down in my head. I was still young compared to a lot of the women there, for one thing, and I was in a rock band. So many of these women had really high stakes losses they were facing, such as custody of their children. I'd listen to their sad stories and their justifications and have no problem seeing their denial clearly. A woman who worked the night shift in a factory, and therefore only drank during the day to avoid the stigma of drinking on the job: *that* was denial. The eating-disordered woman who chose alcohol over food when it came to her daily allotted number of calories: of course she was an alcoholic! The woman who'd resorted to petty scams in order to make enough money for one more fix: glad to hear the one about the rolls of quarters, but none of these were my story.

I said what I knew I had to say to get through each conversation, except when Annie showed up. I guess she thought she'd be my ride home, but after weeks of built-up rage I blew up in her face, which made for a classic rehab breakup scene. She ended up storming out. After "graduation," Mom drove me back to Seattle. As we exited out of the long, winding driveway of the treatment center, a series of signs revealed themselves. "THIS IS THE FIRST DAY OF . . ." I turned on the radio and regarded the first pop song I'd heard in weeks: "Lump," by the Seattle band the Presidents of the United States of America. *Ugh.*

"Mud flowed up into Lump's pajamas . . ." the singer shout-sneered.

"What is *this* shit?" My mother was trying to give me a pep talk about not letting the unpleasantness of this breakup with Annie interfere with my sobriety. I changed the station to Sophie B. Hawkins, "As I Lay Me Down" and found myself preferring it. And in the next moment I wondered what that meant about my sober taste. We'd finally reached the gates out of hell, and I switched the radio back off. The exit sign was clearly prophetic.

"THE REST OF YOUR LIFE."

IN THE END, I came home sullen and sober and told Annie to get the fuck out. She begged me to let her stay one more night, claiming she had nowhere left to go.

"Why don't you go to the Sheraton with the Gimp!"

"He didn't play the Gimp, I told you—he played—"

"I DON'T GIVE A SHIT!" Just then the phone rang and I answered. It was my mom. I didn't let on, though, and instead answered as if I were receiving my welcome home phone call from the supermodel, hoping to lay it on thick for Annie.

"Oh, *hi*. God, I've missed you. How are you?" I walked out of the room and got all whispery. My mother bristled on the other end, probably sensing something was up.

On the other end of the line, the voice said, "Pat, are you okay?"

Annie pretended not to be listening, but I knew there was no way she couldn't hear. I moved into the kitchen.

"It sounds like you're in the middle of something. I'm going to hang up now—call me tomorrow." Even after our call ended, I was in the other room for a good ten minutes, laughing and flirting with my imaginary friend.

ANNIE MOVED OUT of the apartment, then left Seattle altogether. I managed to stay clean for a few weeks all told, from October to November, including the three weeks in rehab. The breakup wasn't even a factor in the relapse, it was more like a lifestyle choice. I hadn't wanted to get clean in the first place, and now that there was no more ball and chain to deal with, I simply decided I would live my best life, with heroin.

It was strange having been on the road for a year and a half with three other bandmates, and now we were all in separate places. Courtney was in L.A. making a movie, and Eric bought a recording studio in Koreatown where he'd disappeared. Melissa moved to New York City where she rented an apartment, dated boys, and posed for photo shoots and wrote songs. My routine? Sleep through the morning hours, wake in the afternoon, go score, come back home forty minutes later, turn on the TV, eat a little something— maybe cereal—and shoot up.

The very best part of the day was when the mail came. The mail was my friend! Because I was still in the scene, because rock stardom was still fresh, I never knew what presents might be coming my way. Packages filled with drumsticks or new equipment, important-seeming FedEx envelopes that needed to be signed for, checks (always a surprise), big glossy magazines shipped from England, rolls of film I'd sent out to be developed, and best of all, gift baskets. There was nothing like a free expensive candle and a shot of heroin to make my life complete.

By March I was back out there, mingling. I started dating Lisa, a triple threat: a multimedia artist, a tattoo artist, a musician. She was another person I'd known from the scene in the late-1980s. Legendary for playing an oven-rack with two forks in an industrial noise band with electrical tape on her nipples. She also art-directed the first Nirvana record and designed their logo. Whatever she wanted to be, she just became it. I guess heroin user wasn't on her list because she didn't really catch on to what I was doing with a belt in my hand while I waited in line for the bathroom at the bar.

Within a couple of months she'd caught on and began to try am-ateur tricks like taking my glasses with her when she left in the morning so I wouldn't be able to drive. Please! I could walk for hours in a blur if it meant there would be a shot and some contact lenses on the other side, and my apartment was only a fifteen-minute-walk away. I'd put Lisa on that pedestal just as soon as we hooked up, and then I started shooting up behind her back. I needed to have that secret life to hide from the person who was normal. Lying. Inserting myself into a relationship I couldn't add anything to but a big, dark blanket of depression and fucked-upness that covered everything.

ONCE LISA AND I started arguing, my reflex was to get back in touch with Annie. We hadn't spoken in months, but I had to conjure that specific dramatic energy that only we shared—I was just as addicted to that. I told her I wanted to try to be friends, and we started talking again. She'd moved back to L.A. and reconnected with her family, then done time in a sober living house, and had managed to stay clean for the last three months. I knew that, but I still asked her to meet up when I was in town for a few days. I realized we'd get high together just minutes into our reunion. You know, "one last time." We went to her apartment. We sat down on her bed and took out the kit. I cooked her a shot, and she stuck the needle in, and pulled back the plunger and emptied it into her arm. And almost immediately turned blue. Annie slumped onto the bed, her eyes fixed on the ceiling. I rushed out of there and pounded on her neighbor's door.

I remember what happens next in flashes coated in shame. The men who lived next door called 911. Paramedics came and gave her the shot of Narcan and she was revived, but looked terrible. I followed the ambulance to the emergency room. But as soon as I got there I felt too sober; I remember thinking that I had to get high again before I saw her. I was the creepy drug addict lurking in the hospital, the one who should have been the one to OD, but instead was shooting up in the public restroom. In the hallway I saw her parents and her sister and felt even worse. Annie had been the apple of their eye—she came from a good family in Orange County, had sisters she liked and parents who never missed a swim meet. It was hard enough that she'd turned out to be into girls, and now there was this addiction to contend with. There was no way around my bad reputation; I was trouble, toxic to others.

I wish a friend's near-death experience would have been the thing that pushed me into treatment, but in fact our band was being summoned to Memphis where Courtney was shooting the movie *The People vs. Larry Flynt.* We would all meet there for a long weekend to write and record during her off hours. On the one hand, I was happy to have the paycheck. On the other, I would need to donate it all to getting clean, my absolute least favorite thing to spend money on. Keeping up the facade at work was the only inspiration for my sobriety.

| 21 |

THE ART OF THE FOUR-DAY DETOX

I waited to detox until there were just five days before I had to be bright-eyed in the studio in Memphis. I checked into Swedish Medical in Seattle for a four-day stay. That's how I rolled—putting off wellness until the last possible moment, 5K on the Mastercard for rest and meds so I could pass for a person who had her shit together in public. Medical detox is not rehab—it is unconcerned with your spiritual life or your future at all, beyond safely ridding your system of toxic substances. That's the appeal for people who can't devote weeks or months—or many thousands of dollars—to a rehab you're not quite sure you're ready to work that well yet. I was no stranger to the process; it was yet another occupational hazard that went hand-in-hand with being a junkie.

When you check in, it's very clinical. A technician or a nurse in scrubs takes your vitals and there's a straightforward interview. What do you take and how much? (More on this in a minute.) How many hours go by after you use before you start to feel the early effects of withdrawal? About six. How do you feel now? Like I'd like not to remember this day by the end of the week. Do you ever share needles? "No." (Sometimes with friends.) Would you like us to test for HIV and Hepatitis? Sure. Are you experiencing suicidal thoughts? Not yet, but ask me in a couple days.

What makes the difference for a more comfortable medical detox is to be honest with your healthcare professional about the size of your habit. Often the tendency is for the addict to minimize the amount and frequency of her own use. And by being honest, I mean *double the actual amounts* so you can get as many sedatives as possible. Kurt was the first person to clue me in to that trick, and having now completed detox probably more than a dozen times, I can personally recommend medical tapering and sedation versus the cold-turkey-with-supervision method that some meaner rehabs employ.

These days you can opt for a more comfortable IV infusion that flushes out the opiates while you're unconscious, but back in the 1990s I was given some Ativan so I could sleep for forty-eight hours in a bed in a wing off the psych ward. There's nothing comfortable about the experience beyond how fuzzy the memories are. A nurse came to check on the patients every so often, and I have a memory of slurping down scrambled eggs straight from a Styrofoam cup, as we weren't allowed access to plastic cutlery.

On the third and fourth days, I'd started to come out of the fog and began to get used to the different sensations in my body. I began a regimen of Naltrexone, a daily pill that blocks your opiate receptors. As long as you keep it in your system, you can't physically get high from taking heroin. (That would buy me five months clean time.) I was given Clonidine to lower high blood pressure, and

Trazodone, an anti-anxiety medication, to help me relax at night. After detox, it usually took at least a couple months for me to get any meaningful sleep and forever to adapt to a normal schedule. It's a special kind of hell to be wide awake at 4:30 a.m. on a tour bus, lying there in silence while the rest of the world softly snores, and you're fretting over the memories of highs gone by and the fear that you'll never feel good again, the fear that you're too far gone.

| 22 |

SISTER

In May 1996, we all convened in L.A. to record a cover of Fleet-wood Mac's "Gold Dust Woman" for *The Crow* soundtrack. Ric Ocasek was producing, and we'd been given a big budget for the video. They put us up in the Wyndham Bel Age Hotel for two weeks while we recorded, and while there Melissa and I found a house to rent in the Silver Lake neighborhood. We filled the big blue house on Kenilworth Ave. with our instruments and a stationary bicycle, which we both used but never discussed. The area was (and is) known to attract musicians and artists, and it was a place where a lot of people we knew lived and played—Butch Vig, Mike D, and Tim Armstrong right nearby.

Today it's pretty expensive to live in Silver Lake, and the two-bedroom houses on the street where we once paid less than 2k a month to rent, now sell for millions. Back then, if you wanted expensive cheese or jeans, you would have to leave the neighborhood to go to Melrose Avenue in Beverly Hills or West Hollywood—these days you can find both in Silver Lake, no problem. In those days, that part of Sunset Boulevard had only a couple of things going on—Millie's Coffee, which is still there (ditto the 7-Eleven on Effie), and the kitschy boutique called You've Got Bad Taste owned by Exene Cervenka from the legendary punk band X. We often went to shows just down the hill from us at Spaceland, a decent venue.

Melissa and I went to so many shows together that we'd gained a reputation for it; if one of us was spotted without the other it was notable. I knew no one could mistake us for a couple—we were both very out about our individual sexual preferences—but we were both single and looking, and I felt pretty disconnected from the community of gay people in L.A. One night I went by myself to the Troubadour in West Hollywood, and this guy Randy from the scene called out to me, "Hey Flea, where's Anthony?" (his nickname for us, the other inseparable pair in town).

I explained that she had gone back home to Montreal to take care of her dad, who was ill. Making small talk, I observed that all the rainbow flags were out—was Pride weekend upcoming? Or were the flags permanent fixtures and I was just too used to blending in that I'd forgotten to notice? Randy was an A&R rep for a record company and had been in the scene forever. And though it wasn't exactly *cool* to be gay in 1996, West Hollywood was, and is, the most gay-friendly neighborhood in L.A., and indie rockers hanging out at the Troubadour were a pretty safe bet, as far as tolerance was concerned. But in the face of these benign questions, suddenly Randy turned angry and defensive.

"I don't know! How would I know? *I'm* not gay," he practically spat at me and stormed off. (He would come out of the closet several years later.)

At that time in my life, I never had a problem meeting women, and I never had a problem telling people I was gay. I didn't care if it pissed someone off that I wasn't their idea of a traditional lady, but it often surprised me that it bothered anyone at all. After that first year of touring, there had been a couple of incidents where I'd be reminded that some people really cared. My ten-year high school reunion coincided with our European tour, and I obviously couldn't make an in-person appearance. A couple months later I heard from an old friend who had gone that I had been the topic of much conversation.

"Did you hear about Patty Schemel?" He mimicked someone saying.

"That she's a drummer in that band Hole?"

"No, that she's a *lesbian*!" After all the criticism leveled at our band that year, the scandal was that the drummer—someone these people had grown up with—was simply gay.

Then when I was dating Lisa, I stumbled upon some gossip about me in a forum I wasn't expecting. Lisa was working at the Seattle paper *The Stranger* at the time and had a computer with the Internet. (Remember dial-up service?) In 1996, the World Wide Web was still a relatively new and exciting way to connect with strangers with mutual interests, and not having a personal computer of my own, Lisa's office was where I often used it. One day I was lurking in some kind of alt rock chat room and came across my name. Someone (possibly a guy) said that they liked my drumming. Someone else thought I was hot and wondered if I was taken. Someone else said they thought I was wearing a wedding ring in the "Violet" video. Then the inevitable, "I heard she was gay." The conversation stopped there. This was confusing on a couple of levels—I couldn't believe that any amount of celebrity could be attributed to me when

I had tried so hard to fade into the background or that my sexuality would be a topic of discussion.

We'd been on the cover of *Rolling Stone* by then, so I was glad that I'd come out in print instead of following what was maybe my natural tendency—to keep my opinions to myself. But I would never forget that feeling of being a freak as a young person, and I wanted to bring the punk ethos to the kids in the middle of nowhere who maybe hadn't yet found their people. That was the power of music and, I thought, the power of our band, especially for young women. I felt a responsibility to them.

THERE WAS THIS girl in the scene who seemed to be everywhere we were, all the time. I'll call her Alice. I began to notice that she went to the same shows and parties that Melissa and I attended, and we often saw her walking in the neighborhood. None of this was particularly unusual in and of itself—she did work at a prominent record label, and making nice with musicians was part of the job. And she apparently lived in the neighborhood. I couldn't put my finger on why, but Alice gave me the creeps. She had such an air of desperation about her—she made no secret of the fact that she was a Hole fan and, by extension, each of us. She could never get to Courtney, who had a policy against hangers-on, but at some point that year Melissa started calling her a friend. I don't think it was anything serious for Melissa, but here was this person who was charismatic and helpful enough not to be a bother, so why not hang out with her?

That spring when we were staying in the hotel during rehearsals, we went to see Stereolab, and Alice came up and introduced herself after the show. I didn't think much of our exchange until we got back to our hotel later that night and the front desk let me know that someone had a left a message for me while we'd been out. When I held out my hand to collect the note, I saw that she'd dropped off a lighter to accompany it. In the elevator I unfolded the piece of paper like a schoolgirl.

"Will you light my fire? –A."

That is 100 percent stupid, so you could say I ignored a lot of warning signs when I kept talking to her after that.

BEING OUT-OF-WORK musicians meant Melissa and I had a lot of time on our hands to socialize with friends around town, make little videos of each other, and work on some music when we felt like it. The plan was for Courtney to take more time off to promote her movie, and we weren't sure exactly when we would reunite to work on the next album in earnest. Melissa and I tried to stay fresh by starting our own no-wave side project, which we called Constant Comment. The recordings were very undefined and sound collage-y. We mixed a lot of synthetic keyboards with sampled audio from found-footage and kitschy recordings, instructionals for the American secretaries of the 1950s on how to type a letter, snippets of "Young Johnny Learns the Proper Way to Cut Meat" layered over some hooks and melodies. We played a couple shows, one in both our hometowns.

What struck me about Melissa—always—was her unquestioning fearlessness when it came to making something. She was the opposite of neurotic about her talent and her right to be there. If she wrote it and worked it out musically, it was good. I envied that confidence as much as I couldn't relate. This was probably the middle child in me and the first-born in her. She was the product of adoration and praise, whereas I was the product of uncomfortable silences and a bitchy older sister. Even when Melissa came home humming a tune she thought she'd written (but was actually the first bit of Muzak that played when we boarded United flights that year). Still, I liked the camaraderie we shared—I liked both the idea of us living together and the actual experience, too.

Melissa spent a lot of time in Montreal that year. When she was gone, I was restless, and when I was restless, I wanted to drink and do drugs. I had managed to maintain a steady near-sobriety on the opiate blocker for six months, but later that fall I had that familiar feeling that I might slip up. The opportunity came one day when my sister, Susan, called with an urgent message: Larry was strung out in Seattle and he needed my help. She had to work a normal job and couldn't get away—besides, it was my turn.

I pleaded with my sister that I was still on shaky ground myself. "I don't think I should go to Seattle," I said. "I can't be around that environment right now."

Susan lost her temper. "Our brother is living in filth, and he can't take care of himself. You need to go find him and pull him out of there!"

A part of me knew that I had no willpower over the mother lode of temptation I was about to encounter, and that's the part of me that decided not to take the opiate blocker when I flew to Seattle the next day.

I knocked on the door at Larry's place to no avail. The windows were blacked out by curtains or sheets. His car wasn't out front—I thought maybe no one was home but figured it would be worth checking out what was going on inside. I had once lived with Larry in a different part of this same duplex, so I knew the landlord lived in a neighboring property. I tried to act casual as I knocked on his door and ran through a script in my head of what I would say.

"Pete! It's great to see you. Do you remember me? I'm Larry's sister—"

The landlord looked concerned. "Is everything okay over there?" I could tell he knew why I had come. I assured him everything was normal—I'd just forgotten my key and had to pick up some stuff. He studied my face for a moment and wordlessly went to produce a spare.

Inside, I found Larry lying on his bed in nothing but a pair of jeans, scrunched into the fetal position, almost catatonic from dope sickness. The apartment was trashed. Everywhere I looked a surface was covered in garbage or stuff; the kitchen sink was so overflowing that the bathtub was also full of dirty dishes. *I guess no one is showering on the regular.* It was clear to me that other people were living there, likely a dealer. By that time, Larry's phone had been turned off, and someone had rigged a telephone line by splicing the wires from a neighbor's apartment and feeding it through a window. I guessed this was how the dealer was able to answer his pages. Susan had been right—this was worse than I'd imagined.

I got Larry to the dealer's, and while I was there I shot up, too. Even seeing him in that condition wasn't enough to stop me from picking right back up. I still had a long way to go before I would let myself get so low, so I pushed away the thought of any comparison between our two habits. As soon as the drugs hit Larry's system, he was reanimated and we could talk.

"So, what happened to your car?" I asked him. I'd given him this classic Ford Fairlane before I moved to L.A.

Larry sighed. "It was impounded weeks ago, and I can't afford to get it back." The tickets and tows he'd accumulated had now made it so the bills associated with losing it cost more than the value of the car itself. "I also had to pawn all the guitars."

We talked about a practical plan for the future, but I knew that he wasn't ready to quit just yet—some things had to come together, and money saved, and arrangements made for treatment. I'd been there myself, obviously, so I did what I'd have wanted my brother to do for me—I gave him money and told him I loved him. I would be there when he was sick, and I would be there when he was well; I would be there.

| 23 |

SHUT THE DOOR

Melissa came back from her trips home to find that I had changed. "You started to shut the door," is how she put it, referring to the door to my bedroom, which we both used to keep open so we could shout across the hall to each other. Literally and figuratively, I shut her out. What had once been a sisterhood now felt merely polite. I was so glad to see her when she got back, but I was in the thick of a binge and I knew Melissa couldn't know about it. But she did, of course. I couldn't hide the obvious. I wanted to be high so I avoided talking with people who might require an upbeat demeanor during our conversation, or expect sophisticated answers to complicated questions, such as, "Where were you last night?"

Oh, I gave it my all anyway, always projecting my voice in an over-the-top greeting (how I imagined a sober person might sound, like I was auditioning for the school play). I kept it simple with Melissa.

At the time I was doing my best Pat Kingsley impression. (She was the most powerful publicist in Hollywood, working for years with Tom Cruise and Ellen DeGeneres.) Pat Kingsley projected a kind of elegant, butch exterior that I was definitely going for that year: Jil Sander suits, Prada shoes, lots of navy, maybe a striped Oxford here or there. Perhaps I was still riding the wave of Courtney's influence, but I had become accustomed to the finer things. I was a rock star after all, and I had an image to protect. If I wanted to get out of the house and treat a girl to a good time, I'd spring for a room at the Peninsula in Beverly Hills, even though it was just twenty minutes away and cost half my monthly stipend. I was desperate to impress, and I constantly felt inferior and increasingly invisible. Ultimately I wouldn't be able to fake that I was monied, cultured, or sober.

Lisa called and told me she'd recently checked in on Larry, and she didn't think he was long for the world. This time I was very matter-of-fact about it when I told him the plan. He would take enough dope to get through the flight, then he would come to L.A. to stay with me to kick while Melissa was gone. Lisa took him to the airport, all his things in a pillowcase, and walked him to the gate.

A few days later we were back at the house in Silver Lake, and Larry was out of his mind while I was just fiending for the next dose. I was just thinking about our predicament when there was an unexpected knock at the door. It was Alice. I was relieved to see someone so willing to improve my quality of life. I explained the situation: Could she get us something to tide us over, just till we got over this hump? She could indeed. When I gave some to Larry, I don't know if it even phased him. He just went back to bed. A few days later he'd move on to convalesce in Palm Springs where our mom lived, and I picked up where he left off.

It wouldn't be long before Melissa told the band about what she characterized as a change in my personality, that she suspected I was using again. A month before recording was set to commence, I agreed to a thirty-day stay at Las Encinas, a mental hospital in Pasadena that specializes in treating addicts with a dual mental health diagnosis (yay!). It was very old Hollywood, the kind of place where movie stars would go to dry out. When I was there, Dr. Drew Pinsky was on staff. The campus had bungalows, acres of landscaping, and a separate medical wing for psych patients. It was hard to ignore the fact that electroshock therapy was available right up the pebbled path past our bungalow. I would see those patients in the cafeteria, the zombies; they had slack expressions and were slow to respond to questions, if at all.

It's important to make a friend in the bin. I always tried to zero in on one person who could make me laugh and normalize the situation, someone I could relate to. It was lonely as hell in there, despite Courtney's care packages stocked with novels, music, and cozy pajamas.

I got lucky when I met Keni, another drummer who had played in the 1980s in a band called Autograph. They had a hit song in 1984 called "Turn Up the Radio," had metal hairstyles, and wore leopard-print leggings. Keni had toured with Van Halen, Motley Crue, and Heart but got less work when the rock landscape changed in the early 1990s in L.A and Seattle. He had the best stories and a spiritual optimism that didn't annoy me. His was a classic tale of addiction: a drummer with back problems falls off a stage and gets hurt badly enough that he's prescribed narcotic painkillers. After he got addicted and could no longer afford the pills, he'd turned to the much-more-affordable street version. Like so many of the musicians there for treatment, ours was being paid for by the Musicians Assistance Program (MAP). Keni was more gracious about the whole concept of treatment than I was. He was the type to make a go of it his very first time out, not wanting to squander MAP's investment.

It made my life easier that this hospital didn't separate the genders—my room actually shared a wall with Keni. In the middle of the night the insomnia was so bad that all my senses were heightened—too alert but physically exhausted, with the hearing of a wild animal (or so I thought). In the quiet of the dark I would lie there listening to the rustling next door and repeat to myself that everything would be okay if Keni was awake, too. (I found out too late in my stay that the rustling I heard was a broken air-conditioner.)

| 24 |

I'M DRUMMING AS FAST AS I CAN

In September of 1997, after a four-year hiatus from recording (aside from "Gold Dust Woman"), the band convened at Conway Studios in L.A. to make *Celebrity Skin*. It was a new era for Hole. By then Courtney was dating the actor Edward Norton, her co-star from *The People vs. Larry Flynt*. Sometimes I'd walk in to rehearsal and there he'd be in the booth, strumming a guitar. Edward was a good guy and he mostly stayed out of the way, but it was always a crowded room. Another presence for the next couple of weeks was Billy Corgan, Courtney's sometimes-friend and collaborator. He was brought in to help her focus and write some melodies and bass parts. It was always an issue for our band—making more material, trying to get enough songs to fill out a set or a record. We'd often have rehearsals where we'd play the same riff for an hour or two, in hopes that something would emerge.

Courtney saw this record as our most melodic and pop yet and wanted a slicker sound this time around. It was rumored that Billy would stick around to produce it, but he ultimately declined. We had a lot of options, but strangely (to me) a decision was made to go with Michael Beinhorn, the notably arrogant producer of inconsequential albums by Aerosmith and Ozzy Osbourne and one decent one by the Red Hot Chili Peppers. This definitely seemed at odds with Courtney's roots in Echo & the Bunnymen, because Beinhorn is probably the Michael Bay of record producers—he's just there to blow stuff up. Everyone in the band had heard the rumors that he was notoriously hard on drummers and generally talked to women like they were all his ex-wives. I expected long days and lots of takes, and I made sure to prepare accordingly. Knowing what I was likely up against, I made it a point to stay clean.

I was first in line to record. During rehearsals, Beinhorn had set up the studio like I was there to go through athletic conditioning, like I needed to relearn to play. Every day I came in on time, and every day he would work me, take after take, for eight hours. Unlike the *Live Through This* sessions, there were no supportive bandmates in the room there to play along with—this time it was all business, just him and me at basic training. Nothing was ever good enough, there was never any praise or specific direction from him besides "Do it again."

It became clear to me that he was trying to wear me down. I had written these drum parts, and this asshole was telling me I wasn't executing them enough, or something. One of the techs told me that Beinhorn read the newspaper in the booth with the sound off while I played. Every night I was frustrated and anxious, sober, and in pain— my back, my hands, my ego. No one was giving me any feedback.

Day after day was exactly the same. I'd get to the studio, and he'd be sitting in the control room with a Moog modular that I'm pretty certain was never used on the record (but probably cost the price of a used car to rent every day), eating his premium takeout sushi and going on about his favorite Fellini film, *Amarcord*. He tried hard to cultivate the posture of the artistic genius who works out, but when he insisted on cigars for his smoke breaks, I couldn't help wonder if he got his tucked-in dad jeans from the juniors section at Bloomingdales.

I couldn't understand his relationship with our music. It seemed to me that when people connected with our sound, they weren't thinking of the precision of the fucking beats per minute. That 15-year-old-girl who listens to our music in her bedroom while she contemplates how much she hates her life, is not going, *Oh my god, that snare!* The truth is, he was always going to push me out, just like he'd done to all the others.

At the time, I still believed we were a feminist band, and Courtney would never have thrown me under the bus based on the opinion of this one guy. And yet, after Beinhorn played her some takes and told her I got red-light fever in the studio—that I'd forget what I was doing once he pressed record—she approved my replacement, a goateed session drummer named Deen Castronovo. He'd been on deck and ready to step in the whole time.

"You just dropped the ball, Patty. I'm sorry—you're out," was how Beinhorn put it to me when I wouldn't concede.

Even as I knew in that moment that this had been his m.o. all along, it was a massive blow that I never saw coming, compounded by the fact that Eric and Melissa didn't appear to have an opinion one way or the other. I'd been dealing with a week's worth of averted eye contact. My faith in Courtney was dead. My confidence as a performer had now been replaced with a question mark. I wasn't going to show it, but it shook me to the core.

I seem to remember storming out of the studio. Fuck you, motherfucker. *Fuck. This.*

| 25 |

ONE WAY OR ANOTHER

It took about five minutes to get un-sober again after that. I stormed back to my house and Alice was there within minutes, balloon of dope in hand. It was as if she'd been waiting all along for a moment like this. All I cared about was numbing out my intense anger. Images of Beinhorn's arrogant face, Courtney's indignant one, and Melissa's above-it-all indifference competed for space in my aching brain. Every instinct told me that Alice was a terrible person, but she was a terrible person who would do anything for me, exactly my type at the moment. I was never more alone. I'd done that to myself.

I raced home to pack a bag and called Alice. I explained what had happened and that I was going to need a pile of drugs and a place to use them as soon as possible. This was Alice's favorite kind of crisis, a real woman in peril story and an opportunity to be useful, and this time I'd come to her.

On the drive to her house I was shaking with rage. *How could this have gotten so serious, so fast? What was going on? Was I out, or was this some kind of test? I was sober. I'd abstained before and during!* And then deep sadness in the pit of my stomach. *How could Courtney, of all people, do this to me? She loved my drumming. Kurt loved my drumming. We were family. Melissa . . .* All of it was painful, and I couldn't stand to hear the thoughts in my head.

Within minutes I was at Alice's. Did she have the stuff? She had it. We'd have to smoke it—she wasn't an IV user. Fine, fine, whatever. Just then, her house phone rang and she picked up. I looked at Alice to gesture her over. She pointed at the phone and mouthed the words, "It's Courtney."

"I don't want to talk to her."

"She wants to talk to you." I could hear her talking through the phone. "She's calling from your house."

What? Courtney didn't go to people's houses. She had certainly never been to our house before. She must have been there with Melissa. I imagined her looking around our living room and making the observations she always makes about a person's living room. Some version of, *"Oh, look at that painting of a cat—you're such a Neo-Romantic. Is that a Tiffany lamp?"*

"How did you get this number?"

"I took an educated guess that this might have been the last call you made before going over there. I hit redial." (Goddamnit, Courtney and her phone games.) "Patty, this is business. It isn't personal."

"Not to *you*! It's pretty fucking personal to me."

"You have a choice, you know," Courtney said. "You can use right now and throw this tour away, or—"

"I haven't had a CHANCE to get high yet, so once again, you're just wasting my time. BYE!" I slammed down the phone and got straight to work on the task at hand, smoking that heroin off a piece of foil. As soon as I was done with that, I went down the hill to the pharmacy on the corner to get the little needles for diabetics and went on a proper bender.

There's this concept of using *at* another person (or the world). It's that *I'll show you what high looks like, bitches!* mentality, and I knew it well. I used at my girlfriends, my family, society, and Earth. But that day I used at the horrible producer, Eric, Melissa, and Courtney.

KENI AND I had kept in touch since we both left Las Encinas, and I told him about what had been happening with the record. In September, when my replacement was finished with basic tracks, I exercised my right to come into the studio and hear him play the drum parts that I wrote. I brought Keni to Conway with me so we could A/B (listen to my parts as I wrote and played them, then the other guy's). Of course they were so different. One was slick and shiny and void of emotion, and the other one was me, playing the songs as they were meant to be heard. The vibe in the studio had changed, too. Beinhorn had a new hairstyle—it had been cut short, bleached, then dyed blue in the places that weren't yellow cheetah spots. (Maybe it was leopard—I always get those confused.) Synthesizers and film equipment littered the studio; a girl I'd never met before was playing guitar in the booth—this was the stuff that was taking up all the space that I'd used to.

Keni's advice to me was not to give up. He told me that this wasn't my fault, that this is just what happened to drummers. So many of them didn't play on their own records—their value was in the live performance. To prove it, he insisted I meet his friend Fred who had been the drummer for Cinderella for years, and Fred told me a similar story. Producers liked to use their own session players; it allowed them better control over the overall tone of the record. As drummers, we were the most replaceable of all band members. I shouldn't take it personally, and I should never walk away. Keni had a mantra. "You're not done."

There's a practice space in Hollywood called MATES, and Keni arranged for me to use an empty rehearsal studio there. I'm not sure if he'd suspected I'd relapsed, but I kept going even after I had. I'd get high and go there by myself, setting up the Beat Bug, a metronome to count the beats per minute. I had to prove to myself that I could keep time (and keep time while under the influence). I needed to know I wasn't crazy.

IN OCTOBER, COURTNEY sprung ye olde intervention, Hole-style. For this one, she'd arranged for catering. Maybe the sushi was supposed to make it feel like less of an ambush/official firing and more of a business lunch. In fact she had summoned me to her house to discuss the album art—that should have been my first clue—Courtney never asked anyone to share in creative decisions, or at least no one in our band. As soon as I walked in, there was my brother, Larry, and my mom and Buddy Arnold, who notoriously ran the Musician's Assistance Program for rock star addicts that I'd just utilized a couple months previous.

I practically spat at Courtney. "Really? Because this worked so well for you when you pulled it with Kurt."

I couldn't believe her hypocrisy. Why wasn't she ever the one ever getting intervened upon? This time they wanted me to go straight into a sober living house, a place where I could be "safe" for a while. It sounded like the rest of the band were the ones needing protection. Neither Melissa nor Eric attended.

I immediately threw a tantrum, "Fuck you, I'm not going!"

"If you do this, Pat, you've still got a shot at the tour. You're still on the cover of the record, you'll do press . . . " Courtney was doing all the talking. "But you'll need to do this now. We need you healthy."

Healthy. Safe. Clean. Out of the way.

Eventually I amended my answer to, "Well, I'm not going *tonight*."

I knew I was in bad enough shape that I wouldn't be able to resist treatment for long, but I felt strongly it was every addict's right to one more night, one more blowout. But for some reason, I could never seem to get enough drugs in my system to get high on those nights.

Insulted and indignant, I reported for duty the next day, as directed, to the all-female "Liberty House." (Ugh.) Liberty's was a sober living situation made up of about a dozen wayward women and an old alcoholic den mother named Bette Albright, who was something of a celebrity in the sober community. The setup was two women per bedroom, a shared kitchen and bathroom, chores, therapy, group therapy, AA meetings, more therapy, exercise, and work.

The house had strict policies, but the rules would bend for me. Rule number one: under no circumstances should an addict who has used anytime in the last seventy-two hours be admitted. They need you to be alert enough to receive the tough love. Plus they're not equipped or licensed to deal with any kind of medical intervention. In order to qualify for a slot, you'd had to have kicked on your own or at another facility. Most of the residents had already completed a thirty-day program somewhere else. But because my intervention was sponsored by MAP, and because the house had an empty bed on short notice, and because my band was affiliated with an extra-famous person, I was delivered to them still high. Which was unfortunate, since I then had to kick cold while trying to hide it from whispering women: *Why does she get to sleep in?*

It would take me a month just to begin to come out of the fog. Stripped of my defenses, privacy, and any hope of a good mood, I found that my anger was back with a vengeance. Every year there was a gala fundraiser for the House, and every year the housemates had various responsibilities in service of the event. Mine was to stuff gift bags with donated moisturizer. One day Marge called me into her office to check in on my progress. After the usual pleasantries and bullshit update about my ongoing efforts to get my life back on track, the conversation went like this (paraphrasing):

Marge: "As you know, we rely on celebrity attendance to the gala. It raises our level of visibility and makes an impact on our fundraising. I understand you're in a band with Courtney Love?"

I quietly seethed in my chair as she continued on and considered all of the things I wanted to say. *Would there be an open bar at this gala? Because nobody I know, addict or not, is going to want to go to an event without booze. Courtney Love—the obvious poster child of health and sobriety—at a fundraiser to benefit fallen drummers, junkies, and drunks in Los Angeles. Would the media be there? Cause if not . . .* I shifted in my chair awkwardly as she spoke, showing with my body what I couldn't say out loud: This was inappropriate. I was so uncomfortable.

Me: "I'll see what I can do."

There was another issue she wanted to discuss. She'd seen that Alice had dropped off some clothes for me the day before.

"I'm going to assume you don't know that Alice has been a visitor here in the past and directly interfered with another resident's treatment. I told her a long time ago that she is not welcome here. Now I'm telling you."

I had not known that, nor was I in a position to care enough to protest.

"Sorry, I didn't know—it won't happen again."

A FEW WEEKS INTO MY FIRST MONTH IN, I was granted a visit home. I decided to go to the house in Silver Lake. I couldn't imagine going back there after everything with Melissa, but all of my possessions were still there. One day when I suspected she would be out, I broke into my old bedroom after climbing up the back of the house like some kind of paranoid ninja. A quick walk around revealed that Melissa's friend Rufus Wainwright had moved in. I left a passive aggressive note on the refrigerator: "Please let me know when the house will be empty so I can move out."

I managed to trip the alarm on my way out, so my plan not to talk to anyone had been thwarted. For the first time in weeks I spoke to Melissa on the phone. Where was the rest of my stuff? She told me that she'd had everything packed up and I could find it all in storage at Drum Paradise. And that was that.

THINGS STARTED LOOKING UP when I began spending quality time with Hannah, a recovering crack and everything addict who had been at the house for more than three months by the time I'd arrived. She had her own room, a car, and all the extra privileges that came with having more sober time under her belt. We got to know each other in the meetings where everybody in the group shared her story. We were the same age but didn't have much in common beyond that, though she did have great taste in music. Otherwise, she was straight, and her boyfriend had been the one who had saved her from the streets. Her addictions to crack and heroin had come on hard and fast. Just hearing her talk about it made me miss life on the outside.

Unfortunately my roommate, Maya, was a bit of a drama queen, and six weeks into my stay, she told on Hannah and me. Engaging in sexual relations with another resident is generally forbidden in rehabilitative settings, so when Maya went to Marge to confess what she knew: that she had seen us fraternizing, which had made her uncomfortable, and the whole thing was a threat to her treatment. We were both immediately kicked out.

Hannah's car made for a convenient exit. We were out of there in no time, and on our way to buy some dope, first thing, then drive to the Valley to pick up Hannah's friend Dawn, who was in a rehab there—bust her out, and take some drugs. Dawn wanted crack and heroin, and that worked for us. She had a hookup and an apartment in Reseda. That's when I smoked crack for the first time. I'd have tried anything at that point anyway—I didn't hesitate. There's nothing to it, really. You just inhale. Then there's a palpable jolt of electricity shooting straight to your brain, if getting hit by lightning came with an explosion of pure euphoria. It made me feel numb and tingly at once. And weightless. The first time I smoked crack, it was so overwhelming that I vomited. That first time in the car with Hannah after my first hit, two moments later and I'm opening the car door, ducking into an alley to throw up, wiping off my chin, getting into the front seat, turning to her and saying, *That was amazing.* I couldn't wait to do it again.

And so began this love affair with a new drug; the new girl was part of it, but mostly it was about the chase for that Feeling. I felt it in my heart, and not metaphorically. I heard bells ring, but not from music. Sometimes if I got a big enough hit, I'd hear a high-pitched chiming sound go off in my head. We called it "a ringer." I knew I'd get addicted to this after that first time, especially because it complemented my dope habit so nicely. I figured out that if I alternated the two of them, they accented each other's effects. The tendency when you're doing crack is to take it over and over—it only lasts a moment, maybe a minute, then subsides. So the heroin helps diminish the cravings. I also believed that this combination evened me out, made me appear stable to the outside world. It was a more hardcore version of the "hippie breakfast" of coffee and a joint. Crack is just coffee for dope fiends.

So the poor man's crack pipes: I got these little glass vials you can find at any mini-mart. They're usually sold as a decorative container for a tiny silk flowers, a gift for ladies and children. It's got a cork stopper at the other end; it costs about a $1. You take off the cork stopper and chuck it on the ground. You remove the flower and flick it up in the air to see if it blows away. Then take a Chore Boy copper scouring pad—the bare bones original; it has to be Chore Boy, nothing else will do—and take a bit of the wire from it, and stuff it into the bottom of the tube using an old-fashioned wire hanger that you've straightened to a point. This is your filter and will collect the resin. Next you put a piece of crack on the end of this makeshift cigarette, light, and inhale. After a day of smoking your stash, it's time to "push your pipe," which is when you take your collection of the day's Chore Boy filters and push them back in the pipe to inhale all the resin. It was a horrible smell all around, like chemicals and toxins and burning metal.

We'd been hanging with Dawn for about two weeks, getting together daily to get high at her place. One day the three of us were in her bedroom. Dawn shot me up with dope, and I guess I just fell back on the bed and immediately turned blue. They dragged me to the bathroom, and I came to in the shower, as freezing cold water rained down. Once I came to, hoisted on two pairs of shoulders, my friends, who were trying to keep my blood circulating, trying to help my body remember what it was supposed to do, I thought to myself, *Why are these people fucking with my high?* Then I smoked some more crack to bring myself back around.

I'd learned to live with the possibility that I would actually leave my body like Kurt or Kristin, and not come back. But the risk wouldn't stop me from doing what was going to make me feel good, if only for a moment. If I'm unaware that my life is in jeopardy, would I even know that I'd died, or would I just fade out on a grey cloud?

I OBVIOUSLY WASN'T going to live with Melissa anymore, and Larry was who I'd always lived with when I wasn't with a girlfriend. My brother was the only person I was sure I loved and loved me back. But he was newly sober and working the program and taking it very seriously. When we did see each other, it was just for an hour or so. He mostly stayed away, and I stayed away back—the part of me that loved him of course wanted him to be healthy and happy, and I was relieved that he hadn't given me an ultimatum. More than anything, I didn't want him to see me like that, so skinny and sick and obviously about to lose everything.

I had a little money so I rented an apartment in Koreatown and stocked it with all the things that Melissa had put into storage. Hannah broke up with her boyfriend and moved in. I told myself I deserved to have a little privacy again. I deserved to feel good about myself. I deserved to feel good.

| 26 |

USE ONCE AND DESTROY

I had committed to participating in the shoot for the album cover of *Celebrity Skin*. It would be the first time I'd seen the band together since storming out of the studio two months prior. I prepared by shooting dope and smoking crack every hour until I had to be on location. In keeping with the record's theme of California's broken dreams, the cover image was meant to look like we were on the beach at night in front of a bonfire but in black and white with a high contrast. But instead of the beach, we were on location way the fuck near the Angeles National Forest, a good hour drive from the city. Apparently because of fire codes or something we had to be in a wide open space to light this palm tree on fire. And we had to accommodate everyone with trailers and wardrobe stations, etc. I was going to have to be "on" after a night of extreme partying. Well.

This was the first time I had seen Melissa and Eric since I'd left the studio. It was painful to fake it when I was already feeling so uncomfortable, and I could feel they were angry, too. When I got there I went straight to the wardrobe trailer, where our stylist Arianne Phillips (also Madonna's long-time costume designer) had things all picked out—tops, leather pants, boots, jewelry, all the details you'd never be able to pick up in a photograph. Everything fit me beautifully because I was so thin, a real sample size. I'd probably lost another 15 pounds since picking up the crack habit. Inside I was completely checked out, so rather than try to make painful conversation while the crew was setting up the shot, I found myself drawn to Courtney's trailer.

Inside she was watching *Sister Wendy*, her old favorite. In this episode the nun was visiting the Sistine Chapel and commenting on Michelangelo's masterpiece on the ceiling, "The Creation of Adam" (which I always think of in my mind as "The Finger").

"Hi," I heard myself say quietly, as we both stared at the television. "You know, it's not about the fingers touching, it's about the space between the fingers."

For the first time Courtney turned to address me, "Yeah! You're so right." Oh my god, I'm losing my mind, I thought, but pushed it out of my mind. I'd think about that another time.

We made small talk about the photographs we would take. I was going to ask if this cover was meant to look like the Gun Club's *Miami* from the early 1980s, but an assistant came to fetch us before I could; the photographer was ready for us. I stuck close to Courtney so I wouldn't have to interact with Melissa and Eric. It felt terrible just to stand next to either one of them. Courtney knew more of what I was going through than the others, and yet she had betrayed me. I couldn't forget that part, and I was still mad about all of it.

We took our marks, and I looked far away and to the side and straight into the camera. I thought of the drugs I would do when this awful day was over and tried to make that translate through my eyes. I had brought some crack, but I worried that it would be too hard to smoke in a mobile home because everything you could inhale would be expelled through the hole in the roof. I'd have to fake a sudden craving for incense, and even then I couldn't be sure that would mask the intensely chemical smell of the crack. What I really wanted was some dope, but it was all gone—I'd finished it in rest stop bathrooms en route to this place. And now I was fiending for the invisibility I got from heroin, that feeling that I'd disappeared inside myself, where I couldn't feel the fear or the shame.

A fan blew my hair away from my face, and I wondered if it was apparent in my eyes that I'd recently gotten high. Someone behind us was shouting, "Light it on fire!" Then the palm tree went up in flames. I felt the heat on my back. This would go on for hours until the fire tech got hoarse from yelling.

It was a relief when Courtney offered to give me a ride back to my place in her town car. I was obsessing over the thought of getting home to Hannah, getting in the car, driving to the dope dealer's. Using.

This would have been a great opportunity for us to lay it all out on the table and really talk about next steps, what happened at Liberty House, the future of our band, and how to move past the anger. Instead, we talked about anything else. Courtney did ask me where I lived now so the car could drop me off.

"In Koreatown, on St. Andrews."

"St. Andrews, Pat!

"What?"

Courtney laughed and pointed out the irony of the address, as if I'd chosen the apartment in homage to a lyric in a Jane's Addiction song about a junkie, "Jane Says."

"You're strung out, right?"

"Yeah, I am. I smoked crack and shot heroin all last night and this morning," I said. What was the point in lying.

"You're smoking crack now?" She kind of chuckled.

"I don't discriminate."

We were quiet for a long time, but as we neared my place Courtney surprised me by asking me to come over to her place in Hancock Park that same night. "I have a lot of clothes and I need to purge. Come over? Bring your friend if you want . . . "

I knew just what she meant.

I collected Hannah; we hopped in my car and drove straight to the dealer's to stock up. Then we took it over to Courtney's very nice rental house, and then we all shot some dope.

This was notable for several reasons.

One: the irony of my firing, by Courtney, due to my perceived drug abuse that wasn't actually happening at the time of the firing but clearly instigated my most recent downward spiral, had now brought me full circle to shooting heroin with the person who fired me.

Two: I had maybe only seen Courtney shoot up once before, and I couldn't remember if that memory was real or imagined. The truth was we never did heroin in front of each other. I had seen her car outside the dealer's, and I knew she'd used needles with Kurt, but not openly—it was something to be done in private.

Three: She needed me to do it for her. It's a pretty intimate thing—the ritual of tying off, finding the vein, cooking the drug, and preparing the syringe. You either really trust the person or you're desperate. I did it all, and when it was time to pull back the plunger, I pushed it in and pulled it back again so that her blood mixed with any residual contents of the syringe, then pushed again.

"Look at you, Patty—double booting," She said.

"I don't like to waste any."

Four: Hannah and I totally smoked crack in the bathroom but kept that to ourselves. It would have been disrespectful to the hostess to partake in a drug she didn't. Plus crack wasn't "cool," it was some street level shit, which was proof that I was out of control. Once we were high the three of us retreated to Courtney's massive walk-in closet, stocked beyond capacity with racks and racks of designer clothes, many (most?) of them brand new or never worn. Comme des Garcons, Alexander McQueen, Dolce & Gabbana, Marc Jacobs, Gucci, Helmut Lang—she gave it all to us! I still have a pair of Versace shoes she gave me from that purge. Courtney did this a lot—gave beautiful things away to people. As soon as something went out, more would come right back in. It was a cycle. Receive, give, take, repeat.

Five: We never acknowledged how notable any of it was, which is what made it feel normal.

| 27 |

SOON

Would you believe that my burning love for Hannah didn't last very long on the outside? Even before I was far away from crack and L.A., I realized there was no way to continue the drama with this straight woman I'd only known for a couple of months. "She's using you," was the refrain from anyone associated with the program, and of course that was obvious, as I was guilty of it myself—users use. Drugs, people, opportunity. She'd stayed at my place for as long as I'd had it, and already I was over it. No more drama.

The decision to end it was reached in my 1971 brown Mercedes sedan, which I drove around Echo Park so I could think and contemplate my next moves. I was a total player with my Motorola StarTAC cellular telephone, with its calculator buttons and adjustable antenna. My cassette player featured a removable plastic face that could be stored in the glove box, so as not to entice thieves. I had my own stash of heroin and crack. What could be better?

I hadn't spoken to Alice since I left the halfway house, but somehow we started talking again just in time for me to need her help. I told her about Hannah's latest mess: she was still seeing her boyfriend, she brought shady characters to the apartment, I couldn't deal with her, and it was no longer fun. Alice told me not to worry—she knew how to take care of it; she had a plan.

After the shoot, I was cut off completely from the band. I heard only from Hole's lawyers. The gist of that conversation was that I could not expect to see anyone, much less rehearse with them for the tour that I couldn't join, if I didn't finish another thirty days of treatment. I still believed then that we would reunite at that point. I'd made it six weeks, and I hadn't been kicked out for using, but for fascist, anti-gay house rules. But then the lawyers repeated that I wouldn't receive any money that I had coming to me unless I completed thirty more days. And since I was out of money, I had to do it.

This time I'd be going to the dreaded Hazelden, the Minnesota institution, the rehab of choice for the desperately out-of-control, where celebrity addicts went to fellowship with poor people and get serious about their recovery. Chris Farley had been there just the year before, and then he overdosed and died. (They say Matthew Perry had a better outcome.)

I took as many drugs as possible in the hours leading up to the intake, as was my way whenever I'd have to stop taking them for any length of time. Even as I was traveling to Minneapolis with a professional escort, aka "sober coach," hired to get me there, I got high several times in the bathroom on the plane. Everything I needed to smoke or shoot was in my pocket. It turns out there were no good times to be had in an American Airlines toilet. It was never enough when I knew how much I was about to miss it.

I've seen the inside of a lot of treatment centers, but I've never had the touchy-feely experience you hear about in Malibu or on some private island with full spa services and equine therapy. I've never looked out over the ocean and contemplated the changing seasons of my life. I'll never associate an attempt at sobriety with a scenic body of water or a smoothie. Hazelden did have an Olympic-sized swimming pool that had been gifted by Eric Clapton and some lush walking paths, but the place was also dorm-like in its bare bones simplicity and featured all the same glum decor I'd come to expect would populate every rehab in North America.

The ubiquitous white plastic chairs on the patio from Costco/Lowe's/Kmart, you'll find 'em there. The same marbled glass round-table with its sad green umbrella and standard-issue restaurant ashtrays, back when ashtrays covered every tabletop, as essential to your meal as the salt and pepper. Hazelden methods were old school—medical detox, followed by constant twelve-step group work, and tough love. After I detoxed, when life came into focus through sober eyes, the familiar fear and overwhelming panic set in. As any fleeting conviction to wellness started to dissolve, I would be pulled back to the blurry numbness. *I need this thing back!*, my body was screaming. *Soon*, I would reassure myself through gritted teeth. In just a few weeks I could crawl back into my drug dungeon and live my life again. I bided my time listening to the shares, the notable speakers, and alumni, and clutching my Patient Pat doll, just waiting.

THE DAY I GOT OUT, Alice was waiting to escort me home in person. This was another time she could swoop in and be a hero. While I was gone, she had gotten to work making sure Hannah moved out and stayed away. She changed my locks and put Hannah's things in storage—I'd never have to worry about her coming around again.

"I hope it's okay, but I brought some of my stuff to have at the place—I don't think you should be alone right now, and I can be there for you when you get back on track with the band. You know, help out with the day-to-day."

Honestly, it was a relief to hear it. I thought in that moment, generally speaking, that Alice did have my best interests at heart, or at least my *interests*—she was never going to question my judgment or priorities or keep me from what made me feel good. Was "feeling good" too much to ask for?

"Okay," I said to Alice, not feeling like I had a choice, but I had bigger problems that needed my immediate attention. After another thirty days clean, all I cared about was getting home and holding drugs and their associated paraphernalia in my hands once again.

| 28 |

TAKING CARE OF BUSINESS

Now that I was back from the requisite thirty days, I felt ready and able to get back to work. I called Courtney and didn't hear back. I called management and didn't hear back. Then I received a letter from Hole's lawyers informing me that in fact I wouldn't be coming back—the band had made its decision, and I would be replaced on tour. The tone of the letter was all business.

"Can you believe this shit?" I threw the piece of paper at Alice. "After two rehabs; after all I've been through!"

Alice, as always, had an idea. She knew a lawyer who she thought I should consult about getting a settlement from Hole for my pain and suffering. Damn right.

EVEN IN MY altered state, I could tell my new lawyer was a hack. According to a plaque that hung above his desk, he'd passed the bar exam, but he was junior varsity level, clearly. But I was on a budget, and I needed someone to help me extricate myself from the band, contractually. Though, to hear this guy talk, I deserved a windfall. I had to admit I enjoyed hearing the words, "You should have more . . ." "Don't let them get away with this . . ." "priceless contributions . . . " "You have a right . . . " *You're goddamn right I do.* I looked at him behind his messy desk with its tall stacks of neglected paperwork and last week's coffee mug, still half full of murky brown liquid, and I said the following: "I want a million dollars."

I don't remember his response, like if he laughed or not—but I knew it felt great just saying the words. Of course, I had no idea what I was owed or what was possible. I just knew that I wrote all of Hole's drum parts, and I'd been paid around $40,000 for the Lollapalooza tour the year before. Melissa and I had each borrowed money from our management company to live off until we started touring again (money that would need to be paid back), and my habit had made it so I was constantly broke. Even though Alice was the one who recommended this guy, I took advantage of attorney/ client privilege just to have someone to vent to while extra tweaked from crack that I was sure she was stealing from me. She *was* stealing from me, but I just think it's crazy that I was using these business meetings to tell him that I thought my girlfriend was also fucking someone else. Like, what could he advise? *Let's try and keep the focus on one betrayal at a time, Patty.* Everything just blurred together into a mass of paranoia and persecution.

After weeks of negotiations with Hole's lawyers, we settled on a termination agreement. I would receive a one-time payment of $150,000 for my work on *Celebrity Skin*, and a $25,000 advance against a percentage of publishing royalties on a few songs that I helped write since I'd joined the band. In addition, I would receive copies of any gold and platinum albums of *Celebrity Skin* should

they both perform as expected, as per the original recording contract. (The album did, indeed, go platinum.)

I mean, sure. I'll take it. I had no concept of money. At the height
of the *Live Through This* period I was making considerably less
than that annually but still more than $100,000 a year, which
seemed to me to be a royal sum, considering I was traveling the
world, taking loads of free drugs, and staying in the Four Seasons
for weeks at a time. I think people expect that most musicians in
popular bands are millionaires, but that's not really how it works
for most of us who aren't writing lyrics, and that goes double for
drummers; a drummer is widely considered to be the most replaceable member of any band. You're living high on the hog in some
ways, but it's borrowed money with a borrowed lifestyle. This
chunk of untaxed cash would be what I'd need to live on for the
foreseeable future.

So the day of the final negotiation, I needed to be present at my
lawyer's office for a phone meeting so I could agree to all these
terms. Lawyers for the band would then fax over the agreement for
me to approve. This was to be the culmination of weeks of back and
forth, so I had to be on my very best behavior and as clear-headed
as possible. But because of this pressure—and because I'm an addict—my instinct was to get as fucked up as possible. I certainly
couldn't handle this shit sober, not a business dealing. I'd already
been up all night doing drugs, and I was out of the stockpile before
the sun rose.

So I drove to my usual spot where I'd cop on the street in emer-
gencies, and no one was there. Trying not to panic, I decided to try
another location that I wasn't as familiar with on the corner of
Wilshire and Alvarado, right across from MacArthur Park. I parked
the car a few blocks away and headed out on foot. It's a heavily
trafficked area—a lot of shops, bodegas, a swap meet—and here I
was wearing hospital scrubs as pants and the same ratty Melvins
T-shirt that had been stuck to me for the last couple of days. No
thoughts given to the fact that my exposed arms are covered in

track marks. I'm just like, *I've got a very important business meeting to get to, so I've got to get fucked up first.* TCB, Schemel style.

Copping on foot is never ideal in L.A., but in a pinch I knew the drill. It helped that I stood out from the usual addicts; a redheaded white girl wouldn't have to wait very long. I scanned the crowd of people on the sidewalk. Most were minding their own business or looking down as they walked, but I looked for the drug dealer, the only stranger who would look you in the eye. It only took a minute to spot him and exchange mutual eye contact, before he gave me the nod. I nodded back in recognition, and we approached each other. I handed him the money I had folded in my hand, like a handshake between good friends—one 30-year-old white girl in pajamas meeting up with her old pal, a Puerto Rican teenager. So easy.

I turned around to start walking back to the car and suddenly felt this hand on my shoulder.

"Excuse me," The voice said, as I turned around to find it belonged to a cop. "Give me your hand and don't drop what's in it." He grabbed my hand, and I dropped the drugs. Then there was another cop, this one a woman, and together they escorted me down the street a little ways before he pushed me up against a brick wall and handcuffed me.

"We watched that whole exchange. You're under arrest for buying narcotics."

They walked me down to the corner and put me in the back of an unmarked Crown Victoria. The backseat was made of plastic, which made me feel cheated somehow, like it's a set piece and not a real car. They take me to the Rampart station (at the time notorious for a massive police corruption scandal), cuff me to a bench, and I get processed. When I got fingerprinted, the cop made a comment about my hands. When you're a crackhead, your thumbs are calloused and thrashed from working the lighter, so it's pretty noticeable—you've worn it down so much, your fingerprint is more of a smear.

After the mugshot, the protocol is pretty degrading. They make you take your clothes off, and it's supposed to be clinical, but it's not like any other physical examination I've ever experienced. For one, there are too many other people around when an officer tells you to bend over so they can make sure you're not hiding anything in any of your orifices. Except the person examining you probably doesn't have much more than a high school diploma. They're wearing Latex gloves and putting their fingers in our open mouths to do a sweep for contraband. I tried to remember the last time I'd brushed my teeth.

After booking they put me in a holding pen with all the other women who were waiting to be arraigned or released. That's when I knew it was real, when I was locked in a cage with mostly other addicts, all withdrawing from our drugs in front of each other. After the first ninety minutes in there, I felt a wave of panic: *I'm going to start getting sick.* I hadn't managed to get any new drugs in my system for several hours, and things would be moving in a bad direction as the hours passed. Pretty soon my stomach would be making my intestines an offer it couldn't refuse. Next to me, an emaciated woman in full sex-worker's makeup lay on the ground shitting out her balloons of heroin, and she wasn't quiet about it. Talk about a buzzkill.

Instead of heading to the lawyer's for the power meeting, I had to call him from jail for a referral. "Hi, it's Pat. I'm not going to make it this morning cause I just got arrested. Know any good criminal lawyers?"

He did. The lawyer told me he would get in touch with Alice, who would hopefully be there shortly. I could handle another two hours, I told myself, but not much else. *It won't be an emergency until the sun goes down.* After the call, I was moved to a smaller cell, where my assigned roommate knew the ropes. There were bunk beds, so at least we could lie down, but they were hard plastic, with the standard issue wool prison blanket that depressed me.

The one I'd inherited had holes in it. For lunch we finally received a meal of grey Beefaroni. I contemplated what looked like human guts on a paper tray before me. The dish was gussied up with a slice of white bread and a pat of butter. Unappealing, but I ate it.

Six hours later I was getting pissed. What could be taking Alice so long? I decided to lie down and was able to manage some sleep before finally being released in the middle of the night.

When I saw Alice, I was relieved because it meant I would be able to do drugs again soon, and I was mad as hell that she'd taken almost twenty-four hours to show up with bail. This wasn't the first time she'd performed this particular duty—she regularly bailed musicians out of unpleasant situations for her job, and she had access to my money.

"I feel like you could have gotten here a little faster," I said to her, realizing just then how much I needed her to survive right now. Alice was craftier than I was and more sober.

She started to apologize, making a list of all the things she'd had to do that day in order to get to me. I tuned her out and then back in when she said, "Don't worry, Patty. Everything you need is waiting at home."

| 29 |

WALKS UP ON ST. ANDREWS

I read somewhere that 35 percent of all the people at an A.A. meeting are court ordered to attend. And not all of them are even addicts—twelve-step meetings are seen by the courts as an alternative for jail when jails get too crowded, so that leads to all kinds of offenders mixing it up with some of the world's most vulnerable people in a church basement near you. Mine was now one of the court cases. I was given a mandate of hours I'd need to spend at a meeting per week, which I resented completely, feeling a horrible sense of déjà vu from all the rhetoric and rituals I'd grown up with. Now I was one of the sad sacks who put their court cards in the donation basket for signature, having to provide proof that I'd taken my daily communion with a higher power, talked to strangers I had no desire to talk to about subjects I had no desire to examine or explore. It would be a losing proposition for all involved.

In addition to the meetings, I was also sentenced to attend "drug and alcohol school" twice a week. This program was like drivers-ed for addicts; we watched short films produced by Mothers Against Drunk Driving. There were endless PowerPoint presentations about what would happen to our brains and bodies if we continued to mis-use substances. We heard many testimonies of recovering addicts who did hard time for their fuck-ups, who had stories of redemption I wanted no part of. Good for them, but I wasn't done yet; I was maintaining, I was just buying my medicine when some quota-filling, likely corrupt cops intervened. I wasn't hurting anybody—that's what made me feel so defensive: my body, my choice. The whole experience was a total crock of shit, and I was comfortably high through it all. For some reason I was never drug tested. It was probably random, and I just got lucky, but the drugs I was taking no doubt emboldened my decision not to worry about crossing that bridge.

MY TEETH WERE all fucked up, just absolutely rotting out of my head. Heroin addiction is bad for oral hygiene. It's not unusual for teeth to chip and crack, and there are several reasons why it's as-sociated with heroin. My teeth were ground down from grinding so hard at night or when so high I wasn't aware of what my jaw was doing. When I did get sleep, it was fitful and that contributed. Many addicts crave sugar while high, or always. It has something to do with replacing dopamine in the brain—you take those chem-icals wherever you can get them. The sugar mixed with your dis-regard for old brushing and flossing habits leads to simple gum disease and tooth decay. You generally aren't eating that much when you're using, so you're not getting nutrients like iron and calcium, or biotin and Vitamin D. And if the heroin causes fre-quent vomiting, the stomach acids will further erode your enamel. You experience a lot of cotton mouth, which is bad for gums and causes further sensitivity, not that you care when you're using. If you smoke the drugs, your teeth will turn brown over time.

While I still had insurance, I went to a dentist when I was already so far gone. I was worried and ashamed to open my mouth—it had to be obvious to everyone, but what was worse was getting the work done—fillings and extractions without the benefit of pain relief. Oh, I wanted to be knocked out, but that wasn't an option—a local anesthetic was the usual protocol. But Novocaine had no effect whatsoever. There was nothing to do but squirm and bear it and wait for it to be over.

I was also having severe lower back pain. Some days it was hard to walk, and I couldn't move until I took a shot. It's a common side effect of being a drummer, but I'm sure what I was putting my body through every day with the drugs was a major contributing factor, plus all the emotional stress I was under. Once again Alice had a referral—maybe I needed to see her doctor at St. Vincent's. He was thorough but wouldn't lecture a drug addict. The hospital was right near my dealer's so I decided to give it a shot. The pain was just getting worse.

The doctor ordered an MRI, which revealed osteomyelitis, a disc disease. The heroin had been masking the pain for as long as it could, but now there was no relief without it. With the amount of opiates already in my bloodstream, the doctor prescribed the non-narcotic pain reliever Tramadol to help ease withdrawal and, I suppose, the back pain. No pill was going to cut it for me; even just psychologically speaking, I couldn't wrap my head around the idea of pill-shaped relief. Needles were the only way to stop a feeling fast, and now that I had an official diagnosis, I could justify my desperate need for the bad/good stuff.

THE MORE TIME ALICE and I spent together, the more I heard her memories of us that I didn't share. She remembered meeting Melissa and me in the grassy area outside the venue at Lollapalooza in L.A.; apparently she'd given us a ride to the stage on a golf cart. I had no memory of this, but anything was possible.

When we first started hanging out, Alice was giving me a tour of her house, which sat above ours on a winding, hilly street. I couldn't help noticing that there was a telescope in her bedroom pointed out the window but not at the sky. I got a strange feeling just seeing it. Later, when I was alone, I looked through its eyepiece and was disturbed to see it pointed right at our house.

Alice had lots of stories about her life before she moved to L.A. Sad stories from Cleveland, some memories so traumatic it was hard for her to talk about them more than once. She told me and Melissa that years ago she'd had a fiancé back in Ohio—a musician and pure artist—he had been the love of her life. They were already living together and planning the wedding when he was tragically killed in a fiery motorcycle crash. But later, when Alice was staying with me and we were acting as if we were a team, we entertained two of her close friends, another lesbian couple in town for only a few days. I took one of them aside in order to ask her to fill in some gaps about Alice's past. Specifically, had she known Alice's motorcycle man? Her friend's eyes grew wide. *"Wait, who?"*

Our fights were epic and embarrassing and also heated enough to get physical. Alice would say something to incite my suspicions and paranoid thinking. She had this friend named Dennis, yet another guy in a band, who she called her best friend and spent time with on a regular basis. I was pretty sure he knew all about our problems and all of my secrets. I was also convinced that she was sleeping with him, or had in the past and was lying about the nature of their relationship now. The crack made me extra amped in my anger, and I'd pushed her against a wall at least once before when she'd gotten in my face. I remember screaming, "Why don't you *ever LEAVE?*" before leaving myself. She went to our doctor for an X-ray, claiming she worried I'd broken her elbow. The test came back negative—she was fine. She wasn't going to press charges, she told the doctor, but she wanted "documentation" in case "the violence escalates." Then she got a big bill that I had to pay, which she waved in my face with wild eyes. "Look what you've done! You caused this."

To avoid repeating such an experience, when we'd get into screaming matches, I would storm off. This made Alice angrier still, and if I'd run out to the car she would chase after me, ranting some crazy talk straight out of a bad movie.

"Look at who you've become—this is *your life*!" She fancied herself a creative writer, so she was always spouting lines like that, meant to be wake-up calls. Please. In another three hours she'd be virtually lighting my crack pipe for me. Two could play at the shitty dialogue game—we were in L.A., after all, the home of bad acting.

"You're the last terrible thing that is ever going to happen to me!" I shouted with conviction before getting in the car and peeling out of the driveway.

Eventually I'd return, she'd be asleep on the couch, and I'd go to my bedroom and close the door, and it would all happen again the next day.

I can remember being asked during rehab intakes if I'd ever been involved in domestic abuse, either as the abused or the abuser. I always said no. But I knew that I had changed, that the anger swirling around me sometimes got so intense that I couldn't remember that it wasn't normal to behave that way. Everything was an immediate reaction. I'd heard it a million times in meetings—when you're drinking and using, always put a "yet" in front of all the things you say you'll never do. *I haven't hit my girlfriend in the face, YET.* Another line had been crossed; I was fully capable of hurting another person.

I RECEIVED THE SETTLEMENT CHECK in one lump sum, which was fortuitous timing, as we were evicted from the house on St. Andrews. But I had a six-figure check and a plan for a fresh start in a new neighborhood with Alice and my drugs and my privacy. No one in my ear with criticism, no one to answer to. I was free.

I did not know it yet—though I should have—that this move would be the beginning of a descent into hell that would change my life forever.

| 30 |

BUYING DRUGS IN L.A.

It's pretty easy for famous or monied people to get any kind of drugs they'd like in L.A. I've seen giant pill deliveries sent by messenger or FedEx, of drugs so good you can't even get them in the States, that were then sorted by personal assistants for their rock star employers with the same casual ease used to accept a delivery of flowers. *Would you like the amphetamines on the mantle above the fireplace or on the silver tray on the coffee table?* I didn't bother with pills unless I needed them to help ease the symptoms of withdrawal (or to use them as currency). Even if you weren't rich and famous, the drug culture in L.A. provided a buffet of options for the addict of every class. There's one El Salvadorian bakery I used to frequent that was known primarily as a Valium distributor. You would simply go up to the counter and order "20 blue" with your slice of coffee cake, and that got you twenty Valium in a brown paper bag for $20. No big deal.

The heroin in L.A. was usually a sticky black tar the color of molasses. It's twisted up in a plastic baggie then placed inside a little rubber balloon to protect it and tied at the end. You need that extra layer because dealers transport them in their orifices. The thing with California is that it's sunny all the time. When you buy it on the street, you learn to perform in bright light, which requires a stealth rapport with your neighborhood dealer. There are certain streets users know to drive down if they're in the market. All you had to do is make the turn down the street and hover for a second, and a guy would dash out to your car real quick. You'd roll down your window, give him a $20 bill, and he'd swipe the inside of his cheek and release the balloon. Heroin would be in the sides of the mouth, and crack would be in the pocket behind the bottom lip, like chewing tobacco. You tell them you want a rock, and he'll reach in with his index finger and thumb and pull out a stack of rectangular squares, like ten of 'em, then he'll swipe 'em onto your hand like a secret handshake, transferring them so they stick to you with the help of his saliva.

By far the best way to buy drugs in L.A. is at a dealer's house. My local spot in Silver Lake was a real who's who of notable cocaine and heroin abusers. Because it's Hollywood, there's always going to be that industry element, but I would not have expected to see an autographed photo of Jean-Claude Van Damme inscribed with a personal note to our drug dealer, thanking her for the good times. She hung it in a prominent part of the house so you could see his endorsement, as if this were a dry cleaner on La Brea or a diner wallpapered in actor headshots.

Mary fulfilled a stereotype I'd come to know over the years of the residential dealer. First, she's a junkie, too—she doesn't try to hide the abscesses. They give her an air of altruism, like we're all in this together. And yet there are a series of rituals that must be respected before orders can be filled. First you have to make small talk with her and the other players. *How old is your nephew now?* or *I really like the light-blocking capabilities of those drapes—do they come in different lengths, do you think?* I often took a moment to admire the photo albums and flip through the scrapbooks that she helpfully displayed on the coffee table. Naturally she was an aspiring portrait photographer, inspired all her life by the musicians and entertainers who now made up her clientele. There was a picture of her and Scott Weiland together backstage stuck to her fridge (and it had been there for five years).

Inevitably Scott would be there—he was the type to stay for hours, just getting high and shooting the shit. I loathed having to stay and chat, but it was the only gateway to having my needs met, and I didn't mind him. The conversations junkie musicians have with each other are pretty clichéd—if it's a lead singer, they want to do a side project; if it's the bass player, they've had it with the guitarist; if it's the drummer, they just want more respect. All roads lead to the following conversation—one that I witnessed, and participated in, many times.

Person No. 1: "My band doesn't understand me. I'm just not moving in the direction that I want to be, creatively. I'm so sick of the record company dictating what the next single will be. I just want to crawl into a hole for a while and record something stripped down with a 4-track."

Person No. 2: "You should totally release a solo album as an alter ego persona. You deserve your own Ziggy Stardust, man."

Then the junkies would have the same conversation the next time they saw each other, because inevitably at least one person had forgotten that this was well-worn material (even if one or more of the participants had formerly agreed to help the other with said side project).

Like all dealers, Mary had a strict "cash only/no-trades-for-product" policy though also lived in an apartment full of odd, random shit—usually in the home appliance category—you could tell was either stolen from the back of a truck, or somebody was pawning off their wedding gifts. For the longest time, Mary had an unopened box containing a home foot spa in her living room. I could imagine the scene: Would you like this drill? It retails for $135. (Unless one of Mary's clients worked for QVC and it was swag, which is entirely possible. This was Hollywood after all.)

| 31 |

SIX MONTHS GONE

On August 17, 1998, we moved into a big, new, rented house with a pool on a cul de sac in the Eagle Rock neighborhood in northeast L.A. This was a real house with three bedrooms, a two-car garage, and a manicured lawn. Just as soon as I signed the lease, we started filling the house with all the necessities. Or Alice did. Suddenly we had a new set of silverware, every possible kitchen utensil, dishes that matched, cloth napkins with rings, new pots and pans for all the cooking and entertaining we were going to be doing. A new stereo, a big TV, surround sound.

I had decided to fashion one of the bedrooms into a recording studio. I bought some guitars (that I couldn't play), an 8-track digital recorder (perhaps for the new band I would put together), new amps, and effects pedals. A new power suit for all those public (court) appearances I'd be making. I paid $30,000 cash for a new car—a nice, safe Volvo (because I was responsible). I figured you needed two cars to fill a two-car garage. I rarely even looked at the pool, but I had all the lounge furniture in case I got inspired.

Before the settlement check came through, my habit had cost me about $200 a day to maintain. Afterward, my use skyrocketed to "however much I wanted to spend." I wanted more, always—I had to fill all that was empty—the rooms in the house, my body with substances, and the multiple pockets stuffed with paraphernalia in my Woolrich utility vest that looked like I'd picked it up at John Popper's yard sale. Alice got whatever she wanted too. She had an ATM card connected to my account and was in charge of all the shopping. I don't recall the conversation that led to that decision; it was just another thing that happened. Alice was another proxy to my instant gratification.

I knew I needed help managing my finances. Since I'd joined the band, my sister, Susan, had generously been handling my money for me. She'd set up a diversified portfolio of stocks, mutual funds, and IRAs. I was an early investor in Starbucks, for instance. Now that I'd received this windfall, Alice suggested a money management firm that could pay my bills every month and put me on a budget. Susan was happy to sign everything over to the new firm, and they gave me an allowance of $800 a week for food and incidentals. My incidentals were drugs, gas for the car, drugs, the occasional pizza, drugs, and whatever Alice was buying that week. But no matter how much it cost, I demanded every need be fulfilled, every wish granted.

Our relationship post-reunion was largely sexless. I was Alice's full-time job, and we were always together but kept different hours. She smoked her weed and drank her beer and passed out early in front of the TV. Meanwhile I would stay up all night making things and listening to music obsessively—certain songs over and over— and closing in on a cocaine-induced psychosis, imagining Alice with other people. Was it a coincidence that we moved so close to Dennis's house? Now we were practically neighbors.

For me, the thing with Alice was more about the game of staying with someone I didn't trust and using that drama as a diversion from the pain and the shame over what I was doing with my life. At the same time, I thought I was lucky, I thought I was rich. I'd heard my picture was on a billboard on Sunset—an ad for the album. I couldn't be bothered to drive to Hollywood to see one more reminder of my failure, and my new house was a cocoon wherein I could pretend my life was a success. I couldn't imagine the money would run out, even though I was spending it like a millionaire with low self-esteem.

A MONTH AFTER moving in, a friend called me up and said, "Hey man, I saw you in the new Hole video."

"What video?" I slurred, just out of my mind high at 11 o'clock in the morning, trying to take the edge off.

"On MTV, right now. You're in the video for 'Celebrity Skin'!"

"I am?" I could have sworn I hadn't shot any music videos lately.

So I turned on the TV, and there's Samantha Maloney playing the part of me as the drummer in the video, her hair dyed a similar color to mine. That was kind of the final straw, that moment. I was about to enter the fog, I could just feel it. The I-don't-give-a-fuck fog.

EVERY DAY AFTER that, I smoked crack and shot heroin and sat on my couch fuming, always with a feeling of such persecution. *Who are they to think I can be replaced so easily? After all I'd done for Courtney, been through with Melissa, put up with from Eric's shifty blind allegiance to Courtney's bad decisions.* The more crack I smoked the angrier I became. Courtney told the world on MTV that I had left the band to "take care of some health problems"— *fuck her.*

Alice fueled the fire. "I saw that Hole is going to perform at the Billboard Music Awards," she announced one day. I wanted to throttle her. "I don't *care*." A part of me knew she was baiting me, that she liked to stoke the fire, but I was busy practicing my angry comebacks to imagined band meetings. *I brought those drum parts into the world, and I can take them out!* But when random newspaper reporters called to get my reaction—did I care to share the story of why I left?—I hung up without comment every time.

At certain times during the day I was more lucid than others, but what came with that was a feeling of enormous self-loathing and regret. As soon as that negativity got anywhere close to the surface I knew it was time to bliss out on some black tar. All day long, it was about finding a balance: first there was anger, then brief euphoria once that first drug of the day hit my system, a period of paranoia and fear, and then I had to formulate an action-packed plan for what to do with my high. Next came the inevitable dive into the pit of despair that accompanies a faded buzz, which is when I would experience the strong desire to inject enough heroin as necessary to induce absolute sensory deprivation. Then I'd go on a drug run, feel sick until I got there (but better once the balloon was in my pocket), then back home again, where I could finally shoot up in peace and stop thinking.

The record company mailed me my platinum record for *Celebrity Skin*. I found the framing quality to be surprisingly lacking, and while on a crack binge, I decided to prove my theory that the label sticker on the painted vinyl was fraudulent. I peeled up almost half of it just to prove how cheap it was. Turned out I was right, and unlike Nirvana's platinum record, the record they'd used was not even Hole's—it was an old one by the Saints (and I'm not even sure we shared a label with them).

I'D RECEIVED THE settlement check in the beginning of September, but by March I only had 30K left to my name and could no longer afford to rent the house in Eagle Rock. For the past couple of months, Alice and I had been fighting constantly. Some days I hated the sight of her, but she was my only link to the outside world. I needed someone to help me make this next transition, to keep an eye on the money, and help me stay either high or clean (depending on the day). The only place we could go on short notice was back to Marysville, Washington, where my dad still lived in our childhood home. I called him and laid out my situation, told him that I was desperate to get clean. I couldn't allow myself to look at what was actually happening to my life moment to moment; I simply said whatever I needed to get to the next step in the process. I needed shelter, and I still had a dad, so I'd go there, and Alice would follow, and then I'd figure out what to do next.

| 32 |

BRINGING IT ALL BACK HOME

When it came time to make the move, I couldn't deal with the complicated logistics, so I hired a bunch of people to do it for me. I still
had that now-diminished chunk of money (which I withdrew from
the bank in one lump sum to have easy access to the cash) and
couldn't imagine moving would cost so much that I'd notice a big
difference. Besides, I had become accustomed to just making a call
when I needed anything. I was a success, and successful people
shipped all their possessions up to their parents' suburban houses in
minor towns outside Seattle—everybody knew that white glove service was the preferred method of busy people like me. I needed help
packing and unpacking and putting most of my possessions into
storage near Dad's house.

I don't know why I didn't drive at least one of my cars up to Washington, but instead I decided that the cars should be shipped by professional carriers, and I would fly to Seattle. From the airport I would take a taxi for the one-hour-plus drive to Marysville. Alice would meet me there the following week—first she wanted to go home to Cleveland for a visit with her parents, she said, so I gave her money to get to Washington. She would also be keeping the entire stash of cash on her person at all times, since everyone agreed that I couldn't be trusted not to spend it on dope.

When I saw my father again, I knew he knew that I was coming to get straight, and that meant that I was still using. It was hard to look him in the eye, to feel his frightened arms around me. I knew I had about two days' worth of drugs to tide me over before I had to start kicking—I wouldn't think about it until then. I had the ability to convince myself and my family and friends that this time I would stop. Really I would. Every time I said it, I really meant it. I'd watched friends overdose, lose their children to the system, commit suicide. I'd overdosed, lost friends, and lost my band and my identity. Nothing could make me stop. Nothing. If I could just stay high I would be okay. I became stuck in a state between, *If I don't do this thing I'll probably die, and if I do this other thing, I could die, too.*

And in a flash the two days had passed, and Alice was there, and I was four days into the worst kick—what was supposed to be the last kick—and all I knew was that I was sick, sick, sick, and so desperate I could scream. The cars hadn't arrived yet, and there was no escape from the two pairs of eyes, always watching. I felt so confined to my body and that house, and just knowing that Alice and my father were no doubt talking about how untrustworthy I was, what a mess of my life I'd made, I couldn't take another night. Nothing would get between me and some relief. Nothing.

On the fifth day, while Alice and Dad were in the living room watching television, I sneaked into my dad's bedroom, where I knew Alice had stashed my cash and found the envelope without much effort. I swiped a pile of the money, not stopping to count it, and Dad's car keys off the dresser, and bolted out to his car. Within an hour I'd be in downtown Seattle, hitting the streets and looking for drugs (something I'd never had to do before). I'd been out of town too long and no longer knew any dealers, and I didn't have time to figure out a new system of supply. I would have to avail myself to the kindness of other junkies and hustlers on the street.

I've been in a lot of sketchy situations in my life, but none where I felt I could be murdered until this night in Seattle. This was a new flavor of darkness. Violence hung in the air like a pendulum; every turn of a corner could prove to be the wrong decision. I was angry, but other people were angrier. The street people of L.A. were different—sunnier, you could say, by comparison. It took me two or three hours just to find someone to make eyes with to start the conversation. Then there's this whole song and dance you have to go through: determine if the guy can deliver, or lead you to another guy who can, buy the drug (in this case crack), then you have to invite him to smoke it with you—it's extremely impolite under these circumstances to deny him a few hits and therefore an unwise move I'd never try. This night, the guy invited himself. He actually said, "Now what are you gonna do for me?" You have to hang out a while to make it feel less shady, you know, just two perfect strangers enjoying a cigarette and a laugh.

We smoked crack for a bit, which only made me crave heroin more. Did he know where I could get any? He did, but it wouldn't be easy. This was blowing my mind—who would have believed you couldn't get heroin in Seattle—it was still the 1990s! Eventually, hours later, he was able to bring me some budget tar that was nothing like the stuff we'd had in the heyday, just five years before. Was it no longer a popular drug? That first twenty-four hours in Seattle was spent on the unfamiliar streets on foot, then some time in my dad's car waiting for the man and getting high and getting high with the man.

And then it was the next day and my cash supply was dwindling, so I went to the ATM only to discover that my account had been frozen. I pushed out the image of my father and/or Alice on the phone with a representative from the bank. I put the crack pipe to my lips, inhaled, felt hopeful and wired—ready for anything—and calculated how much I'd need to get back home. I wouldn't leave until I was absolutely out of everything I could ingest, and I'd drive straight back to Marysville having had no food or rest in forty-eight hours.

I felt like shit when I pulled into my dad's driveway after having stolen his car for days—leaving him with none—and made him think that I was dead, or worse. I knew I was a monster and I would be made to pay with real pain, both physical and emotional. When they came outside, their faces flushed with all of their feelings—relief, anger, sadness, disappointment, disgust, exhaustion—I wanted to disappear. I wanted to sleep forever. I didn't want to be back in the sticks, in this house I'd grown up in, the place that had inspired my great escape in the first place nearly fifteen years before. I'd had one last hurrah, and now I'd pay for it yet again.

I MANAGED TO stay clean for a month. Dad and me, and Alice, makes three! But my dad was getting the short end of the stick, to say the least. He was newly retired, and I don't think he had expected that we would be such terrible roommates. We just didn't do anything around the house—we didn't clean enough, we didn't do the grocery shopping, we didn't cook. Sometimes Alice would watch *The Rockford Files* with him on television, and I'd heat up some mac n' cheese for him if I was hungry myself, but otherwise there was nothing happening in our conversations but resentment on both sides. Every time I'd go out, my father demanded to know my exact itinerary. Where was I going? Who would I be with? When would I be back? He threatened to write down the mileage on the speedometer every time I pulled out of the driveway. After five weeks I knew our days were numbered. It was time to move on down the road.

I left the old Mercedes in Dad's garage, and Alice and I took the Volvo and our suitcases to set up in a Marriott in Lynnwood, a city closer to Seattle. We'd stay there until I could figure out our next move. I still had a bit of money in that envelope so naturally it was burning a hole in my pocket. I couldn't resist the pull of hitting the streets again, and now with my own car there was no one to stop me from going.

I try again in Seattle. I go downtown and scope things out in my car instead of on foot. This time I see a woman I assume is a prostitute. Seeing me staring, she approaches my car and asks me if I'm looking for someone or something.

"Something," I say.

"I can help," she says. *What a relief to find a kind soul out here.*

She asks me to drive her to a nearby address, asks me what I need and how much. "If I can take a commission, I'll go get it for you," she says. "He doesn't take well to strangers, but I do this all the time." I give her a $100 bill, tell her to keep twenty, and watch her disappear inside a building.

I waited 10 minutes, then 15, then 20—never taking my eyes off the door I'd seen her enter. *Maybe she had to wait in line. Maybe she was in the bathroom. Maybe she'd used her $20 to buy some of her own and was getting high there.* I tried to calculate how long that could defer her return. *But she'd promised she'd be right back.* After an hour it finally dawned on me that I'd been scammed with the oldest trick in the book. I was back to square one.

Finally I found a street person who had crack, and because I had money to spend and a car to drive, he took a liking to me right away. We smoked for a while before I asked him if he knew where I could get some dope.

He does. This time I'm taken to an actual crack house, a first for me, with its own unique set of rules and protocols. My chaperone directs me to park on the side of the totally normal looking

Me, Larry, and Susan in 1973. PHOTO: COURTESY THE SCHEMEL FAMILY

Disneyland 1972. PHOTO: LARRY SCHEMEL

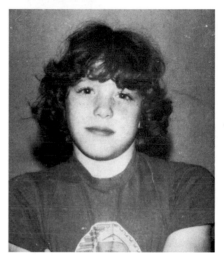

Me at age 10 in my Bachman Turner Overdrive T-shirt. PHOTO: LARRY SCHEMEL

School jazz band, 1982. PHOTO: TERRY SCHEMEL

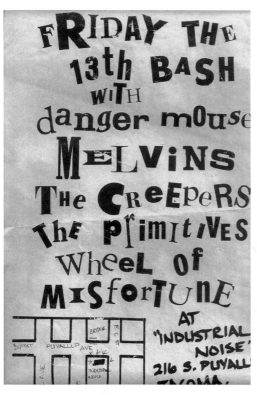

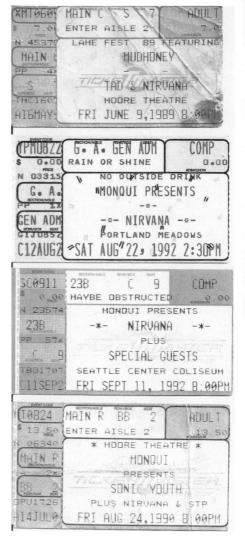

(*Top left*) The Primitives played with the Melvins in 1986. (*Right*) Nirvana ticket stubs 1989, 1990, and 1992.

PHOTOS: LARRY SCHEMEL

(*Left*) Larry and me at Nils Bernstein's apartment in Seattle, 1991.

PHOTO: EBEN CARLSON

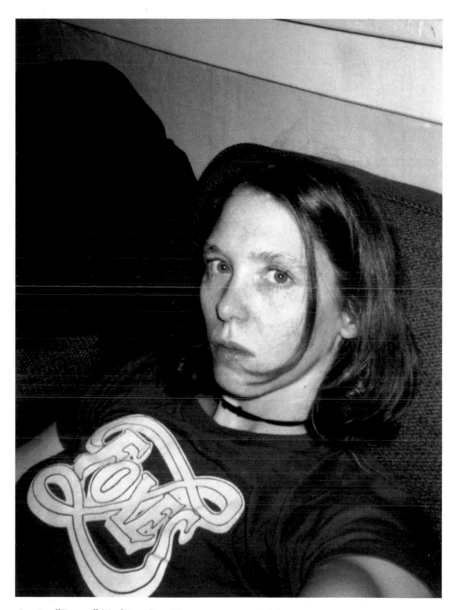

In my "Foxes" T-shirt that Kurt gave me, 1996. PHOTO: LISA ORTH

(*Top*) Kurt, 1992. (*Below*) Kurt onstage in São Paulo, Brazil, for the
Hollywood Rock Festival, 1993. PHOTOGRAPHS: PATTY SCHEMEL

Courtney's hand-drawn drum map for the recording of *Live Through This* that Kurt dictated over the phone.

DRAWING: COURTESY COURTNEY LOVE

Kristen Pfaff promoting "Beautiful Son" EP, backstage in Angers, France, 1993.

PHOTO: PATTY SCHEMEL

Mom and me pose with Courtney and Kristen at the Palace Theater in L.A., opening for the Lemonheads, 1994. PHOTO: TERRY SCHEMEL

(*Above*) Kurt and me with Frances in Seattle, 1993.
PHOTO: COURTNEY LOVE

(*Right*) Kurt and Frances in Seattle, 1993.
PHOTO: PATTY SCHEMEL

At a Kansas City truck stop during the Live Through This tour, 1994.
PHOTO: PATTY SCHEMEL

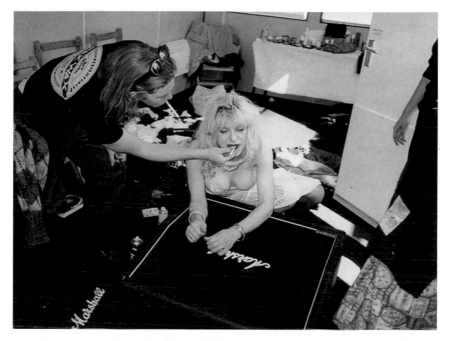

Pre-show cigarettes at Reading, 1994.

Melissa and me on the tour bus, 1994. PHOTOS: MELISSA AUF DER MAUR

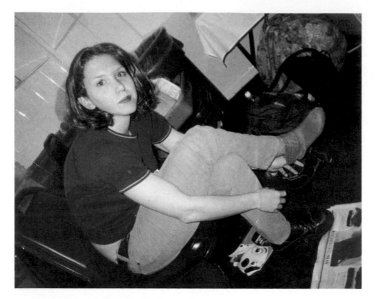

Taking my shoes off pre-show, 1994.
PHOTO: MELISSA AUF DER MAUR

(*Above*) A sleeping Frances and me in the
van, waiting to open for Nine Inch Nails.
Cleveland, Ohio, 1994. PHOTO: PATTY SCHEMEL

(*Right*) Patient Pat along for the ride for the
Lollapalooza tour, 1995. PHOTO: LISA ORTH

(*Top*) Signing autographs on tour in 1994. (*Bottom*) View from the stage, 1994. PHOTOS: MELISSA AUF DER MAUR

(*Top*) Side of the stage just before our encore, in Roseland Ballroom, New York City, 1995. (*Bottom*) The "Violet" video shoot, L.A., 1995.

PHOTOS: MELISSA AUF DER MAUR

The "Violet" video shoot, L.A., 1995. PHOTO: MELISSA AUF DER MAUR

(*Above*) Lollapalooza, Vancouver, 1995.

(*Right*) Photo shoot in an Orlando, Florida, hotel room, March 1995.

PHOTOS:
MELISSA AUF DER MAUR

Arriving in Tuktoyaktuk, Northern Territories, Canada, where we played a show for 500 contest winners with Metallica and Veruca Salt.
PHOTO: MELISSA AUF DER MAUR

Nodding off in Capitol Hill, Seattle, 1996. PHOTO: LISA ORTH

(*Top*) Photo shoot for "Celebrity Skin," 1998. That day would be the last time the band would all be together until our reunion for the *Hit So Hard* documentary in 2013. (*Bottom*) High on set at the "Celebrity Skin" photo shoot, 1998. I wouldn't see Melissa for years after this.

PHOTOS: MELISSA AUF DER MAUR

Christina and Me at the beginning of our relationship, six months clean and sober, September 2005. PHOTO: CHRISTINA SOLETTI

Photo shoot at home for *Hit So Hard*, the documentary, 2010.
PHOTO: PLANET SWAN

My family: Beatrice, Christina, and me, 2011. PHOTO: ANA GRILLO

house—no boarded up windows or anything—but instead of entering through the front entrance in the front, we creep behind the house, which is desolate and quiet. I start to feel nervous when we enter through a less-than-inviting back door. Inside, when my eyes adjust to the scene through the fog of smoke of all kinds, I can see that the carpeted rooms in the house are filled wall to wall with people in various stages of high. In the act, immediately after the act, nodding out, coming to, moaning, retching, laughing, weeping, and waiting. Some people were moving about, going from room to room. I could hear people having sex down the hall.

My chaperone whispers to me not to look anyone in the eye. For a moment I panic. Was I going to be expected to exchange some kind of sexual experience for drugs? I was desperate and beginning to feel sick and didn't have the energy to deal with fending anyone off, plus I could plainly tell that I smelled terrible. I couldn't even remember the last time I'd showered.

"Sit here," says my chaperone, gesturing to an unoccupied space on the floor. I do as I'm told. "I know where I can get some dope, but I'm going to need your car to get it."

I'm alarmed that we're not already at our point-of-sale destination. Surely someone here is holding. But my chaperone disagrees and insists I won't be sorry I came once he came back with what I needed. I can't argue with that, besides I'm going to start getting really sick in about an hour, so beggars can't be choosers.

I say okay and give him my keys and the last of the money I'd brought. I sit there looking at my hands for an hour before I begin to shake and sweat. I'm very aware of my stomach. My body aches in general. I lie down on my own little corner of the carpet and curl into the fetal position, counting my breaths. Hours pass. Hours and hours.

Finally the chaperone returns, and I don't feel any relief, just fear and confusion. I can't think straight and everything is moving too slowly. I see him talking to another girl across the room, and I can't understand why he hasn't come over to save me. I look at him longingly. He and the girl looks back. They have so much energy. *Why is he laughing at me?*

I literally crawl to where they are, where I can see the chaperone unwrapping a bundle and talking to the girl. They don't acknowledge me, even as I am right in front of them. There's really no reason to attempt any pleasantries—they are obviously fucking with me—so I don't bother to try to outwit them or make a case for my car keys or the heroin I'd just purchased. Instead I beg.

"*Please*," I whine pathetically.

The girl speaks to the chaperone but not to me. "Yeah, let's give her some. But me, first."

They give me a pitiful amount, and I get well enough to think straight, but not high. The even feeling gives me back my anger and numbs my fear. I decide to make a break for it—I'm out of money as it is and need to get out of there. I tell the chaperone that I have more money in a bank account, but I need my car to go to an ATM. He begrudgingly gives me back my keys, and I run out of there never to return.

UNTIL I RETURNED two weeks later when we could no longer afford to live high on the hog at the Marriott. Alice and I decided that our only recourse was to go back to L.A. where we knew people and had access to better drugs (well, that was my motivation). Alice had lent her car to a friend there, so the plan was to go back and sell it for cash. We could use that money for a deposit on a new place. We were so low on cash, but I was strung out again and would need enough dope to get me through the seventeen-hour drive to L.A. I hit the streets in Seattle again, and this time I found it in the public restroom near the Pike Street Fish Market. Once again it was a terrible quality tar, so cut that it barely did the job when I tested it out inside one of the stalls.

Walking up the stairs to the market, who do I see walking toward me but the Chaperone, weaving his way through a crowd that happily parts like the sea to avoid him. I could never forget the guy who tortured me two months before. As he came closer I could see that he was muttering to himself. He looked and sounded deranged. Must have been some PCP or dust. *Fuck you*, I think. *Good*. I walked right past him, a small part of me remembering that it could have been me.

| 33 |

THE END OF THE LINE

My only possessions were the Volvo and a little cash—not enough—a toothbrush somewhere in my bag, some clothes, a box or two in the back, and Alice by my side. We didn't know where to go so we went to Echo Park and looked for the cheapest thing possible. We ended up in a one-room flophouse with a disgusting landlord who sweat a lot and made me nervous. Alice got her Corolla back from the friend she'd been lending it to and sold it for $4,000—this would make up the bulk of our estate. Alice hid the money from me and changed its location often.

We slept in sleeping bags on a futon mattress on the floor. We had only the essentials—a folding card table that we found in the lone closet in the room, a few pieces of silverware, a small TV from the 1980s that Alice picked up off the curb, the cheapest house phone on the market. We had almost no money, and I certainly didn't have any career prospects, so Alice and I bickered constantly about it—she resented me for bringing her down by blowing so much cash on drugs, and I resented her for living off me for so long, and taking advantage, and a million other reasons. It was my money so I would spend it the way I wanted—now it was her turn to support us.

Alice managed to get a job as an assistant in an art gallery and had to take my car every day. That meant I was alone to my own devices more often than not and almost always on foot. I'd spend all of my time trying to find things to sell and cooking up financial schemes. Needing to replenish my supply every day meant there was never enough money, and whatever Alice had to her name she would hide from me. On particularly desperate days I would walk long distances to try to cop on the street, just whatever I could get my hands on. I was a criminal, and I was constantly interacting with criminals and sociopaths and junkies and a bunch of other lost causes. I would have purchased a bundle from Charles Manson if he'd had it to sell, okay.

These daily journeys to find relief inspired my discovery that if I just spent a couple of minutes doing something sexual with a guy, a quick hand job behind a building or in a car, for instance, then I could get what I needed and not be dope sick. Turns out this is a common transaction on the street—I wouldn't have characterized what I was willing to do at the time as prostitution, really, I wasn't going on a date or spending any more time with him than was absolutely necessary. If they could close their eyes and pretend they were with someone they were attracted to, I could close mine and count to 180. Before, during, and just as soon as the unpleasantness was over, I would simply push it out of my mind completely, as if it never happened. Living as if no one was watching had become normal. If what happens in Vegas, stays in Vegas, I was Vegas.

That didn't mean I sought it out—it was only to be used as a last resort, and I prided myself on my ability to get out of these situations unscathed. One day I had a little cash in my pocket so I decided to treat myself to a cab instead of the usual long walk down the hill. As luck would have it I realized quickly that my driver was also looking to party. He took me to get some crack, and we smoked it together. We ended up hanging out for hours, and the whole time I could just smell that he was figuring that there would be sex at the end of this, that I would somehow repay him for all the access to drugs he gave me that day.

I told him I knew of another place we could go to get some more crack, and gave him an address a couple of blocks from where I lived. When he pulled up in front of the building, I bolted out of the door and took off running, tucking into an alley and waiting until I knew chances were high that he was gone before I made my way back home. The crack I was using only exacerbated my paranoia, and I was convinced I'd need to look over my shoulder for this guy in case he remembered where he'd picked me up that morning. The next day my fear was realized when I looked out the window and indeed saw the driver parked and waiting at the end of the block. I'd gotten away that time, narrowly, but I was beginning to get used to the idea that trouble would find me no matter what.

I NEEDED SO much money, but had no way to bring it into my life. Whenever I had something I thought someone would pay at least a dollar for, I'd sell it, and whenever I cobbled together enough money to buy any amount of drugs, I'd do the entire haul as soon as possible. I made no attempt to ration the portions in order to stave off the sickness to come, I just inhaled, smoked, or shot it all up, and would worry about tomorrow, tomorrow.

One day I was trolling for some stuff to steal so I could sell it. I swiped the key to Alice's friend Dennis's place. While he was at work I was able to casually let myself into his house, which was a goldmine of valuable shit. Equipment, a large record collection, art on the walls, books. I walked into the bedroom and noticed a book on the bed. Curious, I picked it up to flip through and the papers that had been marking his place fell out. I picked them up. Plane tickets. Or at least the receipt for a recent trip. I noted the destination—Cleveland Hopkins Airport—and the dates, a few days before Alice met me at my dad's in Marysville. *Oh my god, they were together.* Had she passed him off as her boyfriend to her parents? How long had this been going on? I flashed back to the part where I gave her money for her travel expenses. I had no memory of the amount—now I was pretty convinced I'd paid for this clown's plane ticket too.

I put the book back on the bed and grabbed an expensive-looking distortion pedal on my way out.

ALICE CASHED HER checks from work and had some cash leftover from selling her car, which she would always hide from me because it was *her* money, as if she'd never helped herself to mine. There was nowhere to stash it in the one-room we shared, so she'd hide money in the car (my car) and hide the car keys each time she was home. The old hidden keys trick was not a challenging puzzle to solve for a heroin addict. Her hiding place was inside her pillowcase, having obviously transferred the keys from her pocket to this thing that she slept on.

One night Alice fell asleep on the futon with her head on the key pillow. I watched her drift off and waited until she started snoring to execute my plan. With great delicacy I crept around to the other side of her pillow. I could tell from the outline in one of the corners of the pillowcase that the keys were in the farthest corner away from me—I would have to very gently and silently move them to another corner, where I could more easily manipulate their release. I tried not to breathe as I very slowly slid my hand underneath the pillowcase, careful not to alert a sleeping Alice to my presence or disturb her sleep in any way. Then I slowed things down even more in order to push the keys silently toward their necessary destination. Success!

Next I went to the bathroom and found the scissors, returned to the corner of pillow and ever-so-slowly cut the keys out of their hiding place and bolted out to the car without shoes, without anything but the keys themselves and the clothes on my back. In the car I found $500 cash under the mat on the driver's side. *Jackpot.* In a flash I was gone, not stopping to check if there were any shoes in the car somewhere; if I had to buy some new ones, I would do it when I got to where I was going. Or not! It simply didn't matter. I had such a good feeling about my odds for success—tonight I was rich.

I didn't feel guilty; I felt justified and pleased with myself, the picture of self-esteem. I spent all the money and took two days to come home. I knew there would be hysterics upon my return, but I was already angry enough for both of us. Indeed when I walked in the door I was greeted by a shrieking Alice, who pushed me up against wall and screamed in my face. To paraphrase: *You ruined my life! You're nothing but a junkie! I will never forgive myself for loving you!* (Always with the exclamation points!) Looking at her stupid face I saw my own. I must really hate myself if I could hitch myself to this lying monster; I loathed her. How could I have spent the best/worst time of my life in her presence?

When I was angry, my defensive strategy was to storm off (obviously). I enjoyed the fact that I couldn't be stopped. I had perfected the smug smile of a breathing, walking middle finger.

THE FOLLOWING HAPPENED in short order: Alice got fired, leaving us with no money at all; we got kicked out of the makeshift flop house because we couldn't pay the man; Alice stole my Volvo the night after we found out we had a week to vacate the apartment, and disappeared.

| 34 |

PINK TURNS TO BLUE

I had given up my phone number—I couldn't afford to have bills. Even Larry didn't know how to find me. He'd managed to stay sober since the day I'd given him that last dose; I didn't want to drag him down. There was nothing left—no friends, no car, no bank account, nowhere to live, no prospects, no future, no feelings. I'd quickly lost hold of my life and moved willingly, naturally, onto the streets. I didn't have a plan beyond getting dope in my system; where to shoot up became beside the point. I began to sleep among the homeless, preferring a communal mattress on the ground under an overpass to the toxic scene that had been my life with Alice. I was perfectly content to inhabit my one little corner of the side of an intersection, just another place to go to squint into the sun, a place where I could go and twitch. By the time I had graduated to living out of a tent in an abandoned, overgrown field near the freeway, life had become about one thing and one thing only—the quest not to feel it. Like a vampire, consciousness meant I needed to feed, which meant maintaining my drug use every couple of hours. I wore a windbreaker I'd found in a dope house, conveniently forgetting whether or not it had been abandoned or if I'd stolen it outright.

Once you're living in the service of drugs, you don't pay retail. Out-of-towners and newbies, people with cars, and me for the longest time—all paid $20 for a balloon of dope, enough to keep you high for a few hours. But once I went hardcore, my price was $7, which I could then turn around and sell to some rookie for a $13 profit. You learn pretty quickly that two can make more money than one, and so I found a partner in crime. His name was Jimmy, and he was my concierge to the streets—he kept me moving, kept me in crack and dope. A born hustler, Jimmy taught me how to run little cons and steal without being caught.

Jimmy had a hustle at this gas station on the corner—he'd scam people who had car trouble by getting them to trust him to find a cheaper part for a job he could fix quickly, given his considerable experience with auto mechanics. He talked so fast you could barely understand what was happening, but in the end people always drove away happy and gave Jimmy a little extra for his time. Jimmy was also an opportunity provider. If you needed something, he knew the quickest way to get it. Jimmy liked to set things up. He was good at finding guys, for instance, who would give him money to have sex with me.

The first setup was too easy. The guy was practically a kid, a first-timer in the world of hiring-someone-for-sex. But I needed the money and access to a shower, and he was staying in a motel, a welcome change of scenery. Once inside the room, I could tell that he was nervous, which made me feel confident that I had the upper hand. But as luck would have it, the kid made the biggest of rookie mistakes when he left me alone to take a shower and left his wallet full of cash on the dresser. I was out of there before he even got his hair wet. *That was just too easy,* I thought, hoping they would all be like that.

Early on I met a seasoned lady of the evening named Mavis who attempted to show me the ropes. She kind of quizzed me, knowing I was new to the practice, and quickly let me know that I had no idea what I was doing. It's not like I was the type to stand on the street in a miniskirt—far from it. I didn't have to worry, though, because all that was required was to exist—there was always a steady stream of customers.

"Okay, this is number one: Never say you charge $20 for a blow-job," Mavis told me. "Never charge by the act—they're paying for your 'time,' see. Don't ever say blowjob out loud, see? Surest way to get arrested."

I was not a smooth criminal. I was not a born hustler. I was always talking too much, for one thing. One time I'd gone along with Jimmy on a run with this friend, "Doc." Doc didn't have the typical profile of the people we most often did business with. He was white, wore chinos—Dockers, maybe—drove a Corolla. Jimmy was driving the guy's car to a dope house, and I was in the backseat, thinking maybe I should fill the silence with some cheerful banter. I leaned forward and stuck my head between them in front and said to Doc, "So, why do they call you Doc?" That question was met with a silent head shake from Doc and a death glare from Jimmy in the rearview mirror. This wasn't the first time I'd seen that look. Recently, I'd tried to make conversation with a guy whose car's license plate had a trojan on it—by asking if he went to USC.

Later I was scolded by Jimmy. "Don't talk! People are not trying to get to know you, and they definitely don't want you to know them. Get it?"

I eventually did get it, but it took a lot of practice to learn everybody else's scams. Like the one that happens while you're busy doing the work, and the guy is reaching around behind you and taking the $20 they just gave you right back out of your jacket pocket.

When it came to prostitution there was nothing I wouldn't do because I was completely dissociated from the acts themselves. Because I simply was not there, it didn't matter what was happening to my body, what things I was exposing it to, what violence. When I was letting men use my body, in all the ways men can, was I thinking about harm reduction and the importance of condoms? Not even in my top-five priority list at the time, no.

Somewhere inside I remembered that when I'd been a sexual person I had been a gay woman who had no interest in, or experience with, men really. But now that I'd left my humanity behind and was now strictly a drug person, my body was just another commodity, a means to another hit. I didn't care about the old me; I never, ever thought of her.

| 35 |

OCCUPATIONAL HAZARDS

I'd always had good veins. I was lucky that way, but even I had to deal with an abscess once in a while. It can happen if you miss a vein and end up digging around too much. An abscess is a small hole at the injection site that often starts as irritation from the chemicals going under the skin. The first sign is a little hard nub of tissue at the site that feels a little like a b.b. (as in the ammunition) just underneath the puncture wound. If it becomes infected, it hurts like hell. You can tell because your flesh swells up around it and gets red and hot and throbbing. Some get so bad you have to go to the E.R. to get it treated by a doctor with antibiotics. Typically if you see one forming, you find another place on your body to inject, but if you have only one good point of entry and it happens to be the beginning of an abscess, the addict might push their luck and use the b.b. as a guide. I always had a lot of options with veins, so I was never waylaid by an infection severe enough to need hospitalization, but I certainly received my fair share of scarring.

There's this mark you'll get at the injection site called a carbon dot, which I think is from the process of cooking the heroin in the spoon. When you draw it through and it's still hot in the needle and you inject it too quickly, it tattoos a black dot where the needle goes in. I chose to tattoo over all of mine, but because of the subtle scarring, I can tell they're there underneath.

As long as I was using, I was not aware of my own discomfort. It's the absence of the high that reminds you you can feel at all. For those couple of hours or moments, it's total sensory deprivation, but then you come to and realize you're in a sick body. Junkies shit their pants all the time because their bodies are either receiving drugs or withdrawing from them. I've woken up to fevers, sweating, incontinence, cramps, nausea, panic, painful inflammation, or an infection. If I was dope-sick or knew I was likely to be soon, I had to prepare for the condition I referred to as "STOMACH." That's the feeling of anticipation and anxiety that comes with a churning midsection when you know you're going to have to pay for all the constipation caused by opiates—take them away, and the diarrhea can be catastrophic.

And then there's cotton fever—another fairly common risk associated with shooting up that causes hours of acute flu-like symptoms—nausea, the worst headache you've ever experienced, shaking, sweating, and a high fever (not to mention you can't feel your high). Addicts use cotton to filter the cooked heroin (from cotton balls, Q-tips, or cigarette filters), so they can pull the solution through the needle effectively. Once you're using on a regular basis, in order to save money or to have a backup if you run out of drugs, you tend to save up your used, brown cottons, hoping to draw on them again for any residual drugs. There's a particular bacteria that lives in cotton fibers, and if you accidentally introduce an old piece of that bacteria-ridden fiber into your bloodstream, you're all but guaranteed a monstrous couple of hours.

Intravenous drug use is related to the transmission of HIV and Hepatitis C because a desperate addict won't hesitate to share a used needle if there is no other option at the time. When I was living on the streets, it's safe to say I was worlds away from healthy choices of any kind, and I did a lot of things I'll always regret.

There was a flophouse where a bunch of people would congregate to take drugs—the dealer there was gang affiliated and sold the absolute cheapest brown powder in town. There were always people in this house, even though the dealer's girlfriend had a kid there. Sometimes, if I needed a place to nod out, they'd let me stay for a few hours, maybe overnight. One day when I was there, I noticed the girl sitting near me had yellow skin. Her stomach was distended, which I'm sure people mistook for pregnancy, but I knew it was caused by Hepatitis. (Somehow this made her seem a little more sympathetic to me.) The girl had just procured her dope when she turned to me and asked if I had an extra rig. I didn't, but being a feminist I handed her mine. She used, gave the needle back to me, and I didn't hesitate to use it again on myself. Even an incurable disease wasn't enough for me to just say no to needle sharing. I was already half dead by then, I figured—what was one more risk to my "life"?

| 36 |

A DAY IN THE LIFE

I never know what time it is, but gradually I'm coming to, and there's enough available light peeking through the tear in the tarp that I can find the shot I'd prepared just for this moment. That was probably only a couple hours ago. I don't sleep anymore—it's dangerous and takes away from the task at hand. But if I know it's possible I might nod out—usually after I've scored a comfortable amount after a long day's effort—I make sure to prep a new shot for myself to wake up to. My right hand finds its way into the pocket of my jeans to find my wake-up shot. There's a reason they call it "fixing." Fix my state of consciousness, please. Fix me in just one hit. Hit me. There's no pleasure in this first shot—this is just so I can stand up and move around. As things become clearer, I go over my schedule for the day and lay out my goals: meet up with Jimmy, smoke crack, steal batteries from Kmart and sell them to the guy who runs the bodega across from the park, buy heroin, shoot heroin, nod off, come to, sell bags of drugs for a small profit, eat a sandwich from a convenience store, smoke cigarettes, run another hustle with Jimmy, smoke crack, give a disgusting slob a blowjob while vaguely annoyed the money goes to Jimmy—not to me—argue with Jimmy, who placates me with a new hit of crack. This is around the time when I fix myself enough to crash out for an epic two hours then prepare my coming-around-again shot for later, ever hopeful that I'll feel it this time like I used to, back when I used to sprout wings. If I could just get back, get back, get back to that magical chemical formula that could fix everything, how could anyone call this life a failure?

| 37 |

ROCK BOTTOM NO. 1

One morning I woke up in a shitty motel room somewhere in the Valley, easily a half-an-hour drive from where I'd been the night before. As I opened my eyes to adjust to the light peering through the poly beige curtains, I realized I didn't remember how I got there or who I had been with. And now I was totally alone. There had been a man with a car . . . there were drugs . . . I had wanted to come here to take a shower . . . I could still feel the weeks' worth of grime on me, so apparently I hadn't yet. I stood under hot water and rubbed a small bar of soap through my hair, as I thought about what to do next; this wasn't the kind of place that had little shampoos. (A brief flash of memory of the good old days at the Chateau Marmont.) I wasn't sure how I would get back to L.A.—I would have to hitchhike. What if I got sick before I got back to familiar territory? I didn't know my way around, didn't have enough cash to buy anything but a small amount of my next fix. As I was turning my T-shirt inside-out in an attempt at a clean shirt look, I saw somebody pull into the parking lot in a familiar vehicle—it was that moment that I remembered that, yes, indeed, my companion for the night drove a taco truck during the day. *Thank god*, I thought. *At least someone will give me a ride.*

Later, I was hanging out on the steps of a church, which had become a habit—wandering around just looking in windows, sometimes nodding out on steps—and in this church there was a simple Ludwig drum kit, which I beheld with curiosity. I remembered myself, just a glimmer of a memory: *I had once played music.* I knew how to play the drums. When I'm hitting the drums, I'm chasing a feeling. I'm so focused; I'm given over to it, yet in total control. I love that feeling of crashing down on something, high above it. I love sitting behind the instrument, adjusting the kit, playing barefoot. It's the thing that saved me when I'd forgotten who I was. At the end of the world, I remembered I'd been a drummer.

IT WAS PRETTY early in the morning when I left the dope house and saw my old Volvo parked across the street with Alice sitting in the driver's seat. What *the fuck*? I walked closer, and she rolled down the window, and there was fucking *Jimmy* sitting next to her. Was this some kind of setup? Apparently Alice had been driving around looking for me and accidentally stopped in Jimmy's territory, and he'd noticed because he noticed everyone who hovered anywhere near his corner. He'd approached the car, and she'd started asking questions, and Jimmy, being the social butterfly that he was, told her where to find me and also told her how I had been making money for drugs.

They both got out of the car. I told her to give me my fucking car keys, and she wouldn't. Jimmy just stood there and watched. I grabbed her wrist and twisted it until I could get the keys out of her hand. I got in my car and left. I was done with that corner and was never going back. I never saw either of them again.

IT WAS DECEMBER 1999, just after Christmas. After four months on the street, I'd managed to make a "friend" who had a house in Silver Lake and gave me drugs and a place to crash in exchange for regular sex. Mike was a pot dealer who considered himself to be a real Mr. Big. This thing with this guy was a classic power trip. He would get my drugs for me, then he would decide when I could have them. Do this, get that, pretty much every day. Sometimes it was sex that he wanted, sometimes a pick-up or drop-off, sometimes errands or rides. Part of my fee for living there was the use of my car, which was parked in the alley behind his house. Mike was a hoarder—his house was filthy and full of garbage. If there was art on the wall, it was the kind that glowed in the dark. Luckily, he wasn't as interested in a housekeeper.

The night of my escape, Mike wanted me to drive him to his hook-up in Santa Monica. I was supposed to wait in the car for him while he made his usual deal for bricks of marijuana, but as soon as he went inside the house, I took off and sped back to his place. My adrenaline was racing because I knew I had to act quickly and make it through a labyrinth of risk. At his house he kept two terrifying Akita dogs for security, and I was sure they would tear me apart if I entered their space unescorted. I had never been in their presence without Mike, and he'd always assured me they were powerful killers. Sneaking past them proved successful, though, and I quickly made it to phase two of my plan, which involved wading through a thicket of garbage and junk to the place where I guessed he might keep his cash. Indeed I found about $250 in a drawer but for some reason thought better of taking it all. Instead I grabbed five twenties and some clothes, some more drugs for the road, and drove like hell.

From a payphone, I called my father and asked for help (my mother had ceased communication with me at that point)—I'd been humbled by addiction and wanted to come home. *Just one last time, I promise.* He agreed to overnight a pre-paid gas card for just enough credit to get me back to Washington.

When I got to the house in Marysville three days later, I discovered I wasn't the only sick person there to convalesce. Dad's health had been in decline from emphysema, and Larry had moved into the living room to help out around the house. The scene was incredibly depressing. At 32, I was living in my old childhood bedroom, sleeping on the same *Peanuts* pillowcase I'd had since I was a kid, cold turkey-ing it on New Year's Day, my only comfort a rickety old a space heater next to the futon where I lay shaking and grinding my teeth. The withdrawal was brutal, as expected. I had to detox the old-fashioned way, with nothing to ease the misery but my brother's sense of humor and the songs he played for me. After the kick, it takes forever to experience happiness again—months in my case—it's just a heavy slog of sadness plus insomnia. But I never lost my patience with Larry; I respected him too much, and I knew he knew what I was going through, and that made all the difference.

I think Dad was relieved that I was home and alive, but the sickness of withdrawal persisted, and I had no job or plan of action beyond what I was going to eat next. I'd moved the futon mattress into a little storage closet off the garage where I kept an old TV on and tuned to *Friends*, even when I was too unconscious to watch it. I needed some kind of repetitive behavior or noise, even if it was just the sound of David Schwimmer's voice, the laughter from a studio audience, or the whir of the washer and dryer on the other side of the wall. A good day included grocery shopping at the same fucking store I'd grown up with—I never had to struggle to find the popsicles that sustained us all, so there was that—but god how I hated that I recognized all our neighbors. The same shitty people as ever, just older now, all of us stuck in a weigh station for lost, suburban souls.

AFTER WE'D BROKEN UP, Alice had gone back up to the Marys-ville storage unit with Dennis and completely cleaned me out. There was one custom-made green drum set that DW sent to me—it was the best sounding kit I'd ever used. She took it and whatever else I had of any real value, including all the early Hole pressings and merch and personal photo albums. I was still in L.A. when she'd done it, living with Mike. In preparation for my trip home, I called the storage space to inquire about my unit, and the person on the phone told me that a woman had come by not too long ago with a key and had emptied it. That's the thing that gets me the most. It hurt that I'd sold so much of my personal history, but at least it was me doing the selling. But this is what happens when you're an ad-dict and you don't take care of your things. In the program, they call everything you've lost "the wreckage." The only way to get over it is to think of these possessions as things you lost in a fire.

My secrets for sober success during this period? 1. I had no more money, and I was disgusted by what I had to do to earn it. 2. I was physically and emotionally exhausted. 3. I was surrounded by two people who were both also totally clean and on the other side of it. I wanted to believe I was truly invested in my sobriety, but the truth was it was all circumstantial. If I'd had the resources, I'd eventually have used them.

Two months into my stay, I was bored and needed a project. Dad tolerated our music enough to let Larry and I build a little recording studio above the garage. For the second time in my life, Dad gave me the money to buy a drum set. Customizing the space and setting up a new mixing board gave me hope and a sense of purpose—I could play and record at my own pace, I could write songs with Larry, I could do something that didn't involve eating or smoking with my father, while he leaned on his portable oxygen tank. It was there that I broke in my arms again and got my calluses back. I knew I was going to need them.

| 38 |

BACK TO SCHOOL

Hole wouldn't officially announce its breakup until May 2002, but the band hadn't played a live show together since the summer of 1999, so by the end of 2000 I knew it was likely just a matter of time. There had been a disastrous aborted tour with Marilyn Manson, and Geffen went under in the middle of it. Now Courtney was being sued for undelivered albums and had changed her focus to acting in films. In the meantime she'd also turned her attention to the Internet and posting on the band website, which I'd been spending a lot of time on, looking at old pictures and reading her rants and lists of favorite things. There was always a lot of activity on the message boards, and every once in a while someone's question would be about me—what ever happened to Patty Schemel?

It was from the little room in the makeshift studio that I penned and posted a little piece about what the music I'd grown up with had meant to me, and how I always returned to it, no matter what was going on with my life. I kept the focus on those bands and didn't say anything beyond that, but I wanted to let people know that I was still alive. Courtney had read the piece, and tracked me down in Marysville, calling the house the day after I'd posted it. I hadn't heard from Melissa or Eric in almost three years, but somehow it wasn't surprising that Courtney would get back in touch.

She was putting a new band together, she said, and was looking for an all-female lineup, and naturally thought of me. She would pay me to come down to L.A. to discuss the possibilities—she was also talking to Veruca Salt guitarist Louise Post and bassist Corey Parks of Nashville Pussy. Epitaph had given her an advance on a new album. She wanted to call the band Bastard.

There wasn't really an internal debate of any kind. I'd been in Washington six months, and I felt better. I'd been sober and productive, and I felt isolated and bored in my childhood home. This offer felt like a natural next step—maybe I could go back to L.A. and press the reset button on my life. Maybe it was just that easy. Dad was surprised when I announced that Courtney would be flying me down and putting me up for a week. When I was packing up to go he looked sad.

"Don't you want to stay here with me? I thought this was supposed to be a new start for you."

"Stay here? No, I can't stay here. I have to work, Dad—I got a job."

He looked so defeated and was still recovering from pneumonia, but at the time I wasn't able to dwell on anything that would get in the way of my comeback. He hadn't touched another drink since he'd quit in 1968, but the cigarettes got him anyway. I felt a rush of guilt when I saw the panic in his eyes. I knew he was hoping I'd consider starting over in my hometown so I could stay clean and safe and take care of him.

"This is what I do," I told him. I left the next day.

NATURALLY WHEN I saw Courtney again after all that had happened, she was renting a house in West Hollywood. When I got there she was getting some kind of intense, interactive massage that required a small man to walk on her back while she chain-smoked into an ashtray on the floor. So the typical scenario. I'd brought along a tape recorder and played her the songs I'd been working on with Larry. We discussed her ideas for Bastard and made a loose plan to get together soon to rehearse with the band. Great—my schedule was wide open! I'd need a place to stay initially, but I was ready to play again.

Courtney was dating her new manager, Jim Barber, who had been the A&R rep at Geffen during *Celebrity Skin*. Jim was in the midst of a messy divorce, so it was decided that I would stay in his apartment in Larchmont, and he would stay with Courtney. Sounded good to me; I didn't ask any questions. I'd known Jim as a business man who knew a lot about music and repped good bands.

Rehearsals at SIR began a couple weeks later. The band members were different, but the songwriting process was the same as always. It was a struggle for Courtney to come up with new melodies. She preferred to work with producers such as Billy Corgan or Linda Perry, whose style was to sit down at the piano and come up with three melodies in no time. Otherwise we'd end up playing the same riff over and over for hours. We'd been having such a rough time that one of the guys at SIR recommended we listen to some "nu-metal," a horrifying craze sweeping the nation that took the form of bands like Limp Bizkit and Korn. I drew the line when I heard someone say, "Patty's gonna need a double bass . . . "

I liked playing with Louise and Corey, and it was the right time for me to throw myself into something full-on, even if I had my

doubts we would go the distance. If I could just stay busy and productive, I could stay the course of sobriety. But what I wasn't being
honest with myself or anyone else about was that I had simply
transferred my addictive, compulsive, and impulsive behaviors over
to my sex life. Whether or not I was sober, I always had something
going on with a number of women, always had a girlfriend, and
always had something on the side. Having lots of sex, and the inevitable drama it caused, was a way to stave off the soul-crushing
boredom of sobriety or soothe the loneliness of addiction. I could
never be alone. I always needed someone there to witness, always.
When I was going through a sober period, I felt especially entitled
to do whatever I wanted. The pull of non-monogamy was too thrilling to let go. I had to be bad somehow.

I had been corresponding online with Josephine, who lived in
Paris. She fit the usual profile—good taste, cute, into me, and willing to travel. I was casually dating someone else and flirting with
Corey's roommate when I dropped her off after practice at her
rented house in Silver Lake. (I couldn't seem to stay away from that
neighborhood for very long.) Her name was Shannon, and she had
a girlfriend. She was newly sober, too—from alcohol—so we
bonded over that, even though I considered her demons to be child's
play compared to mine.

I had been sober for nine months. I was proud of myself but definitely not taking it as seriously as I needed to. I wasn't going to
meetings regularly, and I wasn't exactly isolating myself from my
old bad influences like my brother had. I knew that what I'd been
through the year before was serious, but here I was playing music
again, back on track. The concept of truly changing my life hadn't
even occurred to me; I was just striving for normal. I had talked to
Larry a little bit about what had happened on the streets, and it
came up once with Courtney. She said she'd heard rumors that I
had been spotted downtown.

"I heard you had dreadlocks and lived on the street."

"What! Where'd you hear that?"

"Well, that's what Eric heard."

"Not dreadlocks. Maybe I woke up with a scrunchie in my hair one time. I believe that was my wake-up call."

I said a few more things about it, vague things like, "I did what I had to do out there." She nodded. She knew what that meant, and nothing shocked her anyway. Her most burning question was this: Had anyone ever recognized me?

"Oh my god, all the time," I said sarcastically. "The people I associated with were definitely not thinking about the Lollapalooza lineup from 1995, and especially not its drummers."

THE BAND STARTED recording the demo, but not with the original lineup. Louise and Gina Crosley left after the long rehearsal period, which meant Barber had to save the day with some replacement players. For a while it was just the two of us. Courtney went on her website to announce that I looked three years younger and played even better than before.

"Her year of crackheaddom made her even funnier—it's a miracle she came back from that but it's funny it was almost like this choice she made "I'm going to live under a bridge and be a crackhead . . . " (sic) Okay, Courtney.

Since Bastard wasn't coming together the way Courtney had hoped, she decided to line up a performance under the name Courtney Love. The set lists were made up of five new songs, six old Hole songs, and one or two covers. We were booked to debut in Ventura at the Majestic Theater, then with Jane's Addiction at their reunion concert at the Hollywood Bowl a week later. We didn't have any players, so Barber brought in Steve McDonald from Redd Kross to play guitar and two other metal guys with short hair—Kenny Korade and Jerry Best—to flesh out the rhythm section. We'd barely managed any rehearsals together before the shows, and wouldn't you know it, they were disastrous.

The pre-show dressing room scene was ridiculous—some hippie kid painting on henna tattoos, somebody else came by with some kind of herbal elixir for everyone to sample. Thanks, but I'll pass on a tincture. And then there was the appearance of the legendary yoga guru to-the-stars, Gurmukh (just Gurmukh) at our sound check. I can't imagine why she was there—Courtney must have summoned her, but during our sound check I saw an older woman wearing white robes and a turban floating up one of the aisles toward the stage. Courtney stopped what she was doing, squinted her eyes toward the woman, and called out, "Gurmukh! Gurmukh! Can you get out of my eyeline?"

The theater's capacity was eighteen thousand, and about half the house was empty. We played for less than forty minutes before we left the stage and Courtney alone to carry on her rambling (the set officially ended forty minutes after that, when security forcibly carried her off the stage).

THE MOTOROLA TWO-WAY pager was all the rage in 2001. It was basically a very primitive Blackberry that had a tiny flip-down keyboard that allowed you to instant message anyone who also had a two-way pager. Courtney arranged for everyone in the band to have one, and Corey had given hers to Shannon. The two of us IM'd each other constantly during the long hours in the studio, and this was how I effectively put the moves on her. After a couple of months at Barber's, I needed to find a new place. I finally had a little money, so after an extended stay at Roddy's—where Shannon and I started dating in earnest—I was able to find a two-bedroom on Franklin in Los Feliz. After being in L.A. for six months, I was sober, playing music again, and financially solvent. I was back.

| 39 |

RE/LAPSE

Shannon and I decided to live together in the two-bedroom, and Larry moved in, too. It was a good idea in theory—three sober people united in rock. And for a little while it was as normal as could be, each of us taking turns buying groceries and cleaning up, watching television, playing our records. Mostly I felt like the beneficiary of all the love. Shannon was the nurturer, and I was the baby.

Courtney took a trip to Japan or something. The band was on a break. Shannon was at work during the day, and since I was sober and not focused on a project—or obsessing over sealing the deal with a girl—I was idle. Idle was the worst for me; idle meant my brain would automatically lapse back to drugs and a way to justify using them. Responsible adults with jobs, I reasoned, ought to be able to handle their drugs. Witty people who go to parties don't have drug problems; they have the memory of their turbulent twenties. *We all did crazy things back then.* After all I'd been through, I was more mature now, worldlier. That was the only train of thought required for me to casually obliterate my progress by simply buying some crack one night, and making it all disappear.

I bought enough for three days. After trying to be a little casual about it, waiting hours to take one hit if I knew I was going to be around the roommates. I lasted two days without raising suspicion, but then of course I got greedy. I upped the ante until I got more and more brazen, and by the third day I was smoking crack out the window of our bedroom while Shannon was in the kitchen making dinner, and Larry was in the living room watching TV. I sat down on the bed and opened the window, smoked a pipe, and blew it outside.

Shannon's cat eyed me with suspicion and clear judgment. She started chattering as if she was about to tell everyone. I tried to shoo her away, but she wouldn't budge.

"Sorella, *don't*!" I hissed. I decided to go out to the kitchen and act normal. But just as soon as I went to get a glass of water and make my cheerful presence known, it was time to get back to the pipe.

I went back to the bedroom, drew back the curtains, and set about my routine. I didn't even close the door—that's how brazen and sloppy I'd become over the course of an afternoon. So I shouldn't have been as surprised as I was when Shannon came into the bedroom and caught me in the act. The look on her face was pure terror—I knew she had never seen crack before. She gasped and drew her hand to her face to cover her mouth.

"What are you *doing*?" she shouted, and then called for Larry.

My brother appeared in the doorway and took in the scene. "Whoa," was all he said.

I was still waving the pipe around. If we were going to cluster around the window, I'd might as well keep going. "Look, I know what you're gonna say, Shannon; I fucked up, and I'll deal with it. But right now, I am way too high on crack—I have to go get some dope so I can come down, and then we can talk."

Shannon's eyes were huge. "WHAT IS GOING ON?" She started to cry.

I heard Larry tell her to let me go. "Just leave her alone," he said under his breath. It was the last thing I heard as I walked out the door.

Later that night, once I'd done my dope and leveled off, I walked out to the living room to face the music. I had my addict's speech all prepared—*Babe, I know it seems extreme, but it was just a slip-up—a totally normal experience for an addict, if you think about it. Look, I'll go to a meeting if that will make you feel better.* My perfunctory AA meeting attendance was not really working for her, and she wanted me to return once again to a sober living house. "You need help, Patty!" I knew she was right.

The next day after Shannon and Larry left for work, I begrudgingly called Liberty House and asked for the house manager I'd remembered. The woman on the phone said that person no longer worked there, but could she help? I explained my predicament. I'd just relapsed after a year clean, and I needed a safe place to go. The woman on the phone was warm as she took down my name and told me to sit tight for a minute while she went to check on any available beds.

When she returned to the phone a few minutes later, her tone was markedly different, and the message was clear: I wasn't welcome.

"We don't have anything available for you," she said.

"At all, or just for me?"

"I was told that you left Liberty House due to an inappropriate relationship with another resident, and that's just not how we do things here," she said, ready to launch into a verbal spanking.

"First of all, that was years ago, and I'm an addict with a good amount of time clean who's in trouble and reaching out to you for help." Jesus Christ, wasn't the first rule of addiction that relapses could be expected?

She was even more terse with her answer. "Well, we can't help."

"Suck. My dick." I hung up enraged. *So fucking typical of the recovery community*, I thought, *with its fascist rules and judgy, jealous elitism. Excuse my lesbian ass for living in a house with ten women and daring to get laid! Who the fuck were they?*

When Shannon came home to find that I hadn't made any progress, she was adamant I had to go. My options were detox or the street.

I found a reputable place to take me for the initial few days. When the tech started in on her speech, "Well, I've got six years clean myself. I used to run drugs from Mexico . . . ,"

I stopped listening. I would do anything not to go through another in-patient rehab, so I stuck it out for detox and transferred to another sober living house.

This one was memorable for its lack of a cheesy name, or really, a structure of any kind. It was just a house with a normal family in the front and a separate structure behind it meant for six women in recovery. It was more like an affordable living situation whose trade off was the lack of privacy that came with living with five other women. I wonder in retrospect if it was even regulated. Actually, I didn't really have to deal with any of my housemates during the day because either everyone went to their job or their court-ordered community service, and I simply went back to my apartment. I did sleep there for Shannon's peace of mind. I was home by New Year's, just in time for my resolutions.

| 40 |

PRIVILEGE SET ME FREE

I managed to stay clean by staying busy, determined not to let that setback affect my moving forward. I threw myself into Courtney's recording sessions. The demos were endless—every song had multiple versions, an example of the departure away from the Hole sound. One night in the thick of it, Courtney asked me to take her to Linda Perry's house for some inspiration. She was the hit-maker of the day, and Courtney hung on her every word. At one point in the evening we made our way over to her grand piano so she could play some new material for us. She sat down and started in on this slow ballad, "Everything . . . is so wonderful . . . "

I listened politely, as she worked through the melody. Lyrically it was a pop song aimed at people who felt bad about themselves after being bullied, called "Beautiful." Courtney listened intently while smoking. I wondered if she would say something sarcastic about its earnestness when we left. But as soon as it was over, Courtney said that she had to have it, as in she wanted to record it for her new album!

An inspirational pop ballad! On piano! About the virtues of inner beauty!

Linda looked just as surprised. "I've already given it to Christina Aguilera. She's already recorded it."

In a year's time "Beautiful" would indeed become a number one song and win the Grammy for Best Female Pop Vocal, etc.

After we left, I asked Courtney what that was all about—that song was clearly not her style. She said she just wanted to try new things, be more adventurous, and push herself. I could see that, of course, but it confused me. Where was the rock?

LARRY STAYED in the two-bedroom apartment, and Shannon and I moved back to her old rental in Silver Lake. During a break from studio work, I went on a six-week U.S. tour with Roddy's band, Imperial Teen, when the drummer Lynn Perko had a baby. Their songs were very poppy and lighter than I was used to playing, but I'd always been a fan, so it was nice for me to try a new way of playing. It was back to the van—a new, old experience that reminded me of my roots—using maps to find our way to the next venue, loading my own equipment, and bare bones egalitarian rehearsals and on-time sound checks. Not to mention that mellow feeling that comes with *no drama*. Another thing that was new: I'd be singing harmonies. I was pleasantly surprised that I could still learn new tricks, and even come out from behind the drums to play bass on one song. The main thing was just feeling really supported and appreciated, like everything was possible. We did a kickoff show at the Satellite—the same club near the old house in Silver Lake, just with a different name. Same scene, but different, because this time I was clean.

BUT WHENEVER I was abstaining from drugs and alcohol, I always went back to my other distraction—sex—and specifically the high I got from sneaking around with someone who wasn't my girlfriend. My French pen pal Josephine lived in Paris, and as luck would have it, France was where Courtney decided she wanted to finish what would become the album *America's Sweetheart*. In the Spring of 2003, Courtney rented a château in Marsais where we would live and "work." Without telling anyone, I arranged to go to Paris ahead of her so I could have a few days with Josephine. Since something she'd said in 1993, I'd made a point never to tell Courtney anything about my personal life. I had confided in her once about getting busted by my girlfriend for hooking up with someone else. "God, Pat. You're just like your father," she'd said, "A cheater." It was a mean thing to say.

After our clandestine affair, I flew down to Courtney's rented villa as planned. Our tech met me in baggage claim with a concerned look on his face and told me I was in a lot of trouble.

"Your girlfriend has been calling all over trying to find you—she says she 'knows about Paris.'"

Great. This was how it always was, me the fuck-up, Shannon the patient one. Me disappointing her, her forgiving me, waiting for me to be better. I was the fire that she was constantly trying to put out. If I was contributing anything to a relationship, it always seemed to be a crisis.

I stayed at the château for a couple of days, and every day Courtney failed to materialize. She was reportedly in London and planned to extend her stay. A week went by. I played the drums a couple times, but I felt guilty and lonely and drained. I saw the writing on the wall—even if Courtney decided to show up for her own album recording, it felt too much like the past—being made to wait while my own life was imploding. I decided I couldn't be there one more day, idle with my thoughts—I had to face the music back in L.A. I knew I'd be fucking up a paying job by leaving France, but I was already done.

A friend of Shannon's arranged for me to fly home early so I could help put her out of her misery—I loved her, she was in pain, and I had to fix it. Despite our epic arguments, Shannon forgave me, and we decided to try to work it out and stay together.

But once again I was reminded that I was a liar, I was a cheat, I was a broken record.

I FOUND SOME studio work with Linda Perry, who was working with a long list of established bands and pop stars. My first job in the studio was working on some demos for Pink and then the actor Juliette Lewis, who was trying to put a band together. One night, Linda, Juliette, and I went to see Blondie, and I think that's when it was decided that I would join her band, Juliette & the Licks. Backstage, I immediately sought out Clem Burke, one of my favorite drummers and one with high self-esteem about his role. I liked how he knew his value and wasn't afraid to tell you.

Soon Juliette recruited Paul Ill, a renowned session musician known for his super-California vibe; he was a high-energy, walking exclamation point. You'd ask him how he was, and he'd always respond, "Truly blessed!" (and he was serious). Paul was probably the most talented bass player I'd ever worked with—we complemented each other, and he filled the pockets of sound between my hits with an underlying rhythm that I hadn't noticed anyone else incorporate before. The guitarist was Todd Morse, known for his band H20, whom I got along with really well too. Juliette was the lyricist, but Clint Walsh and Linda Perry would bring in a lot of the song ideas, and we'd go from there.

Clint ended up being a good advocate for me, making sure that I got paid for the parts of the songs that I wrote. A right to royalties for drummers is a notoriously controversial idea for some people, but some drum parts I've laid down have absolutely inspired or changed the direction of the song. The argument is that guitarists write, and drummers "arrange." *You don't see Ringo collecting any publishing for Beatles's songs (except the two he wrote lyrics for),* is the common refrain, but I would argue that Ringo made out pretty well financially—it's the difference between being paid for your time versus being paid for your creative contribution.

MY DAD HAD gotten sicker and sicker until he could no longer take care of himself. When he was in the later stages of COPD, and after Larry and I moved back to L.A., my sister would fly back and forth from Texas to take care of him. His brain was still sharp—he could carry on the same conversations as ever, if he could get the words out. But it was excruciating to hear him struggling to breathe, the way his breath whistled and gasped, the cough. He had only a quarter of one of his lungs left. My last memories of him are of his fear, the look on his face as he struggled for air to walk across the room.

He was not the type to say, *If I need a ventilator, I just want you to let me go.* If he flatlined, he wanted all the life-saving measures; he wanted to live by any means necessary. While I was making another mess of things in L.A., Susan had moved Dad into her house in Texas, and he died just two months later. I don't know the details of his last days, and there would be no funeral. I guess I'd been preparing because my first reaction was the relief that comes with knowing that he wasn't struggling to breathe anymore. I had a lot of shame about the fact that when I moved back in with my father, I knew he didn't want me to leave. But for years I would feel very numb to what it meant to grieve the loss, any loss.

For a while after he died, Susan and I talked more often. She sent me a little money and kept in touch about what was happening with the house in Marysville. For a while it felt like this would be the new normal, that the three of us would honor our father by coming together as this tight unit of siblings, but it wouldn't last. When I got kicked out of Juliette's band, I told Susan about it. She was supportive and tried to give me advice, but the space between us would grow once there was no official family business to discuss.

TEMPERATURES RISING

It was September 2004. I did manage to secure some publishing, and we were paid for rehearsals and flights to shows, but it was a shoestring budget, and those flights were courtesy of Frontier Airlines. Still, it was exactly what I needed—to keep working, especially because Shannon and I were arguing almost constantly. It wasn't long after I started recording with Juliette that we decided it was best if I got my own place. Shannon—always the mature one—was very generous. She wanted to stay friends and helped me find and move into a one-bedroom apartment in the Valley.

I tried to think back to a time when I'd gone through a breakup alone—either without chemical intervention or as many hookups or rebound relationships as possible—and failed. I was still maintaining sobriety, but I was concerned about being left to my own devices. Juliette and her manager were lifelong Scientologists, so sensing that I was maybe a little down after the move, one of the band's management suggested I go to an introductory Dianetics course with her. I was aware that they had a program specifically for addicts—Narconon—but I was pretty leery of its effectiveness. I had friends who had tried out its methods for drug withdrawal, which didn't sound appealing—sweating out the chemicals in a sauna, taking large doses of niacin supplements to counteract all the nutrients you'd be losing from the sweating, lots of exercise, and eating like a bird (plus listening to Scientologists). No thanks.

I went to the infamous Celebrity Center a couple of times just to give it a proper shot. It's an old, refurbished hotel with a grand, ornate office off the lobby that is kept in pristine condition in case L. Ron Hubbard comes back from the dead to claim it. There's a normal-looking outdoor café that looks out over a courtyard in the back of the building, and it was filled with actors I recognized but maybe didn't know the names of. There were many rooms, each with a different purpose. I went into one room that reminded me of a high school classroom and got the preliminary personality test and one workbook of Level 1. Of course I didn't make it any further once I learned the prices of the coursework, but in general the whole experience reminded me of elementary school—at one point I was asked to use blocks to demonstrate how I might make an ethical decision. After that, nobody pushed. I liked all of the people Juliette worked with, and her friends, but it just wasn't my thing.

I'd been in that apartment for only a couple of weeks before I went out and picked up all over again. We were still in the middle of rehearsals for the tour. After that relapse, I got a call from a Scientologist who heard that perhaps I needed to "get back on course." I begged off the honest way—"These courses are expensive; I just don't have the money."

The answer to that was, "Is there someone you can borrow the money from?"

Hahahahaha, I would be needing each and every cent of that money for my next steps into oblivion. I looked great, everybody said so. I was thin and knew I would be going home to my stash of drugs every night with no one to get on me about it, so I'm sure I was glowing.

THAT FALL, JULIETTE announced we'd be playing some shows leading up to a two-week West Coast tour, to be followed by another week on the East Coast. Just like always, I tried to scramble to get clean in preparation, but this time I was too in the thick of it to taper down.

After a sound check the next day, I told Paul I'd relapsed, and he thought I should tell Juliette. "No!" I said. "That's not why I'm telling you." Why was I telling him?

I wanted to be sober, but not enough to lose my job or put the tour on hold. I wanted someone to witness my seriousness about doing what was right, and I figured my secret was safe with Paul. As soon as I told him, I promised it was under control and I was taking steps to keep it that way. When we had one three-day weekend before the East Coast dates, I tried to detox on my own. I reached out to a couple of people I knew to tell them what was up. One friend left groceries on my doorstep and took me to Roddy's to detox when it felt too dangerous to do it at home. I was shaky to be sure but needed this job and didn't want to lose it.

I went straight from Roddy's to play the Voodoo Fest in New Orleans, an enormous two-day festival show with a ton of headliners including A Tribe Called Quest, the Killers, De la Soul, Green Day, and the newly reunited Pixies. Maybe not the best choice for a person off crack and heroin for three days, but I was determined to make it through. When I saw Kim Deal backstage with her sister, Kelly, and they asked how I'd been doing, I told them about the recent relapse. "Whoa, Patty Schemel on crack! What's that like?"

"You know, it's not bad . . . " It was almost like how people these days would discuss what it's like going gluten-free—a casual endorsement. "It's not for everyone, but I quite liked the feeling."

Seeing the Pixies again took me right back to the early 1990s in Bruce Pavitt's apartment. The feeling I got while listening to "Gigantic" live was unrelated to a drug-induced high but just as strong. It tapped into something purer and older in me, the simple joy of discovering a new song or album for the first time, and I realized that my love of music had nothing to do with my addiction to drugs. It surprised me.

At that point I felt I had to come clean to Juliette, so I told her about my relapse in her dressing room. I didn't know if she had noticed that I had been off, or if my drumming had been affected (I'm sure it had), but I wanted to be honest with her in case she heard about it another way. She was supportive. She immediately produced a bottle of vitamins from a Scientologist health food store—their patented "drug bomb" had worked for a lot of people she knew.

We played a few more shows down south, and then went home to rest for a few days before we were due to start the West Coast tour with three shows in California. In my absence I'd received a royalty check for *America's Sweetheart*, which immediately made me 10K richer than I'd thought. That was the only trigger necessary to fall off the wagon. Again I tried to stockpile—that old impossible trick, packing enough crack and heroin per day to get me through that first two weeks. I'd worry about how to stock up for the East Coast gigs later, I reasoned—maybe I could ration enough to get me to New York City, where at least I knew how to get what I needed. And that's how I found myself flagrantly smoking crack out of the back of the tour bus (though I thought doing it out of the bathroom window somehow counted as discretion). It was a rude awakening when we'd played only a week's worth of shows, and the drugs were all gone.

When we got to the venue in San Francisco, I was already in full panic mode. At sound check I announced, all casual, "I'm going to

go see some friends for an early dinner. See you before the show."
Our guitarist looked at me—and I could tell, but didn't care, that
he knew—and told me that I needed to be back no later than 7
o'clock. "Okayyy!" I practically sang all the way out the door. My
"friends" was the corner of 16th and Mission where I knew I could
go to score, and sure enough, I found what I was looking for within
ten minutes of leaving the building—enough drugs I prayed to last
me the rest of the tour.

BY THE TIME we got to the next show in Philly, all the drugs were
gone again. I'd used them all in a Starbucks bathroom and my hotel
room the night before. I was starting to withdraw. Because I hadn't
thought about the obvious weather differences between the two
coasts during the deep fall, the coat I'd packed was too thin. It
wasn't nearly enough to quell the shakes, much less the bitter cold.
I was openly a mess. As soon as humanly possible after hotel
check-in, I got in a cab, my wallet full of cash, told the driver to
take me to the worst neighborhood in town, and found drugs while
he waited. Of course I got ripped off—so obvious was my predicament as an out-of-towner—I couldn't procure nearly the supply I
wanted. Once I'd gotten back to the hotel, it was all gone in an
hour.

The next day, nothing. Then it was on to Boston, again with the
shakes inside my windbreaker, the freezing, and the panic. Then it's
the same misery in DC. By the time we got to New York City, I'd
made it through enough of the kick (about five days) that my physical condition was elevated to functional, but I was still miserable. I
was staying with Juliette in the hotel, which made everything worse.
I was trying to act normal, but meanwhile I was walking outside for
a smoke break and calling Larry on my cell. I'd found out that he
was in town to play a show with his band, the Midnight Movies.
All I could think about was how he must have had money, and how
much I needed. He wasn't having it though. "I'll see what I can
do . . . " he said, then never called back to confirm.

We played, packed up, then had to do some kind of MTV spot the next day before we could go back to L.A. By the time we got to that publicity appearance, I was so agitated that I lost it with the guitarist over a missing snare drum. I could feel myself lose control, could feel the judgment of the band, which suddenly got quiet when I began to yell. Everyone was over me—I was the fuckup. I'd been sleeping in the dressing rooms before we went on, passing out in the van right after we finished. I felt the shame of exposure, but I also kept my eye on the prize: if I could just make it to my apartment, there would be a welcome-home bit of crack and heroin there for me to get right again. *I'll feel better tomorrow, I'll think about how to be better tomorrow.* I shared a silent car ride with Juliette to the airport. It was finally time to go home.

The next day in my apartment, I got a visit from Juliette's assistant. She'd come with $500 cash as payment for the last show and the MTV piece and an invitation to meet with Juliette at her house. She had some CDs of mine that she wanted to return, and had some other things for me, too. I pretty much knew as soon as she said that that I'd likely be walking into another intervention.

And it was, albeit on a smaller scale, just Juliette and the band manager. They told me they knew what was going on, that I'd been all over the place during the tour, that they'd seen me call the guitar player an asshole onstage, I was mean to the drummer in Salem.

"No I *wasn't*. I wasn't mean to the guy in Salem," I protested. How dare they.

"Patty, you're out of control, and we're letting you go," the manager said, not unkindly, but firm. The whole time I was just standing in the doorway, taking it, annoyed once again that the rest of the band was too fucking gutless to show up to say it to my face. That old familiar lump in my throat was threatening to break me. As high as I was, the feelings were stronger—that scared me.

I summoned my anger—"Okay, well, I'll be in touch about my publishing!"—and left in a huff.

Five years after being kicked out of Hole, I was fired again, strung out, and broke, and this time I had no one to use with, no partner in crime, no friend to use with. I came home and collected myself, which meant pushing out all the thoughts that this was my fault. I knew they weren't wrong to kick me out—I just resented having to acknowledge it to myself just yet. Instead I got high and took a trip back out to the street.

| 42 |

JE T'AIME . . . MOI NON PLUS

I didn't have anyone in L.A., I reasoned, but I still had Josephine in Paris. I decided to stock up on dope and spend a few weeks with her there. The first thing she said when she found out I was coming was, "Do not bring any drugs into France. My father is a judge, and I've seen what they do to people—even Americans—who are caught. It's just not worth it." *Fuck.*

Oh, I still did it, but I sweated it a bit more. I checked a bag with as much heroin and crack for personal use as I could, putting the crack rocks in a pill bottle and the dope all wrapped up in the armpit of a T-shirt (and no needles, for good luck). I got through okay and went to Josephine's place in Paris.

I ran out of crack in no time, but I still had heroin. Then it was straight up debauchery for days and days, just chock full of sex and drugs, until I ran out of heroin, too, so had to kick in Josephine's bed (never good for the sheets). I got as drunk as possible to get through withdrawal, so naturally once I was through the worst of it I was desperate for some crack. I asked her to find me some more. All she could find was powder coke, which was such a bummer. I was used to freebasing it, so it was futile to snort this stupid powder that didn't even touch the places I was used to going to. For me, life on cocaine is joyless, but it was something to do.

Josephine knew that I loved the writer David Sedaris, and he famously lived in Paris (I just realized those two words rhyme). We'd usually take long walks in the city, and one day we went to Café de Flore in Saint-Germain, the famous coffee house she'd heard he frequented.

We scanned the room and its little, circular green tables, and no Sedaris, but there was Melissa Auf der Maur sitting alone at the window. The last time I'd seen her in person was in 1998. We walked toward her until she spotted me.

"Patty?"

"Hi." I hadn't expected this, but it felt right somehow. I wasn't in any shape to see her, but here we were all these years later—what were the odds?

"What are you doing in Paris?" Melissa looked from me to Josephine. I introduced them.

"Oh, you know, just visiting."

Melissa was in Paris to shake off a big breakup. She'd shortened her long, curly red hair. I could tell that she knew Josephine was just another Alice. The whole thing was awkward, but neither of us knew how to end the conversation. Ultimately we made a plan to get together again that night. She suggested Bar Hemingway, where she was going to watch the piano player.

"So, you're drinking now?"

"Yeah, when in Paris . . . "

"I guess alcohol was never really your problem," Melissa said. I thought I could detect a hint of a sneer in her voice. Was she being sarcastic, or trying to normalize it?

"Nope," I said in acknowledgment, and we left it at that.

Except I kept drinking, and somewhere along the way I lost her. It happened quickly. We'd gone to one place, then moved on to another, music played, possibly jazz, there was a man she was there to meet. The next thing I knew, I was alone again, no goodbyes, just accidental hellos. I woke up the next day feeling as if I'd lost something, but couldn't remember what it was.

| 43 |

WALKING WITH A GHOST

December and January have historically been associated with dark times in the life of my addiction—relapses, overdoses, and raging binges dominate my memories—and January 2005 was no different. Once again, I was a mess. I came home after the three weeks in Paris completely defeated and resigned to my fate—I couldn't stay away from crack or heroin. Most days I'd use the bathroom at the Shell gas station on the corner of Alvarado and Temple to fix, using toilet water to mix. I'd get well and go home and do it all again the next day.

Courtney called me about one week after I got back. She'd put a band together that she was now calling "Courtney Love" and needed a drummer to rehearse with. I agreed to go another round in the studio but didn't exactly put my best foot forward. I was late for the first rehearsal—even Courtney had arrived well before I did, something that had never happened before. I went in several times, smoked crack in the bathroom during breaks, and I used my sick mom as an excuse to leave early. Several days in I realized that all these jam sessions were fucking with my high, so I spoke up to inquire about what and when I'd be paid. Nobody came back with an answer, so that was it for me. I went back home to my tiny apartment and went about relieving myself of all my possessions.

It went in waves—if I was off the street and had just experienced a period of relative calm and functionality, sober or not, it was certainly better than the low I'd once known, which I had experienced and survived. I didn't suddenly slip lower, I just kept not really stopping, or pretending I had stopped if I'd made it a day or two, then rewarding myself with a little maintenance. Still not really wanting to imagine a completely sober life was possible.

I was selling everything I owned, found, or was given as a gift. Even though I was about to be three months overdue on the rent, every day I aimed to make enough money to stay high for the next 24 to 36 hours—it never worked out that there would be more than that, and it often worked out to be less. Larry and Josephine had become my primary sources of fallback income, but I couldn't go on living off of Western Union alone. I didn't have any more money, but I did have one more storage space of equipment left over from the old days. When I'd gotten back together with Courtney for the Bastard project, our tech just casually mentioned it one day––if I ever needed more parts, there was a lot of my old tour equipment in Courtney's storage in the Valley. This was the stuff that had gone on the road with us, the instruments that had survived. On one hand it was great to discover that there were all these things that I hadn't already sold, but on the other, as soon as I laid eyes on them I knew they were going to be.

I sold it all: the drum kit that I used to record *Live Through This* went to a pawn shop on La Brea for $800; I sold another drum kit a week later to the same place, two more to Black Market Music in West Hollywood; I'd been using my floor tom as a dining table—that had to go. There was another pawn shop between my place and downtown, and that's where I sold all my snare drums, cymbals, cymbal stands, and kick drum pedals. The maximum I could get for anything from that guy was $100—it didn't matter that I'd played this thing on *Saturday Night Live*, not a dollar more. But he was close by and reliable, and every day he cheerfully gave me between 1 and 15 percent of my possessions' cash value.

I'd also managed to save tons of CDs and vinyl singles, rare imports and autographed copies, and over a period of a few weeks I sold them all to Amoeba. I spent a lot of time there waiting in line for it to be my turn at the BUY counter. One day I looked behind me and recognized Amra's dad (the father of one of Frances's nannies), waiting in another line. Amra's dad was a veteran L.A. punker who had once owned a record store and now sponsored a lot of people in the program. It infuriated me when one of the guys working the counter called out to Amra's dad, inviting him to move up in line.

At this point I was throbbing with paranoia; I'd reached peak crackhead. Because I recognized Amra's dad, I was convinced he had recognized me back, which meant he knew that I was there to sell my record collection to support my habit, and by calling his name before mine, the Amoeba guys were sending a message to both me and Amra's dad that they knew it, too. *Let's make her squirm by calling his name first, that'll teach her.* True collectors like Amra's sober dad to the front! I scowled and put up my Imperial Teen CDs on the counter. It really fucked up my day.

The couch was the last saleable thing I owned, but it was too heavy to contemplate moving, and I could probably get only $25 for it. (Besides, I needed that couch to nod out on.) Where would I go from here? How many bowls of Matzo Ball soup could Larry buy to keep me alive? Sometimes I was psychotic in his presence. I was convinced I was being followed, I was on a list, the phones were bugged. I said things like, "Listen . . . can you hear them? They're in the alley!" I'm sure my eyes were wide and yellow. My brother responded with calm deflections—"Let's go get something to eat." He'd distract me from myself. He always gave me a little money, or if he didn't have cash, something to sell. There was never any relief, only the vicious hunger for more with no chance of pleasure on the other side. This was the beginning of the end for real.

IN LATE FEBRUARY, Shannon called to tell me that she'd pulled some strings and could get me into rehab at CRI-Help. It was all set. They had a bed for me. It would be taken care of with money from MAP. She and Larry would take me that very evening. She would take care of packing up whatever I had left in the apartment and keep it safe. All I had to do was agree to go. I was high when we had the conversation, which explains why I thought it sounded like a good idea (that old cliché), but I couldn't deny it any longer. I'd already hit what most people would call a bottom a million times. I'd already lost everything and gotten it back, only to lose it again. I'd already asked for help and received it; I'd also resisted help and received it anyway, only to squander it. I didn't have any money or means to make it and nowhere to be. I was about to lose my apartment, again. I had torpedoed every relationship with every girlfriend I'd ever had. I hated everything about my life, and I wanted to be normal. I was 37 years old and had run out of time and chances.

"I need to get high before I go." Shannon nodded. By now she knew the drill.

When we got to the waiting room to check in that night, it was really crowded and understaffed. I'd taken all my dope in preparation for this ritual of giving up and handing over. From this moment forward, I would be sick. There would be nothing but sickness, and then the dull ache of sobriety. From now on I was going to be alone with myself every day. Alone with boredom and shame and regret and feeling lower than Morrissey. I really, really didn't want to go through that agony again. My high was definitely fading; my ability to feel good was gone. I was so done with myself, yet I wanted to live. *Here we go again.*

My anxiety was beginning to peak, my knee vibrating up and down from my restlessness. I looked at Larry sitting next to me. There were a bunch of kids' toys in the waiting room, and they were all on the floor at his feet. He picked up a plush baseball bat and held it like a bong between his legs and pretended to light it. I laughed. Shannon was across the room talking to someone in a loud, urgent voice.

"She's going to run if we don't get her into detox now!"

I'm the "she" she's referring to, I think as I'm sitting there. *I'm the runner.* She was right, though. At that point I was living moment to moment, high to high. I was a shell of a person at the end of my rope. I already knew all the AA slogans. I was gonna keep going back just as soon as I got there.

As I finally said goodbye to Larry and Shannon and turned to walk down the hall to face my fear, I had no idea if it was going to be the last time.

But it was.

| 44 |

IN AND OUT OF GRACE

There was nothing new about this check-in except that I was coming back to this specific rehab for the second time, and after the tech took my vitals and began to interview me, I had to confront the fact of how many times I'd sought treatment in the past.

She: "Can you tell me about your habit?"

Me: "Which one?"

"You tell me. How often do you use, and what are we withdrawing from today?"

"I'm shooting about four balloons a day and smoking uh, *a lot* of crack cocaine. I shoot up in the morning to get well and try to smoke as much crack as I can till I need to make money to buy some more."

"Anything else?"

"I've been drinking since I was twelve. I've tried pretty much everything at least once. I've snorted, smoked, and injected crystal meth several times. I've abused various pills, but they were never strong enough, and I barely consider marijuana a drug, and it's never appealed to me. I've smoked cigarettes since I was a teenager."

"And for how long have you been using crack and heroin?"

"Heroin since 1992 or '93, crack for about six years."

"Any periods of sobriety?"

"A few. The longest amount of time I've stayed off heroin was two years."

"Ever sought treatment before?"

I had to count. "Do you mean detoxes? Or rehabs too?"

"How about both . . . if you can."

I was still counting. There were so many short stays and failed attempts over the years, weekend cold turkey stays at a friend's place for privacy, using opiate blockers or benzos to taper down or off, the drinking binges in between. The number of times I'd tried to get sober for any length of time seemed as long as my life.

"Ballpark? 22 detoxes and 14 rehab facilities for varying lengths of time."

There was no judgment from the tech—these people had heard it all before. She wrote down her notes, gave me some meds, and I went off to detox hopeless and depressed. I emerged three days later in a twin bed with a plastic mattress that made noise every time I rolled over, its cheap poly/cotton sheets sticking to my sweaty skin in the room I shared with a stranger. Now I was exhausted and depressed, and I couldn't sleep.

I was worried about what crack might have done to my brain long term and the way it had affected my moods. I just *missed* it so much. Would I ever be able to get out from under the grey cloud or the fog of shame that followed me every time there was an absence of drugs in my body? It takes such a long time to feel better physically, and I had to face it, I'd never lasted long enough sober to prove to myself that I'd ever feel better emotionally. I never cried. I couldn't feel anything really at all, just the heaviness of re-emerging back into the world. My senses were waking up; life was becoming loud again.

Every morning I'd wake up to the sound of the tech opening the door at 7 a.m.—time to get up to shower during the allotted time slot. Everything is scheduled—a structured existence is the cornerstone of rehab. The shower room reminded me of what you'd see in a YMCA, groups of women lined up for her turn. At check-in you receive a small garbage bag of essential toiletries. Everybody gets a dresser drawer and a hook to hang a jacket on. A tiny bedside table for your book. Every day I'd wear multiple layers—I could never get warm enough. I was very thin and always shaking and grinding my teeth.

After our morning showers, we would be dispatched to the cafeteria, which resembled any public high school's. We'd get in line with our trays for French toast and overcooked eggs, sit down at a communal table, and eat mostly in silence. No food was allowed in the bedrooms, so you had to cram it all in at mealtime. Next there was a daily N.A. assembly in a meeting room—that's where the genders are allowed to mix. I think there were about forty of us. We opened with different twelve-step prayers, and then a speaker would focus on one of the steps that we might be struggling with.

One morning about a week into my stay, I was at one of these integrated group meetings when I looked up to see I recognized the speaker, "John." He was reading "Just for today . . . ," and I saw that John was Blackie Onassis from Urge Overkill, who I hadn't seen since I had done dope with him at Lollapalooza. Later, we locked eyes to acknowledge each other, which I recognized as the same look I gave to strangers on the sidewalk I thought might be dealers. I resented the familiar speeches and the constant presence of all the techs (aka the newly sober graduates of the program who needed something to do). They were always trying to give us unsolicited advice.

This time around an anesthesiologist took me by the shoulders, looked me in the eyes, and said, "You're going to die."

Thanks for your support. I thought I'd fine-tuned my rehab act by now, but this woman knew my shtick because she had the same one.

After the first testimony an experienced member of the staff talked about how addiction affects our bodies and brains. Someone else would offer their sober testimony. We would talk about our feelings. Afterward, we'd shuffle back to the women's wing where we would meet in three groups of six. This was the infamous sharing circle, where we could more deeply deconstruct our reasons for being there and tell our sad stories about the various ways we'd fucked up our lives. A lot of people had dual diagnoses—bipolar disorder, anxiety and depression, PTSD, eating disorders—anything that might cause someone to self-medicate.

We learned about the roots of our addictions, the dysfunctional family dynamics that kept us feeling too much, then our quest to self-medicate so we could function without weeping in public, so we could feel good, feel something else. We explored the other areas of our lives where we'd been compulsive or obsessive. Did we gamble a lot and get an adrenaline rush from the terror of winning and/or losing? Did we have sex with a lot of people while also preferring to be in a relationship at all times to avoid being alone? Did we spend money we didn't have? Did we keep eating after we were full, or deprive ourselves all nourishment so we could remain empty?

In one group, I remember abandonment issues coming up as a common thread for people, and realizing that might also be true for me. What I looked for in a partner was someone to take care of me, to commit to sticking around, even if I needed to set the schedule and back out if another opportunity presented itself. I couldn't stand to be alone with myself, so I had taken up drinking and treated it like a friend, someone I could spend my quiet time with or take along to the party where I'd have more confidence to talk to people. Once I got into a relationship, it would feel incredible for a while, but never incredible enough to experience sober.

I finished my share, and the counselor looked at me very seriously and said, "This is going to take you a very long time to unpack." That caught me off guard. Wasn't I unpacking it now? How did she say that so confidently? Wasn't this my major malfunction, or just another issue to add to the arsenal? Of course I wanted to run to the answer and not accept that it could take years. (I guess that's why they tell you to take it "One day at a time.")

THERE'S SOMETHING ABOUT N.A. in the Valley—it's hardcore. In the off-site meetings, I met a lot of women on the six-months-in-jail/six months-in-a-residential-treatment-center track. Gang members, criminals, people who had had every disadvantage. There was a shocking amount of overt racism on display, which was a wake-up call to me but absolutely normal for some. It seemed to carry over from jail, where different groups often self-segregated.

Early on in my stay at CRI-Help, my new roommate and I were being driven to a meeting by one of the alumni volunteers—I was in the backseat, and she was in the front with the driver. I have no idea how their conversation began, but suddenly I heard a string of racist slurs thrown about casually in a tone of voice plenty loud enough for me to hear. It was like the air they breathed. *Holy shit.* In that first moment I was stunned into silence, but it wouldn't be long before I had another chance to confront someone directly. During one of the morning group meetings, I saw that the guest speaker was standing in front of the room wearing a Skrewdriver T-shirt, which was a neo-Nazi hardcore band from the U.K. I confronted her after the meeting—why was she wearing that?

"Oh, this?" She said, gesturing to her T-shirt and sweats.

"That shirt," I said. "I know who Skrewdriver is."

She suddenly, finally looked a little sheepish. "Oh . . . well . . . I didn't think it mattered here . . . But, yeah, I probably shouldn't have. But do you think anyone would even know?"

That's what it was like.

ONE CONSISTENTLY POSITIVE experience I had in rehab was that I'd always somehow manage to make a friend about two weeks in. And usually I picked that person because she had a great sense of humor. The very best sober experience I ever had was laughing—really laughing—for the first time after a detox. It was the feeling of my spirit remembering the punchline. A group of us were outside one day when some alumni volunteers came by to drop off a box of donated clothes. I looked at Gray, one of the women from my group whom I respected, and she silently responded with a look that said simply, *Ugh.*

A week later it became a running joke between us: "Why do you look so happy, the donation box isn't even coming this week." Drug addicts are inherently misanthropic, especially when newly sober—the definition of the word is actually "A person who dislikes humankind and avoids human society." Pretty much.

Because my father had recently died, I was assigned to additional grief counseling. Though I dutifully attended the sessions, I found that I simply didn't feel sad, just completely numb and disconnected from it, from him. It felt like they wanted me to cry it out, that weeping over something was the only way to deal with it. I think I was more angry than sad. *Why couldn't he have quit smoking? Why couldn't he see this coming? Did he think he would live forever, that we would take care of him, that we had the skills for that?*

For me, the first thirty days were about regulating my body to the point where I could sleep peacefully for a few hours. My brain and body were still leveling out, still just getting into the routines, beginning to process the therapy, acting as if. Thirty days is not really enough time for anything to truly sink in—more like I was just getting used to talking about myself in general. *Hello, my name is Patty, and I'm an addict and an alcoholic.* At that time, it was just too soon for me to see or feel the death of my father. I was listening, though, trying to appreciate that it wouldn't always be this way, that at the end of the rainbow there was another world of hurt to contend with.

MARCH 1, 2005, is my official sober birthday. Since that detox at CRI-Help, I never drank or did any drugs again (not that I knew then that I was really and truly finally done, but still). The difference this time: I did what they told me. I did the exact opposite of what I thought I knew. The warning I'd been hearing in meetings forever—"You are going to end up losing everything"—was finally becoming true for me. My father had died, I wasn't communicating regularly with my mom and sister, everybody who loved me obviously had my number. I was unhireable, sick, exhausted, and desperate. There was no band to return to, no dates to play. Whatever possessions I hadn't sold or abandoned were all packed away in a storage locker I didn't even have the key for. This time wasn't about going to rehab because I had an intervention or getting clean because I had to get back on the road, or to please someone else. It was real surrender.

| 45 |

A NORTHERN SOUL

They wanted me to stay longer, but I couldn't afford to. I'd been so lucky that Shannon had reached out for financial assistance for that first thirty days because I'd run out of any other options. After CRI-Help, I transferred straight into a sober living house and made a vow to commit for real. The place was in Van Nuys. There were four women to a room, and my roommates were Gloria, Brenda, and Zoe—women just like me and nothing like me, all at once. The first two became my closest confidantes. I related to them because they were junkies, too. Gloria was from the Valley. For her, smoking pot led to smoking heroin, which quickly accelerated to shooting up in the bushes of a public park. Brenda was in her early fifties, a mom, and had been through recovery earlier in her life. She'd stayed sober for years and had even been a drug and alcohol counselor for a decade when she relapsed, and once she did, she moved right back out to the street. It happened that quickly. Zoe was the youngest, kind of a daddy's girl gone bad—a serious cocaine habit was all it took to bring her to her knees.

I HAD JUST transitioned to the house when Courtney called with a line on a job. Not music-related, but a cash gig that only required me to be sober and aware of my surroundings. After being court-ordered to treatment, Courtney had recently completed a discreet rehabilitative experience in a Malibu beach house with a private chef and an acupuncturist on staff. That stay had been arranged for her by one of the elite Hollywood fixers that I'd learned about almost a decade before. His name was Wade.

When Wade wasn't busy counseling celebrity addicts, he was a drug treatment consultant, a bounty hunter in the field. For a fee, he would go out on the streets, befriend strung-out teens, give them money, start to mentor them, and offer housing. Then he would encourage them into a white van, which he'd use to transport them back to their terrified, desperate, and wealthy parents. Some people would call this kidnapping—it certainly isn't legal. The whole operation requires a number of subcontractors in order to keep up the illusion of efficacy; if the team is on it, it must be serious. That's where I came in. Wade told me about his latest case—a widowed mother had hired him to befriend her only daughter, a 22-year-old meth head who had been panhandling in Venice. Wade would handle the work of snatching her off the street and getting her to a secluded hotel in Huntington Beach. What he needed from me was someone to babysit in the hotel room while she was mostly sedated. I'd get $1,000 for four-day stretches and all the room service I could stomach.

On the first day, a doctor came to the room and took Caitlyn's vitals and sedated her. He prescribed sedatives and talked me through the routine—meth withdrawal is not like heroin withdrawal. The main side effect of coming down off speed is profound depression, so it's best to sleep through the days until the body and brain stabilize. After a few days, Caitlyn's mother came to visit. She seemed thrilled by this progress—here was her daughter, whose death she was sure was imminent, now sleepy and vulnerable and there in a posh hotel being jailed by strangers. I got the sense that she had no idea this wasn't an ideal scenario; all that mattered was Caitlyn was alive and not using that day. Her mom would settle for alive.

Just a couple of days after her mother's visit, Caitlyn tried to escape. She didn't get far, but Wade hired another minder in the form of a brawny guy to stand by the door and look big. After working for Wade for a month, I stopped. I just couldn't feel good about what I thought was a futile effort with little chance of making a difference in the long run—I knew you can't force anyone to get the treatment if they don't feel in control of the decision. I saw the kind of cash being exchanged, and I didn't want to get any more cynical about humanity than I already was. A couple years later, Wade would be played by Benjamin Bratt in a TV show based on his life.

I STAYED IN the sober living house for six months in all and started my first real minimum wage job (since the one I had painting houses back in 1994) a couple months before I left. I heard about the opportunity at a meeting—someone mentioned they saw a posting for a dog groomer/walker at a nearby boarding facility. I wasn't looking for anything in particular—I just knew I needed something to occupy my time, provide a structure to my days—and this intrigued me. *Dogs. Not people.* Yes.

The place was full of characters, both customers and employees, human and canine. One of my favorites was this older Russian man who wore an Adidas tracksuit and gold chains—he was the full-time groomer. Every day we worked together I would watch him and try to figure out his backstory—how does a gangster-of-a-certain-age become the preferred hairdresser to a Bichon Frise named Itsy-Bitsy? One day he's in the middle of giving a Shih Tzu a blowout, when he suddenly asks me, in his thick accent, "Do you know what stars mean on hands?"

I was stumped. Did he mean tattooed stars? "Decoration?" I guessed.

"No, no, no . . . . In Russia, it means you are in the mafia." Oh.

He continued. When you put a ring around your finger, it's supposed to represent how much time you had in the mafia, apparently. So one year equals one tattooed ring.

As luck would have it, I also had a ring tattooed around one of my fingers. "Does this mean I spent a year in the Soviet Gulag?" I asked. He laughed heartily. "Cause I might have and just forgotten." We were fast friends after that.

It was a motley crew. There was the stoner kid who showed me how to brush out the skittish dogs before stepping outside for his second joint of the shift. And the sweet woman who took great care to be so gentle, wrapping the dogs in a hot, fluffy towel so there would be no shivering after their baths. And the Thai movie star who had moved to L.A. to make it big in Hollywood and insisted that dog grooming was a hobby for her. She brought her own toy poodle to work every day—the most impeccably dressed dog I'd ever seen, truly—I never saw Trixie without one of her spotless dresses and matching shoes on, and some days she and her mistress would match! The actress was so popular with customers that she had her own clientele and a waiting list.

There was plenty of work to go around, though—the facility was open 24 hours a day, and I'd typically see about thirty dogs pass through during my shift alone. This being Hollywood, most of the people who utilized our services worked in entertainment—movies, television, music—and kept crazy hours and travel schedules that meant their pets needed a place to go in their absence. My personal favorite was a border collie named Louise. She was the *sweetest* dog, who sometimes stayed for a month at a time. I'd never caught a glimpse of her owner, but I always imagined that Louise must have lived with a sweet older couple.

The healing benefits of having a pet or just spending time around animals are well documented. Dogs in particular are very accepting. A dog doesn't care if you have a hit record or if you were to blame in your last breakup, if you've gained 15 pounds, or if you don't have any money. A dog is just happy you're there. I found myself reading everything I could about animal behavior. I began to work with them as a way back to myself, to accepting myself as a person deserving of love. I was starting to feel things again. Flashes of joy and gratitude—that rare kind of uncomplicated love. I felt certain that the dogs were raising my oxytocin levels in ways I had probably never experienced without the use of synthetic chemicals. That fact alone was miraculous, so I knew I needed to listen to that if I was going to stay healthy. I loved being able to apply what I'd learned to their training and handling, and just generally making them feel as good as they made me feel.

After a couple of months it was time for me to move on, both from the sober living house and the part-time job. On one of my last days, someone came to pick up Louise, and I just happened to be there to see it—she was a young woman, an assistant to the owner who lived in Bel Air. I sang the praises of Louise to her and told her how I'd miss her most of all now that I was about to move on. The assistant took me aside and told me that her owner traveled constantly and was looking for a more personal caretaking experience in her absence. Would I be open to taking care of her outside the boarding facility? Because her owner, Meg Ryan, had to spend the upcoming summer in New York.

And that's just what happened. I moved back to the same rented house in Silver Lake where I'd lived with Shannon. She'd moved out by then, so it was just me and another renter, but I felt comfortable there and could get back to basics. I started hiking regularly with

Louise, then started walking a bunch of other dogs, and because of my connections in music, my client list mostly included the dogs of musicians I'd worked with. Almost instantly it was a business, and because all businesses that have to do with animals have to make use of a pun in their name, I called mine Dog Rocker.

| 46 |

SOMETHING ELECTRICAL

I started seeing Christina after only six months clean, which is quite ill advised for an addict in recovery, but it has worked for us. I was hanging around with a group of sober lesbian friends, and one night we went to see one of our circle DJ at a club. I noticed a girl across the room and realized I'd been seeing her around for years. Christina had a memory of us meeting back in the 1990s, to which I joked that I currently couldn't remember anything from that decade (though I could, and I'd always thought she was hot). We exchanged numbers that night, and it was pretty on after that.

My sponsor was pretty vigilant about calling me out: What did I have to bring to this new relationship? I was still picking up dog shit for a living and slowly coming to terms with a brand new life born of a last chance. They're not trying to punish you when they strongly recommend you not get involved with anyone until you've been sober at least a year—it just makes sense. New relationships are risky and tangled up in an addict's biggest trigger—failure. In the past, a fight or a breakup—pain or discomfort of any kind—was the quickest road to heroin town for me. Healthy relationships require that both parties have good self-esteem, and that was un-questionably a new thing for me.

Let me be clear, when it came to this area of my life, I was going to do what I wanted to do. My issues with love and sex were well known to me, but abstaining from drugs and alcohol was the very best I could do at the time, and it was never my intention to join a convent. We all just have to do the best we can, and the best I could do at the time was to hold out from connecting with another woman on that level for six months.

One thing that helped make a difference was that although Christina had never been addicted to anything, she was already going to Al-Anon meetings when we met (that's a support group for people who have an addict in their lives). She'd seen that tendency in herself to always seek out the person she could take care of, and we both have that same crazy antennae for each other's opposite. She's a planner and a fixer, always organized, and has a knack for anticipating a problem before it becomes one—very Type A. It's safe to say that I'd never made a plan in my life at that point unless it occurred to me five minutes before I acted on it. Christina needed to help, and it was my job to admit that I needed it. When you plug into each other's defects, and everyone's aware and getting outside support or therapy, it can work (but that last part is important).

Christina had a real career working in film and TV production, and I was still just getting my life back on solid ground. She didn't seem to mind that I was starting over, though—she knew I was an artist and had that faith in me that I would find my way back. I'd never imagined I'd be in the kind of relationship where we'd both start the day reading a daily meditation from the Big Book, but that's what we did. All of our friends were in some kind of program, and that helped too. Plus she had good taste in music. For one of our first dates I took her to see this band I liked, High on Fire, and afterward she said that she'd liked the show, but she still preferred their former incarnation, a band called Sleep. The fact that she knew that those two bands were affiliated was so cool, the fact that she knew about *Smash Hits* magazine.

When we first started dating I didn't have very much money for big nights out. My grand romantic gestures came in the form of little notes and drawings, analogue style. One night we were hanging out at her place in Echo Park when we both heard a loud boom. Outside we could see sparks flying off a telephone pole, the sky lit up in orange fireworks. "What do you think that was?" Christina asked. "Looks like something electrical," I said and drew her a picture of the scene. Her birthday was coming up, and that framed drawing was the first gift I ever gave her.

She didn't ever push or probe and let me come to her. She's like that with everyone—when you're ready to talk, she's a great listener. I'm sure she had to resist the urge to do some things for me, especially things that came naturally to her, like getting one's finances in order, and within other relationships I'm sure it's not a big deal for one person to just do things for the other. I had been with a couple of very good partners in my life—or they were good, but I obviously wasn't in a position to give them the kind of things they could give me; I was giving it all to my addictions. With Christina, it's not about either of us rescuing the other person; it's more about holding each other accountable. That, mixed with the reality of my sober vulnerability, built up an expectation of trust between us that stuck.

In the early days, she would go away for jobs sometimes for three months at a time, and it was fine because I had my own work and life to attend to. It just felt different to me right off the bat. I wasn't playing music again yet, just taking care of the dogs and going to my meetings. I was still too scared to play. I still thought I sucked. But once the fog began to lift, I knew I had to hit something if I was ever going to feel better.

Since we met, we've each maintained our own communities of support, so we can better meet in the middle from a place of understanding. I call Al-Anon the "none of your business meetings." That program helps give people the tools to pay attention to their own shit, instead of getting caught in a cycle of worrying about what the other person is doing. Bottom line: if I didn't learn to get back on my feet on my own, I would never be able to build back the self-esteem I'd lost (or never had in the first place) when I was trying to fill that empty space with drugs.

When I was a kid, I used to dream that I'd grow up, fall in love, and have a wife. But I could never have envisioned a world where that would be possible out in the open—I figured we would have to live in secret. But in 2004 gay marriage had been legalized in a couple of states, and California had begun to give out licenses. By 2008, when we were ready, it had been legalized in California and then was made illegal again, but legal or not, nothing was going to stop Christina and me from going through with the ceremony. We were committed, and we wanted the world to know.

A few days before the wedding, my mom texted the news that the ban had been overturned. "Congratulations—you've been recognized!" We got married in the backyard surrounded by friends and family, human and canine alike. Roddy and Larry were my best men. Friends sang songs. No one from Hole was there—we were still a few years from a reunion. Three years clean wasn't quite long enough to move past all the resentments, but I had a feeling they'd be happy for me and that was enough.

There's a photo from that day of my mom and me that I love— she just looks so thrilled and happy to be alive in that moment. She always told me that I'd find someone. She just believed it completely.

Like when I came out to her as a teenager and she told me it was okay, there was a community of people just like me. "You'll fall in love," she'd said, "and someone else will love you back."

AS OF THIS WRITING, Christina and I have been married twelve years, and we have a 6-year-old daughter named Bea. Our days are filled with music and schedules, and we play in rooms that resemble forts with mattresses everywhere and places to fall, just like back in the days when Frances was little (though now that I'm a mom myself, it's awful to remember that I used to do things like smoke around a baby). It's astonishing to realize how little we knew about taking care of ourselves back then, much less how to be a parent to a developing infant.

When I was at Liberty House there had been another resident who was pregnant and about to give birth when I got there. I remember thinking that this was the first pregnant woman I could remember spending any time with in person since Courtney was pregnant in 1992. My life was so far removed from what normal adults were up to by the time they were in their early thirties. By the time I was in a position to become a parent, Frances had graduated from high school.

We researched our options for a long time. Christina wanted to experience being pregnant, so that part was easy. We met with all our friends who had done it—something lesbians love to do: sit down with a pot of tea with other women and share their birth stories. How did you get pregnant? Was the experience different for the partner that gives birth versus the one who doesn't? How did you come to the decision to adopt? Everybody's experience was unique—what was universal were the warnings that our financial situation would change significantly and that we'd never sleep again. Before we set about trying, we took my mother to Ireland and tried to stock up on all the travel we'd realistically be able to do for the rest of our lives.

After talking to all these women, we decided on a plan similar to what one of the couples we knew had done—one parent provided the egg and carried the baby, and the other's male family member made the donation. So Larry helped out in that department, which made it nice because both our families are represented. The first time I told anyone Christina was pregnant was at my Thursday night women's meeting. My focus had shifted to seeking out other moms who'd had experiences like mine. My life now is about asking for help on a regular basis.

Bea was born on Christina's birthday, September 13, 2010, five years to the day after I gave her "Something Electrical." Christina took the better part of her first year off from work, and after that she went back full time, and I took care of our daughter. Each year brings new challenges, and each of us has her own style. Becoming a parent is like getting married and then opening up a small business together. It's a lot of charts, meetings, and negotiations; it's a 24-hour-a-day job.

My life today is my baby and my wife, my sobriety and my music. They say in the program that you live your way back to your life—I did that and built even more on top of it. Having a family really drives home how much I have to lose. I think back to those struggling women in the rehabs over the years and the fact that some of them were facing losing their children. That's why it took me so long to get the message about how bad it had gotten. Losing my career or my status in my community of musicians is nothing compared to losing a baby; that's a pain beyond pain.

Having a kid makes me think so much about my own parents and all the good things they did for me. Like how my dad and I put the engine in my first Volkswagen together, and the way he encouraged me in my drumming and never coddled us. The other day my daughter's toy box lost a screw, and I decided to use it as a teachable moment—we would fix it together. I took her to the hardware store and showed her what we needed for the repair, and when we got home I laid out the tools—the wood screws, the Phillips-head screwdriver. Bea got out her own plastic toolbox. I showed her the difference between the Phillips and a flathead, the sizes of the different screws, and making sure it's secure. She got it right away—when something is broken, you can't wait for someone else to fix it for you.

My mom died just this year, and I'm so grateful that she got to see me sober and got to spend some time with Bea and also see me as a mom. I am the woman she'd always hoped I'd become. Most importantly, I was able to be present for her in the last few months of her life. Something I'd heard other alcoholics talk about in meetings, how sobriety helped them show up for their families. Today I carry on my mom's example of encouraging my daughter that she can be anything she wants to be, that there's no such thing as "girl interests" and "boy interests," only "interests." Bea is her own person, and I respect that the way Mom did for me.

Science seems to support that the disease of alcoholism is partly hereditary. I'm sure it reveals itself in people in different ways. The person that hasn't ever picked up a drink might have problems with food, shopping, or gambling. I grew up hearing my parents talk about the relief they felt when they picked up their first drink, and I recognized early on that feeling for myself. There wasn't anything they could've done to stop me from searching for the relief, the cord that plugged me into the world.

But I was lucky to also find that same feeling by playing music for hours—my parents gave me that, too. I learned there was a healthier way to integrate my arms and legs and heart all together. As long as a kid gets the message that it's okay to talk about our physical, mental, and emotional struggles openly, they have a better shot at a happier, healthier life. Parenting in the 2010s is a lot more child-focused than when my parents were raising me in the 1970s, but I don't regret growing up aware of their struggles to stay healthy. I recently hosted a women's AA meeting at my house on a Saturday morning. Moms brought their children, and they played outside, just as I had as a kid. Those are good memories for me; my parents were happy. I know Bea will be okay, and she will know women can recover. She sees it everyday.

LARRY IS STILL my favorite guitarist, and we continue to play music together. We were both in a band called the Death Valley Girls. Bea knows all the names of the people in the pictures on our bookshelf—"Kurt" she says and points to a picture of him, grinning in his pajamas. She knows "Courtney" and "Eric" and "Melissa." She refers to any band I'm in as "Mom's Rock and Roll," and she asks for it by name. "Let's play Mom's Rock 'n' Roll," means she wants to hear the Upset record *She's Gone,* or *Street Venom* by Death Valley Girls.

I was talking to Melissa the other day, and she pointed out that I'm the only member from the glory days of Hole who still plays music regularly. For the last few years I've been playing with a band called Upset with Ali Koehler, Lauren Freeman, Rachel Gagliardi, and Nicole Snyder—we play shows in small clubs pretty regularly. I'm 50, usually the oldest person in the room. Sometimes I get "rockegnized," either at shows or every once in a while out and about in L.A.; someone will come up to me to say how much *Live Through This* influenced their life or how they were teenagers when I came out in *Rolling Stone* and it helped them feel less alone. Mostly I get a lot of, "I can't believe you're standing here at the Smell" (a club in L.A.). Me neither . . .

But I still like playing—it keeps me in shape and on top of things mentally, and I love the music and need it in my life. There are a lot of differences—the girls in my band grew up listening to Blink 182. For the kids these days, Nirvana is classic rock. Sheryl Crow is their Joni Mitchell, and they take Marilyn Manson pretty seriously, like he was doing something political. One of my younger drum students is fascinated by Slipknot. I'm not surprised they're so connected to a slicker sound. A lot has changed with the invention of software that makes it possible for almost anyone to make music in the comfort of their own bedroom, no drum kit required. These days you can mic an old shoebox, bang around a little bit, run it through Pro Tools, and it'll sound like Neil Peart. Seeing what people are up to when it comes to technology keeps me inspired, but I'll never stop teaching the basics.

| 47 |

THE DIFFERENCE

A few days ago Christina sat on the edge of the bed and told me gently not to look at the news. My habit is to read the headlines compulsively every morning while still in bed. I rolled over and hung on to one last precious moment of ignorance.

"What happened?"

Chris Cornell had just been found dead in a hotel bathroom in Detroit, she told me. It was being reported that he'd committed suicide, possibly after overdosing. My heart sank: *not again*. His family, his kids.

Soundgarden was born in the same Seattle as Nirvana. And Alice in Chains and Green River, Mother Love Bone, Mudhoney, Screaming Trees, Pearl Jam, and Hole. We were so young but felt so old on the inside. On the outside, everyone's hair was long then, Chris's especially; he was known to whip it around on stage in a dramatic display of circular head banging. When I first became aware of him in the mid-1980s, he was still playing drums in his band. But a drummer with a four octave vocal range should probably be up front.

I'd always liked him—really everyone did. I felt a kinship because of some similarities in our stories. He'd been sober since 2002, still played music, and seemed so happy. He was one of the success stories, both professionally and in his sobriety.

The news was physically crushing. That morning, my daughter could tell I was down and asked what was wrong. Christina told her my friend had died and I was sad and feeling quiet.

"Sometimes people want to be alone when they're sad, and sometimes they want extra hugs," Christina explained to Bea.

Christina answered Bea's question—"Which one does Mom want?"—by looking straight at me for emphasis. "Let's give her a little time to feel ready for hugs." And then Bea got a little emotional.

"We want Mom here with us."

Her tone was adamant and tender, but I could hear fear in her voice. I knew that meant, *Be here now,* and also *Don't you fucking die on us.*

There are still so many hard days. It scares me when people who've come so far are able to succumb to their disease so suddenly. I am careful to remember that one bad mood could be enough to flip the switch—my body would remember if I'd let it. But I don't want to go back. It's the not wanting to feel differently than you do all the time that is why you have to be vigilant.

And I worry sometimes about getting older, and I don't love that I don't have that same familiar, skinny body anymore. I struggle with the quest for perfection, and I don't want to admit that I sometimes have a compulsive relationship with food. Lately I've slacked off on going to meetings; I have to remind myself to maintain a spiritual connection to the work of recovery. I hate that I'll need to keep Chris's death in my mind whenever I think about the ongoing commitment to my health and sanity. I know Chris wanted the same things all those years he was able to stay clean—nobody chooses this struggle.

WHEN PEOPLE ASK me if there was an event or moment that finally made it click for me, I can't say that there is. It wasn't waking up one day clean and sober and ready to shine. Recovery is a series of moments. I have moments of gratitude when I remember that I don't have to sort out my lies today. And I have moments of what-the-fuck whenever I find myself engaging in some kind of exercise in wellness, such as hiking, or exercise in general. Or when I find myself not changing the station when the Indigo Girls come on the radio, or the all-female country group Wild Rose from 1988. (But maybe that just has to do with getting older.) I've never had the moment where I think I'm cured, or even if I know it's all going to be okay. I didn't even begin to touch the real shit underneath my shit until two or three years into recovery—that's been my experience, anyway—there's a *lot* of work to do, a lot of feelings about something, or someone, to analyze. The whole family dynamic—I'm still looking at that stuff.

Once I started to engage in therapy, and reading about addiction and the various theories about what causes it, I began to see the fuller picture of what was going on with me. In my case, I'm an all-in addict. I finally understand how powerless I am against the pull of drugs and alcohol. Before, I never wanted to accept that I couldn't control it. If I'd just been given the right circumstances, I believed—more money, a steady gig to keep me occupied, the right girlfriend or band—maybe I could juggle the dual responsibilities to my drugs and my life. I've obviously tried all the sober-lite compromises and alternatives one can over the years, trying to train myself to drink socially and take drugs casually.

We've all met those people who have had a drinking problem for a while—even years—and can successfully modify their behavior later. And I've known people who have tried heroin a few times but didn't get addicted. Or maybe heroin was a problem for a spell, but they've kicked it and years later can have wine with dinner without connecting the two experiences (they're probably the type for whom diets work, too). Some substitute pot for everything else. No judgment whatsoever to these people—and maybe a little envy—but that will *never* be me, and it's key to know that about myself.

I wish I could blame coming of age in the 1980s, but I was a child born of addicts who went on to start getting drunk at twelve— that fact suggests a genetic link. I also felt like an outcast, another predictor for some people; gay kids often turn to substances to medicate their social anxiety, feelings of freakishness, loneliness, or stress from bullying. A widely reported study from 2009 found that between 20 and 30 percent of LGBT adolescents are likely to abuse substances, while the statistic is 9 percent for their heterosexual peers.*

Being a gay kid is the perfect training ground for an addict because secrets and lies are how you survive (or don't). I got the message that I should be ashamed of myself early on—not as much from my family as from the culture itself, though the messages in the recovery movement I grew up around could also be confusing to a kid: if you're part of a group that meets in secret and has rules to never reveal its members, it drives home the message that there's something wrong with you that outsiders shouldn't know about.

What if, like being gay, we looked at addiction as something that a person is born predisposed to and is therefore deserving of our

---

*Marshal, M. P., M. S. Friedman, R. Stall, K. M. King, J. Miles, and M. A. Gold, et al. 2008. "Sexual Orientation and Adolescent Substance Use: A Meta-Analysis and Methodological Review." *Addiction* 103(4): 546–556.

compassion and support for the challenges that will invariably arise as the person comes of age? That's my hope when telling my story and listening to those of others; I want to constantly remind that person who is ashamed of themself that it doesn't have to feel that way, and no matter what your challenges in life, you're in good company.

It makes sense to me that my brain reacts differently to drugs and alcohol—once I took that first sip, my physiology changed forever. That's how I wanted to feel all the time, my brain was sure of it. It's that combination of chemicals and life experiences. I understand why some people have it in their heads that addicts are weak—they cannot relate to that same feeling of healing that comes when the alcoholic finishes that very first drink. Normal people work through feelings of inadequacy and stress in a healthier way, like going for a run. They make better choices, like not casually breaking the law.

The moment I always go back to is that clichéd promise I'd heard in all the rehabs and recovery meetings along the way: "Eventually the drugs just stop working." In all those years of using, I never believed this could apply to me, never. After all, I had given up everything for heroin, just everything. It had been my friend, my family, my music, my whole world for so long. I traded my sexuality and my career for the chance at more time with it. Clearly the fact of that meant that the drug worked for me. Sure, I had a disease. I could admit to that—I needed help. And heroin was the only thing that helped. Besides, losing what I'd already lost had to be worth it.

But that last year in that shitty apartment in North Hollywood, the drugs did stop working. I'll never forget how intensely that last shot of heroin failed me. For one thing, when I put the needle in my arm and waited for the familiar release, instead there was nothing. No rush, no numbing, no difference. All the problems that I was running from were still with me in that room, sitting with me on the couch, and suddenly the drug wouldn't let me unsee all that was gone. I was alone, scared, sick, and empty. I knew the only things left to lose were what was left of my sanity and my life.

Even now the fact of it keeps me clean: heroin is an ineffective painkiller for someone who has abused it for years. It will stop working and start hurting. I see now how sick I was (mentally, physically, all of it), but at the time my body was making all my decisions for me and I couldn't see beyond my immediate need to keep the sickness away. The pull of it outside of the physical is the idea of those first highs. Your body remembers and your brain remembers, and compulsion takes over.

I know that if I ever went off that ledge again, it would be over for me in less than two days. I would obliterate my life. I know that a heroin-addicted crackhead is not a mother or a partner or a good musician or a contributing member of society, and now I can't unknow it. And a relapse wouldn't be wasted on beer either. People are always asking me if I'm okay being around alcohol. Fuck yeah, I'm okay with it, because if I was going to throw in the towel, I wouldn't go out on something as basic as a gin and tonic. Because of this, I know I'm always vulnerable.

You can try to reset your brain every day, make that daily choice to stay the course, but there are some impulses you never forget. Where we live in L.A. is not very far from my old stomping grounds. There are days when I'll be driving my daughter to school, and I know there's a shortcut if we don't take the freeway, right down the same streets where I used to buy and sell my soul. I know if we take the back roads, I'll see them—the man in the hat who just stands there, the newbie pulling up in the car, the casual lean into the window, the obvious exchange of goods. But Bea's school is also at the foot of some mountains, and I try to focus on those instead. I think of the way that my dad always told us to look at the mountains, to just meditate on the bigness of the landscape, the history, and the metaphor. Now I wonder if he looked at mountains to forget alcohol.

IN MY BIG BOOK from those early days of sobriety-for-real, I took a lot of notes in the margins. This time around, I was struck by the serenity prayer in a new way: "God grant me the serenity to accept the things I cannot change, the courage to change the things I can, and the wisdom to know the difference." It is the motto that addicts have been reciting since before my parents' time in the program. As if understanding how this applied to my life for the first time, I wrote underneath in all caps, "Alice."

They say that in order to keep it you have to give back. It means you have to remain humble in the face of your recovery, and you do that by sharing your story to try to help other people forgive themselves. It's like that old gem by Anthony Keidis: you gotta give it away now. (I hate myself for this reference, but I'm pretty sure the song was inspired by the Twelfth Step.) What gets you through is the community part. It's about shining a light on the problems, plural. It doesn't happen right away, but over time you get more comfortable talking about your compulsions and obsessions, and layers of stuff gets stripped away.

I've learned to trust my instincts about new people. Somehow this new layer of insight has gotten stronger the longer I've stayed sober. Of course, the longer you stay in the program, the more you're reminded that if you think you know it all, you're on course for failure. I get the importance of humility in the face of addiction, but in general the wisdom that comes with the gut feeling has been one of the biggest revelations for me and has helped protect me inside the program too. Just because someone has twenty years clean doesn't mean they can't also be a manipulative asshole.

Sometimes I'll hear things in a meeting that will make me roll my eyes internally. Such as recently when a very young man was sharing about the insecurities that contributed to his addiction and said, "You know, I tried so hard to have a father, but instead I had a *dad*." (I hope he was aware that was the exact comparison Kurt made in "Serve the Servants," though this kid probably hadn't even been conceived by his "dad" when Kurt wrote that lyric.) I take what I need and what works for me to get through, and I surround myself with a support system that makes me laugh and think, and I respectfully reject the rest.

Sometimes I see myself in some of the other addicts I've met along the way. A few years ago I met a young woman named Lily, who my sponsor was also sponsoring. She was maybe early twenties and thirty days clean from dope. She had red hair and tattoos, was super smart and likeable. One day we picked her up at her parents' house to take her to a meeting. Before it started, I stood outside with her in the parking lot while she smoked a cigarette, and I drank my coffee. She was in that all-too-familiar place where all a junkie wants to talk about is the dope and its associated rituals. She was still running.

I listened and remembered and had a moment of gratitude that I was on the other side of that beginning stage I knew so well. That manic energy had left me, and I could finally just be calm and still. I remember saying a few things, keeping it simple, validating what she was saying, giving her my number, and encouraging her to call. I could see in her face that proverbial eyeroll: *words, words, words.* I felt for her.

The next day she called our sponsor in the morning to check in and went to a noon meeting by herself. After the meeting, she called some friends, got high in a parking lot, and died.

There is nothing that Lily (or Kristen or Kurt) did that day that I hadn't done countless times before. I don't know why she died and I didn't. She didn't do anything wrong, and I didn't do anything right; I just got more chances.

There's one thing that drives me nuts about some people's interpretation of sobriety in the program, and that is that you're betraying yourself or "cheating" if you go on psychiatric meds to treat an underlying chemical imbalance or mental illness. Speaking from experience, the right medication can make all the difference between relapse and one more day for a clinically depressed person. That's what I mean about trusting your gut—it's not about perfection or purity—it's about getting through and getting the help you need. (And believe me, you can't abuse an antidepressant.) When it comes to your neurological health, there's no substitute for legitimate medical advice.

BECAUSE IT'S THE twentieth anniversary of many seminal albums produced by my contemporaries, I've been going to a lot of shows lately and seeing a lot of old friends I haven't seen in decades. Recently I found myself backstage talking to an old friend whose band we used to tour with, someone who is still using heroin after all these years. It was hard to watch, knowing what it's like to be so long in that place that you can't even imagine another one. We reminisced about the fun we'd had in this city, the antics backstage in that one, but very quickly the conversation turned to the dark parts of the good old days. I realized as my friend was talking that they were still living in those moments, still stuck in the rivalries and insecurities that fueled so much of rock 'n' roll when we were twenty-six, still stuck in that same physical and emotional place at forty-seven.

"Don't you miss it sometimes, though?" they asked, knowing I'm sober now but still playing music. "Honestly," I said, "It's been so long now I don't think my body could take it." Which I know is absolutely true. The tricky thing about heroin is the way it lies. *I used to be able to handle this much, so I'll need at least this much to sprout the wings. Just one more time for old time's sake. . . .* Every day I'm reminded—when another person I admire dies of their addiction—that we've lost too many artists (whose sensitivity is necessary to the work they produce, often to their detriment). I know all my chances are up. I know the way I know I love my little girl that one more of anything would kill me.

I wrapped my arms around my friend and said goodnight; it was great to hear those songs again. It was late, and I needed to get home. As I pushed my way through the throng backstage, heading out to the staircase that led outside, I felt a hand squeeze my shoulder from behind. Turning back I saw her, the dealer-to-the-stars from way back when, a person on whose couch I'd nodded off more than once. A flood of faces washed over me, the faces of so many dead friends, her hand still on my shoulder like the icy grip of the Grim Reaper. "Hi Pat," she said, expectantly. I shrugged her off and walked out the door, never forgetting how everywhere my past will always be, and how hard-won my future.

Just the other day I was going through an old junk drawer and found a little box of all the chips and key chains I'd received at meetings during my first year of sobriety: I have the welcome chip, the orange keychain marking 30 days, the green is 60 days, 90 days, 9 months, one year—I'd kept every one. When my daughter was a baby, she used to play with them, and when she saw them again as a preschooler, she announced that she wanted them back. I politely told her that they were Mama's.

"What are they for?" She asked.

"They're little trophies for hard work and being brave." I said, realizing then that that's the truth. That's what sobriety is—doing what you're afraid of. For me that's living one day at a time without drugs.

THESE DAYS I'M often asked, after all those years of excess, self-destruction, loss, shame, anger, loneliness, restlessness, and grief, how I forgave myself. After ego-building success and soul-crushing failure, breakups with bands and girlfriends and family members. After the deaths of so many good friends, estrangement from others, the loss of my father, and the irreparable fact that he never lived to see me sober. People ask how I found, and continue to find, the strength to risk the specter of failure that plagues the recovering addict every single day. The lament of every newly sober person alive: How to live with all the regret?

Was it a spiritual awakening? You could say that, and I do. But because I was born into a family of twelve-steppers, my parents never gave us the benefit (or the curse) of defining the divine. All my life I was encouraged to turn to "a god of my own understanding," and of course I never knew what that meant. For a while the god of my understanding was America's god, a bearded Santa Claus god, the man in the sky who got pissed at the idea of two guys kissing. It was the guy who inspired Kurt to scream defiantly, "God is gay."

God certainly wasn't in the details. If I was drunk the details are fuzzy, and when I was in the throes of heroin and crack addiction, the details were too disturbing to dwell on. For me, God didn't come from enlightenment—I've never been able to chant like the Buddhists or pray like the Christians. I guess I would say the god of my own understanding took a lifetime to emerge, first through music, then through laughter, and then through love itself. God is simply a desire to live and to *feel* it, in some ways for the first time.

In the beginning, music taught me how to feel so much it hurt. Twenty years ago, it hurt too much to feel. Fifteen years ago I was so far from feeling, I couldn't even hear the music much less make it anymore. Twelve years ago, I could have never imagined the life I have now, *never* imagined I'd be able to quit smoking, much less be somebody's wife or somebody's mom. That I'd be in a band again—more than one—much less that I'd be teaching kids—boys and girls—how to play the drums. I had no inkling then that one day I'd walk down the street pushing a stroller on the hunt for ice cream in Silver Lake, instead of on foot, scouring the streets for crack.

I think of all the women I've met in the sober living houses, the diversity of their stories, the way they made me laugh, the incomparable strength of women. I think of the sweet dogs that made me feel seen and needed and loved, the easy therapy of their faith in me. I think of the music and the unconditional pull of the drums in my life. The image of that kit through the door of the church: so apt. I think there's a nice poetry in picking the drums as the god of my own understanding. I vow every day to give my daughter and my wife the life they deserve. I vow to allow myself to feel the preciousness of that vow, and how lucky I am to be making it. Lucky, too, to finally know in my guts—when I play, when I work, when I'm home—I have too much to live for.

THE END

ACKNOWLEDGMENTS

I'd like to thank Ben Schafer at Da Capo for his early encouragement, and Erin Hosier for helping me through the time machine and putting it all into words. Thank you, Henry Dunow, for your guidance in the book world.

I owe a debt to every single person in recovery that has shared their story with me and listened to mine, and the Musicians Assistance Program, who never gave up. Thank you, Shannon Del, for being my friend and getting me to rehab on March 1, 2005, and Molly Cleator for your constant support, sense of humor, strength, and beauty. I'm grateful for every single dog that needed me (I needed you more), and every single apartment, band, and relationship I've lost because of my addiction; those were the things that got me clean and sober.

To my bandmates Melissa Auf Der Maur, Eric Erlandson, and Courtney Love: thank you for the music and the friendship. Kristen Pfaff: you made me a better drummer with your bass playing—I miss you. Kurt, I miss your voice, the music, and *you*.

Thank you Seattle and Los Angeles, especially the following bands and friends: the Melvins, MudHoney, My Bloody Valentine, Nirvana, Yo La Tengo, Sub Pop, Bruce Pavitt, Peter Mensch, Butch Vig, Deb Googe, Beth Halper, Dylan Carlson, Amra Brooks, Ali Koehler, Polly Johnson, Lauren Freeman, Nicole Snyder, Rachel Gagliardi, Death Valley Girls, Bonnie Bloomgarden, Molly Schiot, Frances Bean Cobain, Jillian Lauren, James McNew, Kirk Ward, Cecil Castellucci, Jenn Bowman, Roz Music, Sia Furler, Lisa Orth for your photos and inspiration, P. David Ebersole and Todd Hughes for *Hit So Hard*, the documentary, and Joe Mama Nitzberg for all things art, style, music, and recovery.

Thank you to Susan Bordeaux for letting me listen to your records, taking me to see live music, and being my big sister; my father, Larry Schemel Sr., for teaching me that I could be anything I wanted to be, and my mother, Terry Schemel, for loving me no matter what and showing me the humor in the world. My brother, Larry, is my best friend, favorite guitarist, and the funniest person I know—thank you for always showing up for me, even after you got clean and I didn't.

Thank you, Roddy Bottum, always, for everything.

Thank you to my wife and partner, Christina Soletti, for your patience and understanding, and my daughter, Beatrice, for choosing me to be your parent. You both show me a new way to see the world every single day; you are gifts of sobriety, and I love you.

INDEX

abandonment issues, 240
abscess, 197–198
addiction. *See also* drug rehab;
    intervention(s); relapses;
    sobriety
    author's early experiences with,
        1–3
    challenges of, 109–111
    of Cobain and Love, 46
    and drugs' eventual
        ineffectiveness, 263–264
    humility in face of, 265
    powerlessness against, 261–263,
        267
Aguilera, Christina, 218
Al-Anon, 253
Albright, Bette, 145
alcohol
    arrests due to, 19–21, 24
    author's first experience with,
        7–8
    causes problems with author's
        girlfriend, 35, 36–37
    before performances, 44
    procuring, 18–19
    as source of bravery, 16
Alcoholics Anonymous
    author ordered to attend, 165–
        166
    author's early experiences with,
        1–3
Alice
    author meets, 130–31
    author's relationship with, 160,
        167–169, 176–177, 191–192
    bails author out of jail, 164
    banned from Liberty House, 146
    empties author's storage unit, 206
    fuels author's anger, 178

helps author, 156, 157–159
    last time author sees, 203–204
    procures drugs for author, 135,
        141–142
    returns to L.A., 186, 188–189
    as roommate, 183
Annie, 84–86, 89–90, 105, 106,
    115–120, 122
anxiety, 6–7
Arnold, Buddy, 144
arrest, of author, 20–21, 161–164
"Asking for It" (Hole), 66
Auf der Maur, Melissa
    author hides drug use from,
        134–135
    author meets, in Paris, 230–231
    author meets Alice through, 130
    author's relationship with, 128,
        146–147
    becomes disenchanted with Hole,
        99
    confidence of, 131
    joins Hole, 83–84
    moves to New York, 121
    rents house with author, 127
awkwardness, 6–7

back pain, 104, 167
Bailey, Ernie, 53
Barber, Jim, 209
Bastard, 208–212
Beastie Boys, 23
"Beautiful" (Aguilera), 217–218
Beinhorn, Michael, 139–140, 143
Benson, Scott, 6
Best, Jerry, 211–212
"Best Sunday Dress" (Hole), 97
Big Day Out music festival, 91–92
Blood Circus, 34

Bordeaux, Susan Schemel
  author detoxes with, 75–76
  as author's financial manager,
    176
  and author's first experiences with
    drugs and alcohol, 7–8
  author's relationship with, 6, 221
  childhood of, 3
  leaves with father, 10
  personality of, 6
  procuring alcohol with, 18
  returns from Seattle, 13
  sends author to look after brother,
    132
boundaries, 85
"Boys on the Radio" (Hole), 97
Brenda, 244–245
Brooks, Amra, 87, 88, 234
burglary, 190–191
Burke, Clem, 220
Butcher, Raegan, 22–23

Caitlyn (addict), 245–246
Caitlyn (dealer), 56–57
Cantrell, Jerry, 28
carbon dot, 198
Carlson, Dylan, 33, 37, 75
Carroll, Linda, 76
Castronovo, Deen, 140
Cathy, 24–27, 31
Celebrity Center, 223
Celebrity Skin (Hole), 138–140, 143,
    150–152, 160–161, 178
"Celebrity Skin" video, 177
Channing, Chad, 29
chicken costume, 88
Child Protective Services, 13
children, and parenthood, 254–257
Christmas, 87–88
cigarettes, 13
Cobain, Frances, 46–47, 60–61, 88
Cobain, Kurt
  as addict and father, 46–47
  attends author's audition for
    Hole, 39
  on author as musician, 99

  author goes shopping and
    shooting with, 49–50
  author plays with, 51
  author's relationship with, 28–29,
    63
  avoids unwanted attention, 45–46
  commutes to Olympia, 33
  death of, 76–78, 80, 82
  fame and success of, 35–36, 42
  goes to Rio de Janeiro with
    Nirvana, 52–53, 55–56
  helps Make-a-Wish, 43
  intervention for, 72–75
  Love's collaboration with, 97
  relationship of, with Tobi Vail and
    Kathleen Hanna, 100
  shoots up author, 57
  writes new music, 51
cocaine, 54–55, 230
Community World Theater, 28
Constant Comment, 131
Cooper, Agent, 98
Corgan, Billy, 138, 139, 209
Cornell, Chris, 259–261
cotton fever, 198–199
couples therapy, 98
Courtney Love (band), 232–233
crack, 147–149, 153–154,
    213–215
crack pipes, 148–149
"Credit in the Straight World"
    (Hole), 66
CRI-Help, 235–243
crystal meth, 36, 69

Dawn, 147, 149
Deal, Kim, 224
Death Valley Girls, 257
Del, Shannon, 212, 214–215,
    219–220, 222–223, 235
Des Barres, Pamela, 41
detoxing. *See also* drug rehab;
    sobriety
  author's plan for, 75
  four-day, 124–126
  in Hawaii, 115–116

from heroin, 60
before important life events, 73
in Seattle, 181–182, 205
divorce, 8–10
Doc, 195
dog boarding facility, 246–248
Dog Rockers, 248–249
dog-walking business, 248–249
"Doll Parts" (Hole), 66, 67
Doll Squad, 24–25, 28, 29, 31
domestic violence, 168–169
drug and alcohol school, 166
drug rehab. *See also* sobriety
    CRI-Help, 235–243
    in eastern Washington, 117–120
    Exodus, 104–105
    Hazelden, 156–157
    Las Encinas, 136–137
    Liberty House, 145–147,
        215–216
    Sundown, 78–80
drugs. *See also* addiction; crack;
        detoxing; drug rehab; heroin;
        intervention(s); relapses;
        sobriety
    author arrested for purchasing,
        161–164
    author does, with Love, 152–154
    author loses everything to, 193–
        194
    author quits, in Seattle, 183–184
    author's addiction to, intensifies,
        56–57, 71
    author's anger fueled by, 177–178
    in Brazil, 54–55
    buying, in Los Angeles, 171–174
    buying, in New York City,
        112–113
    buying, in Seattle, 182, 184–187
    cause problems with author's
        girlfriend, 36–37
    decreased efficacy of, 108,
        263–264
    desperate means for procuring,
        189–192, 194–196, 204,
        233–235

Kristen Pfaff dies from overdose
        of, 80–83
    physical effects of, 166–167,
        197–199
    procured in Europe, 59–60
    used by Kurt Cobain and
        Courtney Love, 37
drummers
    replaceability of, 161
    royalties for, 220–21
drumming
    author's love of, 203
    back pain caused by, 167
    playing through pain in, 14–15
drunk driving, 24
"Drunk in Rio" (Hole), 55–56, 98
Dumbhead, 35
Duncan, Big John, 53
Dylan, Bob, tribute concert to,
        61–62

Ecstasy, 59
England, 59–63
Erlandson, Eric
    attends therapy sessions with
        band, 98
    and author's audition for Hole,
        37, 38
    gets angry at Love, 85
    getting money from, 64–65
    introduces Hole to Kristen Pfaff,
        58
    Love's treatment of, 91
    professionalism of, 43–44
    records *Live Through This*, 67,
        68
Europe. *See also* Paris
    drugs procured in, 59–60
    Hole tours, 99
Exodus, 73–74, 104–105

Fastbacks, 20
feminist rage, 23, 24
finances, 176–177, 178–179, 186,
        190–191
Flea, 54

flight(s)
   detoxing on, 116
   drug use on, 109–110
   turbulent, 60–61
forgiveness, for yourself, 268–269
Foster, Dave, 28

gay bar, 27
gay pride, 27
geographic cure, 3
glasses, 7
Gloria, 244–45
God, of author's understanding,
   269
Googe, Deb, 59
Great Britain, 59–63
Green River, 31
Grohl, Dave, 42, 53
guns, shooting, 50–51
Gurmukh, 212
"Gutless" (Hole), 66

hang gliding, 55
Hanna, Kathleen, 33, 100–101
Hannah, 147–149, 153–156,
   157
Hawaii, 115–116
Hazelden, 156–157
Hepatitis C, 199
heroin
   Annie overdoses on, 122
   author's addiction to, intensifies,
      56–57, 71
   author's first time taking, 30
   in Brazil, 54–55
   buying, in New York City,
      112–113
   effects of, 103–104, 166–167
   in Los Angeles, 172
   Pfaff dies from overdose of, 80–83
   smuggled into Canada, 106–107
   stops working, 263
   used by Cobain and Love, 37
Hole
   "Asking for It," 66
   author auditions for, 37, 38–39

   author cut off from, 156, 159
   author encouraged to leave,
      118–119
   author questions place in, 140–142
   author's anger over, 177–178
   author's earnings from, 64
   "Best Sunday Dress," 97
   "Boys on the Radio," 97
   breakup of, 207
   Celebrity Skin, 138–140, 143,
      150–152, 160–161, 178
   "Celebrity Skin" video, 177
   "Credit in the Straight World," 66
   "Doll Parts," 66, 67
   "Drunk in Rio," 55–56, 98
   "Gutless," 66
   hires Pfaff, 58–59
   "I Think That I Would Die," 66
   "Jennifer's Body," 66, 67
   Live Through This, 65–68, 78
   "Miss World," 55, 66, 67
   "Old Age," 97
   performs at Big Day Out music
      festival, 91–92
   performs at MTV Video Music
      Awards, 108
   performs at Phoenix Festival,
      62–63
   performs on "Unplugged," 93–94,
      96–98
   plays at Tuktoyaktuk, 107
   "Plump," 59, 66
   rallies following Pfaff's death, 83–
      85
   records *Celebrity Skin*, 138–140,
      143
   records first EP, 42–43
   records *Live Through This*, 65–68
   rehearses for "Unplugged," 93–94
   "She Walks," 55, 66
   shoots album cover for *Celebrity
      Skin*, 150–152
   "Softer Softest," 66
   "Sugar Coma," 97
   termination agreement with,
      159–161, 169–170

therapy sessions for, 98
tours Europe, 99
"Violet," 66, 108
Hollywood Rock Festival, 52
homelessness, 193–204, 210–211
humility, in face of addiction, 265

Ill, Paul, 220
image, of author, 95–96, 135
Imperial Teen, 218
"In Bloom" (Nirvana), 88
intervention(s)
    for author, 144–145, 227
    for Kurt Cobain, 72–75
"I Think That I Would Die" (Hole),
    66

Jabberjaw, 39
Jackson, Michael, 109
Jenn, 34–35, 36–37, 39–40
"Jennifer's Body" (Hole), 66, 67
Jessica, 11–12
Jet Rag, 49–50
Jimmy, 194, 195, 201, 203–204
Josephine, 210, 219, 229–230
Juliette & the Licks, 220, 221,
    224–228

Keni, 136–137, 143–144
Kiedis, Anthony, 54, 74, 265
Kingsley, Pat, 135
Kolderie, Paul, 65, 66
Korade, Kenny, 211–212
Kristofferson, Kris, 62
Kross, Redd, 211–212

Lewis, Juliette, 220, 223, 224, 225,
    227
Liberty House, 145–147, 215
Lily, 266
Lisa, 121–122, 129
Live Through This (Hole), 65–68,
    78
Lollapalooza, 100–103
Love, Courtney
    as addict and mother, 46–47

asks about author's life on streets,
    210–211
attends therapy sessions with
    band, 98
author becomes frustrated with,
    86–87
author feels betrayed by, 140, 141,
    142, 151
author goes shopping with, 49–50
author plays with, 51
author recommended to, 37
author records with, 43
author's relationship with, 63, 90
on author's romantic life, 219
buys Christmas presents, 87–88
and death of Kurt Cobain, 76
experiences turbulent flight, 60–61
gets back in touch with author,
    207–208
goes to Hawaii to detox, 115
goes to Rio de Janeiro with
    Nirvana, 52, 53, 55
hires author, 39
hires Pfaff, 58–59
holds intervention for author, 144
holds intervention for Cobain, 72,
    73
interview style of, 41–42
meets Madonna, 94–95
opposes mixing drugs, 55
performs at MTV Video Music
    Awards, 108
performs high, 85
phone calls and conversational
    style of, 40
and public relations, 45, 110–111
records Celebrity Skin, 138–139
records Live Through This, 65–66,
    67, 68
rehearses for "Unplugged," 94
starts Bastard, 208–209, 211–212
starts Courtney Love, 232–233
takes bus, 70–71
tours with Lollapalooza, 100–103
at Tuktoyaktuk concerts, 107–108
unpredictability of, 91–92

Love, Courtney (*Continued*)
    wants to try new style, 217–218
    watches Sinead O'Connor on TV,
        61–62
Lush, 33

Madonna, 94–95
mail, 121
Majestic Theater, 211–212
Make-a-Wish, 43
Maloney, Samantha, 177
marijuana, 30
Markham, Stephen, 6
marriage, of author, 253–254
Mary, 172–174
MATES, 144
Mavis, 195
Maya, 147
McDonald, Steve, 211–212
medication, psychiatric, 266–267
Mensch, Peter, 108
Metallica, 107–108
meth, 36, 69
Mike, 204
Milkbone, 19
"Miss World" (Hole), 55, 66, 67
Modern Drummer magazine, 109,
    110–111
Molson beer, 105–106
Montgomery, Craig, 53
Moon, Slim, 33
Morse, Todd, 220
MTV Video Music Awards,
    108–109
Mudhoney, 31
music
    author's connection to, 16–17
    author's current involvement
        with, 257–258
    author's early experiences with,
        14
    and author's social life, 19
    bought by author's mother, 11
    drugs and, 12
Music Bank, 28
Muzak, 30–31

Naltrexone, 125
Nancy, 78–80
Nirvana, 28, 29, 36, 52–56, 68–69
    "In Bloom," 88
    "Rape Me," 51
    "Scentless Apprentice," 55–56
    "Smells Like Teen Spirit," 100
    "You Know You're Right," 97–98
Norton, Edward, 138
Novoselic, Krist, 53
Numbers Cabaret, 27

O'Connor, Sinead, 61–62, 102
"Old Age" (Hole), 97
"Olympia" (Sybil), 33–34
Olympia, Washington, 33–34
Onassis, Blackie, 102, 239
osteomyelitis, 167

parenthood, 254–257
Paris, 99, 219, 229–231
Patient Pat, 116–117, 157
Pavitt, Bruce, 30–31
Perfect Prescription, The (Spaceman
    3), 32
Perry, Linda, 209, 217–218, 220
personal riders, 96
Peterson, Charles, 31
Petrucci, Roxy, 111
Pfaff, Kristen
    author's relationship with, 69–70
    death of, 80–83
    goes to rehab, 78
    heroin use of, 71
    joins Hole, 58–59
    records *Live Through This*, 67,
        68
Phoenix Festival, 62–63
photo shoots, 95–96
Pixies, 224–225
"Plump" (Hole), 59, 66
Polly, 41, 47–48, 89
Presley, Lisa Marie, 109
Primitives, 22–23
prostitution, 189–190, 194–196,
    204

psychiatric medication, 266–267
punk music, 16–17

Q-Prime, 105–106

racism, 241
Ramones, 20–21
"Rape Me" (Nirvana), 51
Reading Festival, 83, 84
red hair, 6–7
Red Hot Chili Peppers, 54
regret, living with, 268–269
Rehab Doll (Green River), 31
relapses, 89–90, 102–103, 120–123,
    134–135, 141–143, 213–215,
    223–228
riders, 96
Rio de Janeiro, Brazil, 52–56
Rohypnol, 59–60
Rose, Axl, 46
Ryan, Meg, 248

São Paulo, Brazil, 53–54
Saturday Night Live, 68–69
"Scentless Apprentice" (Nirvana),
    55–56
Schemel, Larry Jr.
    author helps, while strung out,
        132–133
    author plays music with, 206, 257
    as author's drug buddy, 12
    author's relationship with, 149
    checks into rehab, 78
    childhood of, 3, 5
    detoxes at author's house, 135–
        136
    as donor for author's baby, 255
    helps author detox, 205
    reaction to father's new
        personality, 12–13
    as Sybil band member, 32
    understanding of, 234–235
Schemel, Larry Sr.
    author moves in with, 179–84,
        205–209
    checks kids into rehab, 78

    death of, 221, 242, 268
    divorce of, 8–10, 12–13
    fixes author's glasses, 7
    married life of, 2–3
    as parenting influence, 255
    parenting style of, 13
    personality of, 5
    as recovering alcoholic, 264
Schemel, Terry
    death of, 256
    divorce of, 8–9
    married life of, 2–3
    parenting style of, 5, 10–11, 13,
        18
    supports author, 4, 6–7, 16, 21,
        119–120, 253–254
    visits on Family Day, 118
Scientology, 223–224
Screaming Life (Soundgarden),
    31
Screaming Trees, 29
Sedaris, David, 230
self-forgiveness, 268–269
sexuality
    addiction and, 262–263
    addictive behaviors transferred to,
        210, 219–220
    author faces opposition due to,
        128–130
    during author's adolescence, 12,
        16–17, 21
    author's childhood realization
        regarding, 4–5
    author's denial of, 22–23
    and gay activism, 27
Shane, Debbie, 35
Sheila E, 111
"She Walks" (Hole), 55, 66
shooting range, 50–51
shopping, 50
Skrewdriver, 241
Slade, Sean, 65, 66
Smear, Pat, 73, 75
"Smells Like Teen Spirit" (Nirvana),
    100
sober living house, 244–247

sobriety. *See also* detoxing; drug
  rehab; relapses
  beginning of author's, 206–212
  challenges of, 260–261
  at CRI-Help, 235–243
  and dating Christina, 250–253
  and marriage and family, 253–256
  music career and, 217–220
  in sober living house, 244–247
  success in, 261–270
  and working at dog boarding
    facility, 246–249
social anxiety and awkwardness, 6–7
"Softer Softest" (Hole), 66
Soletti, Christina, 250–255, 259–260
Soundgarden, 31, 259–260
Spaceman 3, 32
speedball, 55
Staley, Layne, 28, 30, 54–57
Starr, Mike, 28
Starr, Ringo, 220–221
Stinky Puffs, 49
studio work, 220
"Sugar Coma" (Hole), 97
Sundown, 78–80
Sybil, 32–34, 35

teeth, heroin's impact on, 166–167
Temgesic, 60
theft, 190–191
therapy sessions, 98
Timony, Simon Fair, 49
tour bus, 101–102

Tree People, 34
Triazolam, 60
Triclops, 65
Troubadour, 128–129
Tuktoyaktuk settlement, 105–108
turbulent flight, author survives, 60–
  61

Ulrich, Lars, 107
"Unplugged," 93–94, 96–98
Upset, 257

Vail, Tobi, 33
Valium, 54
Van Damme, Jean-Claude, 172
Vanity Fair, 45, 95
Victoria's Secret catalogue, 87–88
"Violet" (Hole), 66, 108
Voodoo Fest, 224–225

Wade, 245–246
Wainwright, Rufus, 146
Walsh, Clint, 220
Warnick, Kim, 20, 43
Watson, Tammy, 32
Weiland, Scott, 173
Willner, Hal, 93
Word of Mouth, 42–43

"You Know You're Right"
  (Nirvana), 97–98

Zoe, 245